NEVER A DULL MOMENT

A MEMOIR OF
CANADIAN NAVAL AVIATION,
FIREBOMBING AND THEATRE

GEORGE E. PLAWSKI

 FriesenPress

Suite 300 - 990 Fort St
Victoria, BC, V8V 3K2
Canada

www.friesenpress.com

ISBN
978-1-5255-6084-2 (Hardcover)
978-1-5255-6085-9 (Paperback)
978-1-5255-6086-6 (eBook)

1. BIOGRAPHY & AUTOBIOGRAPHY, AVIATION & NAUTICAL

Distributed to the trade by The Ingram Book Company

TABLE OF CONTENTS

NOTE. Titles in CAPITALS follow a chronological sequence starting in 1963, while *anecdotes, flashbacks or flash forwards* are italicized.

PREFACE

Never a Dull Moment is a lively chronicle of how my life changed into an exhilarating Canadian adventure when, after spending my childhood under Nazi and Soviet occupations in Poland, I came to Canada with my parents as political refugees in 1948.

I shall share with the reader remarkable stories of my progenitors' lives, my father's service in the Polish Navy (a rare combination of being a pilot as well as the commanding officer of surface ships and submarines), and my mother's harrowing escape from her communist-subjugated homeland.

Moreover, if you promise to sit on your hands, I will invite you to join me in the cockpit of my navy Tracker to experience the thrill of flying off the aircraft carrier, HMCS *Bonaventure*. After I leave the Navy, you can accompany me on challenging sorties as I bomb forest fires in Canada and California, and witness the hilarious anarchy of budworm-spraying in New Brunswick.

These accounts will be seamlessly interspersed with a riveting chronology of how my passion for theatre led to the founding of Vancouver's City Stage, and the political shenanigans required to keep it going.

This telling is enhanced by a cast of talented, provocative, and engaging personalities whose friendship influenced and enriched the most creative and venturesome chapters of my life, and it's embellished by the debut of a beautiful girl and the start of enduring love.

It is to this girl, my wife, Rita, who became the inspiration behind everything I do, that I lovingly dedicate this memoir.

My narrative commences in 1963 during my last operational deployment in the carrier, nine months before I resigned my commission to launch into the unknown.

Note. Throughout this book I have used American spelling conventions; however, since my theatre studies and work took place in Canada and the UK, I have chosen to utilize the Canadian spelling of the word: theatre.

EXERCISE "MAINBRACE"

In the autumn of 1963, the Royal Canadian Navy (RCN) was on a roll. The replacement of World War II ships, which allowed the Canadian Navy to effectively assume its assigned NATO role as a modern anti-submarine force, was largely complete, and naval aviation was reaching its peak.

Deployed in the carrier HMCS *Bonaventure*, Tracker and helicopter squadrons consistently outperformed their NATO allies during combined fleet exercises, and preparations were in place to equip our frigates with new, state of the art Sea King helicopters.

I was at the apogee of my career as a naval aviator, flying the Grumman Tracker in 880 Squadron, the operational anti-submarine squadron embarked in the *Bonnie*, as she was affectionately known, and I was having the time of my life. My Tracker was a twin-engine, propeller-driven aircraft built explicitly for the anti-submarine role. To carry out our missions required a crew of four, which consisted of my co-pilot, Sub-Lieutenant Dave Muckle (eventually re-invented as an Air Canada captain under a new *nom de guerre* of Dave Benton), and two experienced naval aircrewmen, Leading Seaman Jim Dodd and Able Seaman Paul Legère.

We were equipped with highly sensitive radar as well as with electronic countermeasures, and we could stay aloft for close to six hours. Our suite of thirty sonobuoys was used to detect the general presence of a submerged submarine, the exact position of which we could pinpoint with MAD, a magnetic anomaly detection system that measured the distortion of the earth's magnetic field caused by the presence of a metallic object. Such a fix enabled a precision attack with depth charges or homing torpedoes.

The starboard wing bulged with a seventy-million candlepower searchlight, powerful enough to pick out a periscope at night half-a-mile away. This device could only be lit in flight, because without the cooling stream of air it could burn off the wing, which created a nasty mess on the tarmac. It was operated by the co-pilot and doubled as a source of amusement when, after lighting up a Russian "Elint" (electronic intelligence) trawler, we watched as it hastily pretended to be fishing.

The carrier was scheduled to take part in an extensive NATO exercise that would involve the Navies of six countries in the inhospitable waters north of

Scotland, and the month of September was spent gearing up for that momentous event.

The voyage was to be my last operational deployment in 880 Squadron, because following this trip, along with one of my best friends, Charlie Poirier, I would be transferred to Utility Squadron, VU32, at our shore base, HMCS Shearwater.

I wasn't looking forward to this appointment, since it represented a significant downgrade from the excitement inherent in carrier operations, but I couldn't let this distract me as we were engaged in flat-out preparations for the upcoming war games. These training sessions consisted of day and night Marlant (Maritime Atlantic) patrols, instrument takeoffs, navigational exercises, and a glut of field carrier-landing practice.

On September 25, we watched the majestic pageant of the *Bonnie* as she departed the Shearwater jetty with her crews mustered smartly on the flight deck. A few hours later, we manned our planes, flew to the ship in close formation, and after trapping smartly on board, we completed her complement and fulfilled her *raison d'être*.

The *Bonnie* was a twenty-thousand-ton ship whose flight deck measures 700 feet in length by 107 in width (213 meters by 32). Though tiny by American standards, it's a colossus when seen from up close.

The ship is technically capable of twenty-two knots (forty kph), but none of us had ever known her to go over eighteen, at which speed vibration causes the dishes and silverware to migrate noisily along the tables, permitting neighbors to sample each other's fare.

The hull, built during the latter part of the war, lay unfinished in Belfast until the Canadian Navy decided to buy it following considerable upgrading. These improvements consisted of installing three British innovations accepted by all of the world's Navies: the angled deck, the mirror landing system, and the steam catapult.

The landing area at the aft end of the deck was a rectangle eighty feet long traversed by five wires stretched athwartships twenty feet apart. This was the space into which arriving aircraft needed to fit the hook—tricky business when attempted on a jet-black night in a roaring gale through billowing spray onto a pitching deck.

Our living quarters were also at the aft end of the ship, where pilots of the rank of lieutenant or lower shared double cabins, while four pilots who were willing to allow their bedroom to double as the after-hours party space volunteered to occupy an expansive, eight-bunk compartment known as the "Ay-rab" quarters. This, of course, was precisely where Charlie, I, and two like-minded rabble-rousers chose to hang our hats.

The center of the action was the wardroom bar. Apart from the bar itself, its two chief attractions were a piano and a propeller-hub suspended from the deck-head, whose shape and paint job appropriately reflected its matronymic of *The Swinging Tit*.

The bar-limit for lieutenants was $25 per month, entirely manageable for most considering that a mixed drink cost six cents. Almost nobody drank beer, owing to its exorbitant price of fifteen cents per can, while wine at a buck-a-bottle was a quota-killer. In spite of the prices, the party types regularly reached the limit well short of the month, which unfortunately included some of my friends … in fact, some of my closest friends. OK, me too. At one point, this prompted the executive officer to confront us with the disagreeable reminder that the $25 cut-off was a limit, not a goal. Thankfully, there were several highly popular moderate drinkers who allowed us to piggy-back on their quota.

We wasted no time en route to our operational area to commence an intensive period of day and night deck re-qualification. It was during such concentrated periods of activity that morale in the squadron reached its peak. Pilots worldwide tend to create tightly-knit communities, but naval aviators, sequestered in a ship and bonded by the risk of their unique and often hazardous operations, become a brotherhood lasting a lifetime.

On reaching the exercise area north of Scotland, we worked with combined fleets from France, Denmark, Norway, the US, the UK, and the Netherlands in weather that was uniformly appalling (See Allan Snowie's excellent book, *The Bonnie*, chapter 11), while the overall command was executed from the cruiser HMS *Tiger*.

Our task was to prevent exercise submarines from penetrating through the Greenland-Iceland/ UK gap, the route which Russian subs would need to take to break out into the Atlantic. In spite of the conditions, we accomplished our mission beyond expectations.

The Dutch were represented by *Bonaventure's* sister ship, *Karel Doorman*, along with several destroyers. For reasons that remain unexplained, the Dutch destroyer *Overijssel* developed an overprotective attitude toward our ship, which one evening at 10:00 p.m. forced us to go full astern to avoid a collision.

Returned to its proper shepherding position, this ship unaccountably chose to renew its intimacies two hours later with an advance that resulted in her disappearance under our bows. *Bonnie* had to endure another convulsive reversing of engines accompanied by a violent list to port. We had no way of knowing that the "law-of-threes" decreed that close encounters with the Dutch were by no means exhausted.

With a portion of the exercise complete, we anchored in Cromarty Firth near Invergordon, where I played golf with Charlie and some squadron mates on the famous links at Tain.

Highjinks among the ships in the fleet were a nightly occurrence. I particularly remember one rambunctious evening, when after a *rijsttafel* blowout aboard the *Karel Doorman*, a group of our squadron pilots, along with some Dutch aircrew, terrorized a French frigate from a motor launch that the captain of a Norwegian destroyer had assigned for our disposal. A combined concentration of searchlights and fire hoses eventually chased us away, but not before we plastered the decks and superstructure with an assortment of colorful and sticky foodstuffs.

When we sailed again to complete the last part of the schedule, we did so with two CBC reporters on board. One of these was a gentleman named Cleary, who bravely accompanied me for a demonstration deck-landing, while the other was the redoubtable broadcaster Stanley Burke, whose unlimited access to the bar suited him admirably. Since I was the host of a daily news and music program on the ship's radio, I approached Mr Burke with a request for an interview.

"Why not?" he responded.

He followed me into the radio room, and while I was setting up the equipment, Mr. Burke stretched out on a table and fell dead asleep. This put me in an embarrassing dilemma, because Mr. Burke was the Peter Mansbridge of his day, minus the tact but plus a generous dose of persuasive intimidation.

With much apprehension, I respectfully nudged him awake; he came up graciously cooperative and gave me a memorable interview, which by popular demand I was obliged to replay on several occasions.

The exercise was complete when, on October 24 as we steamed lazily down the east coast of Scotland toward Rosyth, word went out that a two-plane sortie was to be launched that afternoon. On checking the schedule, I discovered that my close friend Bill Nash and I had been chosen to fly it.

Intelligence obtained by the CIC (Combat Information Center) revealed that a detachment of Royal Navy's MTBs (Motor Torpedo Boats) lurked in the fjords with the intent to execute torpedo attacks on the passing fleet. Bill's and my mission was to defend against this treachery by deploying a rarely used weapon, operationally known as PCP (Pulverized Cereal Powder), provided by the ship's bakery in brown paper bags. These were to be launched by our naval aircrewmen out of the back door in a blinding imitation of the famous WWII, radar-baffling countermeasure, "Window."

Recognizing this flight as an official lark, I asked our galley cook to provide me with a clutch of hard-boiled eggs, which I distributed in the nooks and crannies of the undercarriage during my pre-flight inspection, planning t "shell" Bill's aircraft behind me during the catapult shot.

The briefing included the usual items. Weather: unlimited ceiling and visibility. Ships in company: *Karel Doorman* five miles ahead on our port bow, flying stations secured. This was followed by the projected time and position for recovery and known intelligence about the enemy.

After signing out our airplanes, caparisoned in our "poopy-suits," as the waterproof flight suits were called because of the absence of ready-access to the most vital area of relief, we plodded to our assigned machines and clambered clumsily aboard.

Our flight was the envy of all our squadron mates. It promised to be a free-wheeling, informal, no holds barred launch with which to cap a month of intensive and concentrated work. As it turned out, for me this was to be considerably more than a memorable occasion—its consequences became one of the reasons that eventually precipitated my decision to leave the Navy.

HMCS Bonaventure.

My crew. L to R: me, CBC's Creary, S/lt. Muckle, LS Dodd.

Flying companions: L to R, B. Montgomery, Squadron CO Pappy McLeod,B. Hogg, J. Todd, P. Hamilton, K. Miller, USN.

My Fateful Sortie, painting by Jack Ford.

THE *KAREL DOORMAN* SORTIE

With everyone strapped in, I started the engines, completed the run-up, and after receiving the crew's ready status, reported to Flyco: "1597 Ready!"

"1587 Ready!" Bill Nash echoed from the Tracker behind us.

As the light on the carrier's superstructure changed from red to green, the Director, his feet rooted astride the catapult shuttle slot, raised his crossed arms which signaled the pilot to release the parking brake and step on the brake pedals, allowing the chockmen, amicably known as "deck apes," to remove the chocks that they had been physically holding in place and carry them away as they scurried on all fours from under the aircraft.

Responding with bursts of power and touches of brakes to the Director's sharp and deliberate hand-signals, I taxied toward him until the main wheels abutted the positioning chocks. We felt the bump of the shuttle as it slid under the nose wheel and waited for it to be attached by the bridle to our catapult hook; tensioned like a slingshot against the hold-back, the nose lifted purpose-fully off the deck, assuming the attitude for takeoff.

His job complete, the Director turned control over to the flight deck officer (FDO) and disappeared past the right wing tip.

We rechecked the last cockpit items: flaps one third, trims set, hatches open, harness locked, rudder assist on, feet off the brakes, catapult grip down.

(The catapult grip is an inverted T shaped handle that is pulled down from the upper console. When the throttles are fully advanced, the pilot meshes their knobs with the catapult grip, which ensures that power is not inadver-tently jerked back when the catapult fires.)

The FDO raised his green flag and circled it over his head; this was the signal to push the throttles forward and mesh their knobs with the cat-grip.

A shuddering roar drowned everything out.

My practiced scan of the instruments showed all within limits.

"YES! YES! YES!" I shouted to Dave on the intercom, and out of the corner of my eye saw him salute the FDO.

With my left hand on the control column, left elbow buried in the gut, helmet firm against the head-rest, the right arm fully extended with the elbow joint over-center and a death grip on the throttles, we waited for the rush of acceleration to fling us into the air.

As the FDO dropped his flag, the engineering petty officer in the Howdah pushed the appropriate button, which a second later produced a mighty, stomach-crunching and eyeball-uncaging kick. (The Howdah is a retractable Plexiglass booth to starboard and astern of the catapult track which houses the operator who, on the signal from the Flight Deck Officer, fires the cat which gets its steam pressure from the ship's boilers.)

In one-and-a-half seconds from a standing start, after a roll of thirty-five meters, we were airborne with ninety knots (166 mph) on the clock. I loved that masculine thrust that propelled us so positively into the sky.

After briefly relishing a fleeting image of Nash getting pelted with a flurry of eggs, my focus switched to the beckoning gray shape looming ahead to port. There is no need to explain to any self-respecting Navy pilot the meaning of "fair game".

"They gave me a Seafire to beat up the fleet" was a line in a song that was practically a Fleet Air Arm anthem. We belted it out in the wardroom at larynx-lacerating levels, accompanied on the piano by Nick Winchester, Ben Oxholm, or Art Williams. It was an impulse enshrined in our psyche, embedded in our pilot DNA, and its object was now staring me in the face.

I pulled up the gear and flaps, descended to the wave tops, and maintaining a healthy power setting aimed for the starboard quarter of the ship.

We ate up the distance in no time, and when the carrier loomed impossibly above us, I pulled up to bridge level, rolled in 90 degrees of bank to starboard, and yanked hard on the yoke, mooning the Dutch with a bellicose close up of our belly.

I was genuinely pleased with myself as we climbed away when the radio came alive: "This is Highground (*Bonaventure's* call sign). Aircraft that made the pass on the *Karel Doorman*, report your side number!"

I felt entitled to kudos, yet the tone of that voice was distinctly unfriendly.

I was about to answer when Dave beat me to it; I looked at him quizzically, but his posture mimicked the Sphinx. Nothing more was said, but the accusatory inflection caused a feeling of unease to nibble at my senses. *What the hell is going on?*

We had just performed a legendary bounce: a clear-cut- candidate to enter our naval aviators' lore which screamed for a round of Bravo Zulus,[*] not this tight-assed voice followed by a foreboding silence.

---

[*] A flag-hoist composed of the flags B and Z, which signifies "Well done."

I put these misgivings aside to enjoy the MTB pursuit; we intercepted them as they pounced out of hiding, and our attacks were a paragon of crew cooperation.

While I aimed the airplane, one of the naval aircrewmen held the door open against the slipstream for the other to deploy the weapon on Dave's command. Two bombs broke upon release, but we all agreed that the other two fell within lethal range of the target, thus neutralizing the threat.

When it was over, we received a new assignment. Both aircraft were to continue patrol until dark then proceed to Lossiemouth, eat supper in RNA *Fulmar*, then fly a night patrol and trap on board at 2:00 a.m.

After we landed and serviced the airplanes, someone directed us to an austere, ill-lit, barracks-like canteen.

"Am I in the shit?" I asked Bill when we sat down.

"It doesn't sound good," he replied, unwittingly adding to my gloom.

For chrissake, the *Banshee* and *Sea Fury* guys used to drape *gongs* on themselves for less. Was there something wrong with: "They gave me a Tracker to beat up the fleet?" Did substituting the aircraft type ring a false note? Did it devalue the accepted fighter-jock image? And I thought we were *expected* to be aggressive! How the hell else did we disable the Italian fleet in Taranto? Or cripple the goddam *Bismarck?*

We were already fatigued from the just-completed 5.4-hour flight when we launched for the night patrol. Whatever we patrolled is lost to the caprice of time, but the weather deteriorated, which meant we needed to make an instrument approach.

Three and a half hours later, we obtained the ship's course and position with instructions for a CCA. (This acronym stands for "Carrier Controlled Approach," a talk-down by experienced controllers who issue verbal *course* corrections, though the *altitude* during descent is the pilot's responsibility.)

We approached the ship at 1,500 feet and received the "Foxtrot Corpen," the name of the into-the-wind course the carrier needed briefly to assume for the duration of the recovery. (Remaining on a predictable course for an extended period makes the ship vulnerable to submarine attack.)

When we opened to a prescribed distance astern, the CCA controller picked us up on radar and began vectoring us toward the deck. The personal rapport we'd developed with these specialists made it customary for the controller and the pilot to identify each other by name, and it was gratifying to learn that leading us in tonight was the highly-competent Petty Officer Putnam.

With the hook down, hatches open, and landing checklist complete, I remained on instruments, maintaining ninety knots as I followed the vectors while Dave kept his eyes peeled ahead, ready to call visual when we broke out of the overcast.

Abruptly, the blackness gave way to a display of luminescence. An orange ball glowed prominently in the middle of a row of green lights, while to the right of it, a line of white lights made an inverted T with four horizontal reds. This shining array is a dazzle of confusion when seen for the first time, but to an experienced pilot, it contains all the information required for a successful approach. The orange light is called a "meatball," a steering-wheel sized light reflected astern at a pre-set angle off a concave, gyro-stabilized mirror.

In combination with the green datum lights, the meatball provides the pilot with a visual approach slope usually set to 3.5 degrees. The airplane is on the glide path when the meatball appears to the pilot to be centered vertically between the green lights. The airplane is below the glide path whenever the meatball slips below the datum lights, and vice versa. The row of white lights shows the center-line, while the red lights mark the aft edge of the flight deck.

A landing signals officer (LSO) accompanied by an assistant monitors all approaches from a platform between the mirror and the round-down. When the aircraft is on short final, the LSO takes over from the CCA controller and either clears the pilot to land, or waves him off with a verbal command along with an unmistakable cascade of red pyrotechnics. Trying to keep the meatball in the middle with appropriate power corrections while maintaining the center line with ailerons and rudder, we reached the position when the LSO cleared us to land. I held the aircraft attitude to touchdown, and as the wheels slammed onto the deck, a welcoming g-force pinned us forward into our harnesses.

Simultaneously with the stoppage of motion, a lit-up "X" materialized ahead of us. It was time for the abstract video-game of following the dancing wands. The wands were the extension of the invisible Director's arms that, when they cross, mean "brakes-on!"

As soon as a hookman cleared the wires beneath us, the wands uncrossed, and with dynamic back-and-forth movements, urged me to taxi out of the landing area while Dave raised the hook and started the wing-fold sequence on my command. The wands lowered, pointed forward, and extinguished at the same moment that another vertical pair lit up in the distance and beckoned me toward them. It took a considerable amount of power to start taxiing into the wind, which buffeted us with chilling blasts through the open hatches. We rolled through the blackness with the rhythm of the ship, my eyes riveted on the waving wands until we were right on top of them when they crossed into an X.

As I stopped and set the parking brake, we felt the ship altering course out of the wind, which told us that Bill had landed behind us. Though we couldn't see it, our nose was even with the down-curving bow of the ship.

This tightly knit choreography performed on the flight deck day and night requires teamwork and absolute concentration. Unlike the world of general aviation, where the pilot assumes all responsibility for avoiding collision with neighboring objects, on aircraft carriers this shifts to the Directors. These highly trained senior petty officers, buffeted by wind and ocean spray on a frequently heaving deck, become the pilots' eyes. In return, we are expected to match the urgency of their directions by following them expeditiously and implicitly. On disembarking, we often paused to admire the precision with which we'd been parked. It never ceased to amaze us to see that our prop arc had stopped within the horizontal Y of the blades of the neighboring aircraft.

We had enormous respect for these magicians of the flight deck, and it was heartwarming to know that should the pilot taxi his aircraft off the ship while under their control, the responsibility would be assigned to the marshaller.

AFTERMATH

It was my thirty-second night-landing out of a total of a 141, and though I didn't know it, it was slated to be my last.

After removing our poopy-suit tops and hanging our up helmets, we took up our places for the debriefing. As I sat unsure of what to expect as a result of my kiss-and-go with *La Grande Hollandaise*, the squadron ops officer, LCdr. Ben Oxholm, peeked in and beckoned me out of the briefing room. Benny was a swashbuckling epitome of a naval aviator whose exuberance and showy flying amply reflected his fighter-pilot mentality. He looked distinctly low-key as he quietly informed me that I had a rendezvous with Captain Timbrell, the ship's commanding officer, in the captain's cabin at eight in the morning. I raised my eyes quizzically, in response to which Ben could only shrug, but it seemed unlikely that the visit would include breakfast.

A few restless hours later, I reported to our squadron CO, "Doughy" McLean, who led me to the captain's quarters.

"Off cap!" he ordered as we entered.

Dangerously silent, Captain Timbrell paced back and forth on the other side of the table, evidently gearing up for a substantial disquisition. When he finally stopped, he planted his hands on the back of a chair, and after pausing for effect, addressed the enormity of my transgression.

I remember the sight of his whitening knuckles and recall precisely the words he uttered in an icy voice: "Puloski!" He mispronounced my name after searching for it on his desk, "In one thoughtless moment, you have destroyed ten years of goodwill between the Royal Dutch Navy and the RCN!"

I admit this took my breath away.

"Moreover," the captain continued, "I will not have you return to Canada in my ship. You will pack your bags and transfer to the *Algonquin*. That will be all."

I might have been tempted to find this decision somewhat extreme … but who knows? Perhaps the Dutch Admiral had sent a rocket to the *Bonnie*, and this was the result.

"On cap!" prompted Doughy as he propelled me out of the cabin. We walked away in silence, my CO kindly choosing not to add to my discomfort.

When Benny found out, he was boiling mad. In his opinion, which he had no qualms to express, the captain's verdict was outrageously over-the-top. Though

Ben failed in his attempt to have me exonerated, I felt justly proud to have had the anointed master of the hairy low pass himself go to bat in my defense.

The ship entered Rosyth harbor in the forenoon and tied up to seaward of the Firth of Forth Bridge. In keeping with naval custom, to reciprocate for their *rijsttafel*, a reception for the Dutch was scheduled at noon in our wardroom, and they arrived in force. Although my gear was packed, I was still on board because *Algonquin* had not yet entered harbor. Understandably subdued, I kept to one side, surrounded by my friends, who were equally appalled by the captain's reaction.

Everyone was in a jubilant mood; an exchange of gifts followed the post-prandial addresses, during which we presented the Dutch with the customary squadron badges, to which they responded with a pair of wooden clogs with their squadron insignia niftily embossed on the toes. The ceremonies appeared to be over when, unexpectedly, their squadron CO asked: "And who is the pilot who made that pass on our ship yesterday?"

A moment of tense silence followed, after which, not knowing what to expect, I timidly stepped forward. To my total surprise, I received a chorus of bravos, a barrage of back-slapping, and all at once everyone seemed to want to shake my hand. Their squadron CO then presented me with a special gift: a framed photo of the *Karel Doorman*, appropriately a close-up, with the following dedication inscribed on the back: "With the compliments of Commander Air and squadrons H. Neth. M.S. *Karel Doorman*, Oct. 24th, 1963."

Were these Dutchmen unaware of the damage I had inflicted on our Navies' mutual good will?

I nervously sought a sign of reprieve from Doughy and Captain Timbrell, who were present throughout, but eye contact proved elusive. Before long, when the Dutch discovered that I was being flung off the ship, their squadron CO attempted to intervene on my behalf, but his entreaties, like Benny's, also fell on deaf ears.

My pass, I was later told, was a total surprise. A watch of four stood on the bridge, including the ship's captain, who was relaxing in his chair with his jacket off. Alerted by the roar, they were convinced a berserk Tracker pilot was about to enter the premises.

Everyone hit the deck except the CO, whose suspenders became entangled with an armrest. Their first reaction was to exclaim: "Canadian Bastard!" But when they cooled down, they had to acknowledge it was a classic bounce.

Apparently, the accusation of the loss of goodwill did not originate with the Dutch.

Later that day, clutching my luggage, golf clubs, and flight gear, I reported on board *Algonquin*. I was intimately familiar with this ship, because I had served seven months in her as a midshipman in 1956. Though none of her previous complement was on board, the officers graciously accepted me in their wardroom.

The ship spent seven days in harbor. I played golf with Benny and Charlie, and in Ben's company brazenly stole a flag in broad daylight off HMS *Tiger*. Everything was always fair game.

Taking advantage of having no duties to perform, I spent my time ashore in agreeable company and only showed up on board in time for the passage to Brighton, where we stayed another week. I moved to London, saw several plays, including two performances of *Beyond the Fringe*, and came back to the ship only once—to collect an advance on pay.

We returned to Halifax after a leisurely passage, which included a four- day stopover in the Azores.

A few days after docking, as a gesture of gratitude for the hospitality shown me by my erstwhile hosts, I held a reception on board. It came to a premature halt around 1:30 in the afternoon when we received the news. It was November 22, 1963: President Kennedy had just been shot.

Numerous versions of the *Karel Doorman* sortie had been circulating over the years, including one which had me cashiered out of the Navy. In fact, I didn't leave until July 1964, exclusively of my own volition, but that will be the subject of the next section of this memoir.

The decision to leave the Navy eventually proved to suit my interests well, but I am convinced that Captain Timbrell weighed the benefit entirely in favor of the Service.

1964, LIMBO: A TIME FOR INTROSPECTION

Ben Oxholm was still livid.

"Don't let it grind you down, George," he counseled. "Remember that you were flung off the ship by a goddamned fish-head (vernacular for a 'non-pilot'). No captain with wings would ever have done such a thing. Neither Commander Air nor the squadron CO was contemplating any action. Believe me … I know."

Soothing words coming from Ben, our most colorful and undoctrinaire officer, who would reach the rank of brigadier general in the post-Navy armed forces, but they were hardly sufficient to calm my troubled mind.

This event, which a scant few years earlier would have been greeted with caps thrown into the air to salute Navy-pilot bravado, had suddenly become taboo, and I instinctively knew that it was to be a permanent blot on my record. The Navy in which I had grown up, which not only tolerated but expected acts of derring-do, appeared to be undergoing some sphincter-tightening readjustments, and I wondered if it heralded the start of a distastefully calcifying trend.

In keeping with our appointment, Charlie and I reported to VU32 mid-November, where I spent the next six months training naval air-crewmen. That this employment lacked the glamor of my previous appointment was no understatement, even though occasionally it offered some unexpected variety.

One such event occurred when the CO unkindly altered my meticulously laid plans to take a Tracker to New York for a weekend with an assignment to deliver something to Goose Bay, Labrador. My pleas that this meant scrubbing an important date fell on unreceptive ears, and I soon found myself in an ice-locked land, strangled in the sullen grip of winter, where the thermometer registered -40 degrees on both measures of the scale.

Ground control cleared me to the doors of a hangar that opened briefly to let me taxi inside. The moment I shut down, the ground crew installed gas-driven heaters called Herman Nelsons under the engines to prevent the oil from freezing.

As it turned out, the warmth of this welcome was not limited to the hangars. Still in a sour mood from having to change my plans, I was waiting to be served at the wardroom bar when I felt a tap on my shoulder.

"May I buy you a drink?" said a brightly smiling face with inviting eyes.

Taking my stunned silence as a *yes* for an answer, the cheerful lady soon disclosed the reason for this unexpected role-reversal, which stemmed from the surfeit of unaccompanied nurses and teachers on the base.

Entirely sensible, I agreed, and on the following visit to Goose Bay, for which I should stress I happily volunteered, Bob Edey and I discovered that the welcome was even more expansive on the vastly larger US Strategic Air Command side of this complex. It was exemplified by the impressive Officers' Club, where the Glenn Miller Band came to play on the day of our arrival.

These mini-adventures were all very pleasant on the surface, but the monotony of the job and the absence of meaningful prospects gave rise to a gnawing sense of ennui, which shadowed me each passing day.

Fueled by the career-dampening circumstances of my departure from the ship, and the anti-climax of post-aircraft-carrier operations, I spent many a restless night reviewing my future, and my past.

Plawski Family Histories: A Challenge to Credulity

My reveries flitted back to long before 1948, the year when our family arrived at Pier 21 in Halifax as political refugees to start life from scratch in a new country.

It had been quite a saga.

My parents readily succeeded in igniting my interest in the history of the Plawski family because its passage never stopped at flirting with implausibility; instead, it coupled with it lustily, spawning results that are as hard to believe as they are fascinating to recall.

To offer an example, I invite you to travel with me in time to the middle of the nineteenth century to my paternal great-grandfather's country estate south of Warsaw, where preparations are in progress for tomorrow's annual hunt, which will culminate in a tragic accident. Among the guests arriving in sleighs and horse-drawn carriages is my great progenitor's best friend, Count Poroszyn, who is accompanied by his young and only son.

To stage this event, local farmers will be engaged as beaters. They will assemble in file at the perimeter of the property before daylight, while the hunters, along with their guns and their loaders, will be dropped off by sleigh to form a line across the middle of the estate.

Though only shotguns are used, because the quarry is anything that gallops, runs, hops, shimmies, crawls, or flies, the loaders' job is to have the correct load ready in the guns. Once the game has been driven past the hunters, lunch will be served to everyone in the field, which will give time for the beaters to form on the opposite perimeter in preparation to herd the surviving animals back through the hunters' line. At the end of the hunt, the farmers will amass the spoils of the affair, which might consist of scores of deer and wild boars and a countless number of hare, partridge and pheasants, and likely a wolf or two.

Traditionally, guests are only permitted to take home a token brace of pheasant, while the beaters share the entire kill as a reward for their effort, and for promising to refrain from poaching for the rest of the year.

The social part of the event is scheduled for after the hunt, when following a sumptuous dinner, the formally attired guests repair to the ballroom for recitals and dancing.

The following morning, the first snow had already carpeted the land when the distant sound of the trumpet announced the start of the hunt. Soon the air was filled with the beaters' calls, and furious fusillades of fire began exploding from the shooters' redoubts. Once the game had passed and the shooting stopped, all ears tuned into the silence for the eagerly awaited sound of the bell from an approaching horse-drawn sleigh. This tantalizing tinkle announced the arrival of the welcome-wagon, which carried two barrels: one to impregnate the countryside with a mouth-watering bouquet of steaming *Bigos*, while the other was full of energy-restoring vodka. (*Bigos* is a dense mixture of cabbage and sauerkraut slow-cooked with chunks of smoked bacon, meats, and sausages, seasoned with pepper and juniper berries.) According to my father, had Pavlov participated in such a hunt, he wouldn't have had to use dogs for proof of his theory of the conditioned response.

He was convinced that, following several hours of such frenetic activity, the sound of those ardently anticipated chimes was capable of causing a corpse to salivate.

After the beaters assembled at the other perimeter and finished their lunch, the trumpet once again announced the revival of the hunt.

No one knows how in the course of the action the seven-year ol Poroszyn boy blundered ahead of the beaters into my grandfather's line of fire.

Unnoticed in the heat of the barrage, the lad was struck by a stray slug and fell dead in the snow.

Improbably, this accident did not alienate the two friends, who devised a Solomonic solution. Since there were six boys in the Plawski clan, the fathers agreed to appoint Alexander, the boy closest to the slain child in age, to be brought up by the Count in the place of his son. Alexander was the boy destined to be my grandfather.

For reasons lost to time, the Poroszyn family moved to the south of France, where Alexander finished his schooling and obtained a law degree. Intending to practice in Provence, he wrote to his father in Poland requesting some necessary documentation. When the package arrived, it came accompanied by a sobering attachment from the Russian-appointed Governor of Warsaw, which included a warning that if Alexander chose to remain in France, he would lose all rights of visitation as well as of inheritance.

(From the latter part of the eighteenth century, Poland had been in the throes of partition by Prussia, Austria-Hungary, and Russia. The nation was thus reduced to a geographical expression for 123 years until its restoration to statehood in 1918. Warsaw was in the sphere controlled by the Russians.)

Returning to Poland, however, included the disagreeable prospect of having to spend five years as a conscript in the Russian army. To winnow the best deal out of this awkward mess, Alexander inquired if he could enlist in the cavalry. This was approved, and after two years of training in Odessa, where he learned Russian, he received his commission along with a posting as garrison Commander on the east coast of the Black Sea in the friendly resort town of Kutais.

Some thirty years before the previously described accident, two friends in Alsace-Lorraine, on the occasion of their double wedding, made a wager. The prize was to be awarded many years in the future to the husband who sired the most offspring. [The wives, it seems, were mere onlookers of the contest.] When the sport terminated, either because of his wife's exhaustion or his loss of vigor, the father of twenty-two had to settle for the silver medal.

This contestant, the loser by two, was the father of my grandmother, Eliza.

Eliza was an exceptionally gifted girl who was born in 1872 into a family of siblings who would eventually count eighteen girls and four boys. When Eliza was seventeen, soon after she had been accepted into the top class of the Conservatory of Music in Strasbourg, her parents surprised her with an unexpected announcement: they had selected for her a husband. This prospect horrified the precocious girl, who fled from home. In her determination to build as much distance as possible from her intended fate, she teamed up with a girlfriend who happened to be traveling to visit her engineer-father working in Russia. It's not hard to divine from the foregoing that the father lived in Kutais.

To earn a living, Eliza taught French in the homes of the local intelligentsia, where she soon met, fell in love with, and married Rotmistr Alexander Plawski.

The first issue of this marriage was my father, Józef Eugeniusz, whose mother presented him to the world in Novorossiysk in 1895. Since my grandfather was no friend of the Russians, he taught his son to think of himself as Polish. Unfortunately, the boy's assertion of his nationality blossomed at a most inopportune time during an inspection of his father's squadron by a Tsarist cavalry general. With the formalities complete and following a farewell supper, the general hoisted the five-year-old onto his knee and murmured something complimentary about the boy growing up to be a fine little Russian.

"I'm not Russian; I'm Polish," corrected the youngster, which exerted a distinctly chilling effect on the visiting dignitary. The general rose, nodded to his staff, and rode away into the night.

The punitive new posting arrived within a month. My grandfather was being transferred to take command of a garrison at the eastern extremity of Siberia on the Russia-Manchuria border, somewhere between Harbin and Vladivostok.

The journey, accomplished in the winter of 1901 along the yet-unfinished Trans-Siberian railroad, took thirty-two days. It included portages on sledges and a crossing of Lake Baikal along a railway track laid across the ice.

My father remembered this segment for the fissures that, accompanied by thunderous sounds, sped away from the train along the ice like lightning, which terrified the passengers in spite of having been assured that, to date, only a single locomotive on a trial run the previous year had broken through the ice.

When they finally arrived at their destination, the family discovered a land of unbelievable fecundity stocked to the brim with fish, fowl, and game.

My grandfather, General Aleksander Pławski.

My grandmother, Elżbieta Feldman, and her son, Eugene, in the uniform of the St. Petersburg Naval Academy.

The Maternal Side of the Family

During this era, my future maternal family, whose surname was Dyck, lived in Grochów on the eastern periphery of Warsaw in what had been their ancestral home from the early part of the nineteenth century. It was a sizable estate where the family operated a brewery. Barns and stables housed horses and cattle, while orchards and gardens thrived between the brewery and the homestead. There was separate housing for the staff, while my favorite retreat, a reed-encircled and frog-infested pond, nestled in a curve of the tree-lined road leading to the estate.

I cannot help speculating that when my grandfather, Stanisław Nowaczynski, presented himself as a suitor to Helena Dyck, he was thoroughly vetted not only as a prospective groom but as a future director of the business.

Evidently, he was found suitable on both counts, because the couple took over the house in the 1890s, where they started a family.

My mother, Maria, was born in 1901, and along with her older brother, Tadeusz, and younger sister, Irena, grew up in these enviable surroundings, enjoying horseback riding and country living until the outbreak of WWI.

Napoleon may have postulated that an army marches on its stomach, but the Russians knew that for troops to fight, their need for alcohol exceeded all other requirements. Consequently, they permitted the brewing business to continue, from which the family prospered and dutifully deposited their savings in a Russian bank, the only such institution available in Warsaw.

When the Russian armies began to unravel under German assault in 1915, the banks withdrew their Polish investments for safekeeping deep into Russia with such thoroughness that they remain secreted there to this day.

The Germans had no trouble entering Warsaw, but on discovering a brewery, they made one of the many tactical blunders that eventually lost them both wars—they dismantled the brewery's copper and brass installations, and by shipping them home for weapons production, deprived my grandparents of their livelihood, and their soldiers of a vital fighting commodity.

Though the brewery was destroyed, the home survived, and when my parents married in 1923, they moved into the ample house and were still living there in 1939 when the Germans rekindled their appetite for Polish territory and once more invaded the country.

A Pilot in the Tsarist Navy

My father remembered his early years in the garrison town in Manchuria commanded by his father as idyllic. Since there was no school in the area, my grandfather hired a tutor, who lived with the family until my father was ten. Unlimited hunting, fishing, and schooling at home served my father well. When eventually his parents enrolled him in a cadet school in Khabarovsk, his grades permitted him to be accepted to the naval academy in St Petersburg. The train journey westward was now a mere twenty-two days, and each of the four subsequent crossings of the continent shortened the trip by a day. His graduation in 1914, at the age of nineteen, vaulted him neatly into the outbreak of WWI.

His first appointment as a mine-and-torpedo officer in a destroyer in the Black Sea heralded the start of a successful naval career, which was almost extinguished in December when he was severely wounded in an artillery exchange with the Turkish cruiser *Mecidiye*.

After four months in the hospital, he returned to the fleet, where for the next eighteen months he took part in the diverse business of destroyer warfare. This included mine laying, invasive raids of the Turkish coast, the sinking of dozens of freighters, and gun-battles with the German cruisers *Goeben* and *Breslau*.

All this excitement was insufficient to satisfy his hunger for adventure, because as he later recalled, "entirely on a whim, in September of 1916, I decided to push all of it aside and requested a transfer to Naval Aviation." His request was accepted. When he reported for flight training near St. Petersburg, on seeing his naval uniform, the officer in charge made a comment that remained wedged in his memory: "This foolish pastime should only be taken up by expendables like the infantry or cavalry, but if you insist on killing yourself, be my guest; I'm just returning from a funeral."

Training in sea-planes in re-constructed wrecks or rejects from the front proceeded at a snails' pace. At the approach of winter, the entire school—workshops, airplanes, and staff—were transported by train to the ice-free waters of the Black Sea.

One of his early assignments was to fly a reconnaissance flight over the Turkish coast, which he described as follows:

Sometime around the start of March, 1917, I was embarked in a sea-plane tender carrying an airplane, which was lowered to the water with a crane. A downward-pointing camera equipped with a timer hung under the fuselage, which after being started, automatically tripped the shutter at pre-arranged intervals.

I was ordered to fly at two thousand meters and to start the photo sequence over a specific geographic location. On arrival, I decided that though I risked much more accurate anti-aircraft fire, I could get better pictures from a lower altitude. Accordingly, I descended to a thousand meters, started the camera, and brazened it out in the teeth of the opposition without sustaining a hit.

I was very pleased with myself when I returned to the ship and delivered the results.

As soon as the film was exposed, I was called to report to the CO. Expecting a commendation, I was surprised to be met by particularly hostile expressions from the commander and his staff.

"What was the altitude at which you were you ordered to fly?"

"Two thousand meters, Sir."

"And from what altitude did you take these pictures?"

"One thousand meters, Sir; I thought I could get better resolution if I ..."

"Come over here and have a look."

I approached the table and saw the strip of photos. They didn't seem to join up.

"The interval was calculated to provide an overlap from two thousand meters. From a thousand, you served up nothing but a series of gaps!"

I was marched back to the airplane and had to repeat the entire exercise.

The Germans were now better prepared, because a Taube attacked me right at the end of my mission. With luck,

I managed to escape, but on approaching our fleet, I was almost shot down by our own artillery.

At the onset of the October Revolution in 1917, Eugene was in Odessa. He was preparing to fly a mission when, on learning that his airplane was unserviceable, he signed out the executive officer's machine. As he taxied out, he felt that the aileron controls were unresponsive. Returning to the dock, he discovered that the cause was wooden wedges deliberately driven into the rigging.

"What is the meaning of this?" he enquired of the chief mechanic.

"Sorry, Sir," the man nonchalantly replied, "we didn't know you'd be flying this airplane. We were trying to kill the executive officer."

Though the undeniable sincerity of the remark was warmly reassuring, this complication of an already sufficiently dangerous occupation convinced him to abandon aviation and return to the fleet. His first posting was as the executive officer of a destroyer. Russia was now passing through the apogee of the social experiment fueled by decades of hatred of the Tsars. Like all revolutions, it was characterized by anti-authoritarianism, lawlessness, and simple murderous lust, and presently stood on the brink of the soon-to-be-dashed dream of rule by the proletariat.

Anarchy and the settling of scores readily spilled over into the Navy. Ships were now run by revolutionary committees, which elected their officers who no longer merited a salute. When elections were held in his ship, the result was the dismissal of the captain and the appointment of my father to take his place. He was twenty-two years old.

After barely escaping the revolutionary chaos with his life, when the war ended in 1918, Eugene made his way to newly independent Poland, where he enrolled in the just-forming Polish Navy. This was a new experience for the recently liberated nation, and taking an active part in the development of its Navy became my father's full-time occupation.

In 1920, he met Maria Nowaczynska, daughter of a respectable landowning family with a healthy suspicion of sailors. It required three years to melt the family's reluctance before they consented to the wedding. The ceremony in a church in Warsaw was punctuated by a last-minute warning, sounded either by a well-meaning friend or a disappointed suitor, who shouted at the bride as she was being escorted up the aisle: "Maryla! Come back to your senses while it's not too late. Have you no shame marrying a sailor?"

She resisted the advice, and in 1924 the union produced their first son, Witold.

Meanwhile, the sailor was contributing significantly to the expansion of the burgeoning Navy as a training officer and captain of a succession of gunboats.

From Surface Ships to Submarines

In 1925, the Polish Navy decided to expand its fleet into unexplored territory. Lessons learned from the history of naval warfare during the First World War, along with Poland's unfortunate location between the two troublemakers of Europe, convinced naval headquarters to strengthen its force with a squadron of submarines. Since these were to be purpose-built in France, it was necessary to appoint a suitable commander. Choosing my father for the job was a stroke of genius. His leadership skills, experience, cheerful personality, and fluency in French made him a perfect candidate.

The first stage of this appointment involved ten months of preparatory courses at the *École de Navigation Sous-Marine* in Toulon. After agonizing about what to do with ten-month-old Witold, the newlyweds reluctantly agreed to leave him in the care of his grandmother, and laden with presents bestowed by well-wishers, departed by train for France.

If I were given a chance to time-travel to a place and era of my choosing, Paris in 1925 would be the bullseye of my list. Nowhere did people swing with greater abandon than in the city of light between the horrors of WWI and the onset of the depression.

Paris was the center of the universe, the cradle of art and literature, and everybody knew it. Albeit briefly, my parents entered this exuberant atmosphere and saw the raves of the era: Maurice Chevalier and banana-clad Josephine Baker at the Folies Bergère.

On return to Gdynia, my father's task was to supervise the choice and the schooling of prospective submariners. In 1928, the cream of the crop arrived in France for two years of training. Since lectures and manuals were in a foreign language, this considerably complicated the syllabus. With my father's guidance, this hand-picked crew surprised the French instructors by topping their classes, and after manning their boat in Cherbourg, Lieutenant-Commander Plawski proudly delivered the first submarine, ORP *Żbik*, and its finely tuned crew to Gdynia.**

Progressively, the submarine fleet rose to four, while in 1934, the Plawski family also expanded with my birth on July 16.

---

* ORP stands for Okręt Rzeczpospolitej Polskiej, which means "Ship of the Republic of Poland." Żbik means "wildcat."

In 1936, with the rank of commander, my father became the Chief of Submarine Warfare, a position he held until the outbreak of the war. Being remembered as the Father of the Polish Submarine Service was a distinction my father cherished to the end of his days.

My father, Mother on his right, takes command of the submarine ŻBIK.

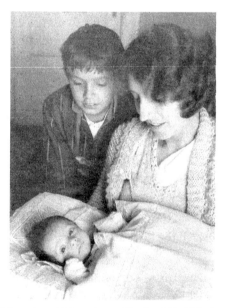

Hello, universe! My mother and brother, Witold, look on.

The German Invasion of Poland

On September 1, 1939, emboldened by British appeasement and the lack of opposition to his aggressive ventures in Alsace Lorraine and Czechoslovakia, Hitler fudged his promise that these were to have been his last ambitions in Europe and invaded Poland. The outbreak of the war found my father on a military mission in France, which prevented his return to Poland and would separate us until the end of the war.

As the German army approached and the daily bombings of Warsaw became intolerable, my mother decided to distance us from the fray. Accordingly, she loaded our 1936 English Ford with as much as could be stuffed into and tied or propped up on its body, and with five-year-old me, my fifteen-year-old brother, Witold, and our faithful German au-pair girl, Fraulein Lily, my mother joined the stream of like-minded refugees heading for the presumed relative safety of the east.

I believe that we spent a week in Mińsk Mazowiecki sheltered by friends, after which I caught a nasty case of tonsillitis, which forced us to hole up in a farmer's house while the car remained cached in a barn under a mountain of hay.

It was then that the chummy arrangement signed in great secrecy by Hitler and Stalin a week before the German invasion, which became known as the Molotov-Ribbentrop Pact, came into play. The terms of this thieves' covenant, signed with scout's honor, guaranteed neutrality between the parties, delineated their spheres of interest, and set out the rules for a joint invasion of Poland.

After making sure that the Polish armed forces were fully involved with the Germans in the west, the Russians executed their classic stab-in-the-back on September 17. This left our family squeezed in a pocket between two fronts.

From a few tattered scraps of memory, I can dredge up the sights and sounds of war: the haunting vision of a burning village at night (Stojadła?), wounded horses struggling in the tangled wreckage of a wagon in a ditch, and the look of abject terror on a young man's waxen face as he was forcibly escorted to some unpleasant fate—guilty, we were told, of espionage. On several occasions we watched open mouthed as an aerial ballet of dogfights unfolded in the autumn sky. It would be some time before we learned the unlikely results of these confrontations, which revealed that the Polish pilots flying ancient machines shot down more of the enemy's planes than their own losses, a feat which the survivors of these dogfights would repeat during the Battle of Britain in spades.

Terrified of the hated Russians and mindful of the German component of our foursome, my mother reluctantly joined the straggling exodus back toward Warsaw. With Witold walking beside the car after having relinquished his seat to a wounded soldier, we reached Grochów two days later.

Warsaw had capitulated and was already in German hands when we finally rolled up to our driveway, and as we rounded the bulrushes which fronted my treasured pond, we caught sight of three chimneys sprouting out of the still-smoking rubble, which was all that was left of our home. The remaining staff, which consisted of the gardener, cook, groundskeeper and housekeepers, who along with their families lived in their own houses on the property, met us on arrival. Presently, they related the story.

A group of Wehrmacht soldiers requisitioned the house, and on discovering my father's uniforms, ever alert to a propaganda coup, decided to profit from the opportunity. Evidence that Hitler's foremost propagandist, Leni Riefenstahl, was involved is inconclusive; nevertheless, an army camera crew arrived a few days later and installed itself for a shoot. To demonstrate to the German public how eagerly Polish workers steal from the owners in their absence, the locals were ordered to evacuate the belongings of the house, which the Germans filmed from all angles with Teutonic thoroughness.

Once the house was empty, the staff were commanded to set the building on fire—an order with which, to forestall the shoot from taking on a more literal character, they were obliged to comply. After the house collapsed, the camera crew stowed their gear and departed.

We were thus left in the unenviable position of having a stableful of furniture but no home in which to put it. As we rummaged through the ruins, my grief-stricken mother occasionally burst into tears on finding a remnant of something of sentimental value.

My turn to cry came as soon as I saw that crushed mass of blue metal under a layer of debris, which I instantly recognized as the pedal-car my father had bought for me in France. It had been my most prized possession, the symbol of my identity, and the sight of its mangled remains brought this war down to a personal level.

My mother had more pressing problems on her mind, like how to deal with homelessness in the middle of a still-roiling war. The staff kindly cleared one room for the four of us in their house, but soon Fraulein Lily's sudden and mysterious departure served to relieve our congestion.

With the car safely hidden in the stables, we laid low, awaiting developments. The first of these was the reappearance of a most elegantly accoutered, coiffed, and perfumed Fraulein Lily, whose revival of her national roots was evidenced by her arrival in a chauffeur-driven German staff-car in the company of a highly presentable young officer. With excessive politeness, they inquired about our health, commiserated about the regrettable loss of the house, and presented me with a box of chocolates. By the way, they wondered, might it be possible to borrow the car?

When we brushed the car clear of the covering straw, the officer took the wheel, and with a smart "Heil Hitler," the happy couple piloted our precious *Fordzik* to its indentured fate, but not before Witold grabbed the chocolate box and threw it into the back seat.

Sometime in October, after the fighting subsided, my mother rented a horse-drawn wagon, which our hosts helped to load with our unburned furniture. Walking next to this teetering pyramid, we headed for Milanówek, a small settlement on the southern periphery of Warsaw, where we temporarily moved into a house owned by an acquaintance.

My maternal grandmother, Helena, eventually joined us, along with the housekeeper, Helenka, who wouldn't hear of being left behind and insisted on staying with us without pay. I remember that she walked with a conspicuous limp and that her jaw was characterized by a pronounced underbite, but I loved her dearly and she faithfully remained with us as a valued part of the family.

In the winter of 1940, my mother rented a first-floor apartment in a house, where we lived until the end of the war.

My schooling was primarily conducted at home by my mother, whereas Witold occasionally profited from private tutoring in teachers' houses. He was a talented artist and a voracious reader, fluent in French. In spite of a lack of formal schooling, after two months of self-study he aced his high school exams.

We rarely saw him in the last three years of his life, much of which he spent in the woods with the underground army, creating maximum mayhem for the enemy.

In May of 1944, with the aim of escaping to neutral Sweden, he and a group of his fellow fighters volunteered to be transported to a German work-camp in Norway. Their hasty escape was poorly executed. Instead of a handful, sixteen men broke out of the camp, and after walking through deep snow all night, they stopped to get their bearings. While the group waited, Witold and a companion made their way toward a settlement to get information and stumbled across a German patrol. Eager to catch the remainder of the escapees, the Germans executed the boys with a shot to the back of the head, then followed their tracks and killed six more of the group.

My mother never recovered from this blow, which in addition to the family tragedy, deprived the world of an exceptional artistic talent.

Witold was barely twenty years old.

After the war, the two German soldiers responsible for the executions were tried for their crime in a Polish court and sentenced to hang. Though this verdict was just, their death, apart from a fleeting sense of vindication, added nothing to atone for the atrocity of the war itself; it merely deepened the tragedy by depriving two young families of their fathers.

What's left of our house in Warsaw, 1939.

Saved from the fire: my grandmother, Elżbieta, and brother, Witold.

Unexpected Visit to Norway

In the winter of 1995, my wife Rita was startled by a call from the RCMP. After assuring her that her husband's liberty was not in jeopardy, the caller explained that someone from Norway by name of Björn Bratbak was urgently attempting to contact me, and they provided the gentleman's phone number. When I made the call, I discovered an amateur historian with a specific interest in Polish affairs.

Mr Bratbak had traced the escape of my brother's group and invited me to Norway for the fiftieth celebration of the end of WWII, which was to include a visit to the place of my brother's execution. I am eternally indebted to him for this remarkable experience.

I flew to Oslo in May, where Björn introduced me to Edward Śledź, a member of Witold's underground cell and a survivor of the shooting. Edward chose to remain in Norway after the war and was a Norwegian citizen.

Several days later, I boarded a ferry for an all-day-and-night trip through the Lofoten Islands until I reached the village of Sörfold, which was near where Witold was killed. Björn and Edward met me on the dock, and it was there that I began to understand the depth of Björn's research. He drove us to a farm whose proprietor, Björn discovered, was a five-year-old boy at the time of the tragedy.

The farmer remembered precisely where, on German orders, Russian prisoners dug the graves to bury my brother and his companion. It was at the base of the hill where the Germans caught the rest of the group. As I looked around the sparsely wooded area, my gaze froze at the sight of two trees growing like twins out of the same stump. It was a chilling facsimile of a sketch my brother had drawn, which depicted twin pine trees next to a wooden cross topped with a helmet. Witold's name was on the cross-piece. I spent some quiet time standing before the two trees, mesmerized by this coincidence.

The following day, the citizens of Sörfold organized a memorial to the foreigners fallen on their land. An honor guard of the local militia performed a ceremony, accompanied by a troupe of scouts who delivered a touching rendition of the Polish national anthem. The corridors of the school, as well as those of the town hall, were hung with the students' imagined recreations of the war-time events. They were the result of a school-wide assignment of the previous week.

That afternoon we all gathered in the school auditorium. The place was filled with the villagers and their children, for whom the mayor had declared a holiday. Edward and I were the guests of honor. He delivered an oration in Norwegian, which I followed in English. It appeared to be widely understood, and there wasn't a dry eye in the house.

The mayor presented me with a gift of an engraved glass flower vase bearing the village's name, for which I resolved to find a fitting reward.

Björn and I then drove to Narvik, where my brother's disinterred remains rest under a monument erected in memory of Polish soldiers and sailors who died in Norway during the early part of the war. Among these are the bodies of those who perished during the sinking of the Polish destroyer, *Grom*, which was bombed in the Narvik fjord in 1940. Coincidentally, many of the surviving members of that ship's crew would soon serve in the *Piorun* under my father's command.

While we were in Narvik, I became involved in an event that could be classed as hilarious if it wasn't for its embarrassing component. To celebrate the fiftieth anniversary of the end of the war in Europe, the Norwegian prime minister was to visit the city.

The Town Hall square where the dignitaries were to arrive was jammed with spectators, and though we weren't sure exactly where the prime minister would alight, Björn suggested that I station myself with my camera near the hotel while he staked out a position somewhere else.

By luck, when the motorcade arrived, the limousine carrying the prime minister stopped directly in front of me. Two persons occupied the back seat. The one closest to me was a woman in a red dress, while the other, appropriately decorated with garlands of badges of honor, sat on the opposite side.

While the chauffeur and an attendant opened the doors, it was maddening to find myself so close to my target, which obstinately remained hidden either by the car, or that woman who almost knocked the camera out of my hand. No matter how I tried to get around her, with that red dress constantly in my face, I only managed to get a picture of the top of the gentleman's head.

After the pair disappeared in the crowd, I found Björn.

"Were you ever lucky, George! You couldn't have been in a more ideal place."

"I would have been if it wasn't for that woman in the red dress."

His silence said everything.

I don't know when I've been so utterly and deservedly embarrassed. The bemedaled man whose head I made such a heroic effort to capture after Prime Minister Gro Harlem Bruntland and her red dress stepped out of the way, was the mayor of Narvik.

In keeping with my resolution, on returning home to Vancouver, I tore out the page from Witold's sketchbook with the picture of the cross next to the twin trees. Though it broke my heart to part with it, after immortalising the drawing with my camera, I sent it to the mayor of Sörfold, along with my expressions of gratitude for the town's sincere and poignant tribute.

Premonition. Witold inscribed his name on the cross-piece.

From my brother's sketch book.

My Father's Service in WWII

Stranded in Paris and unable to return to Poland, my father made his way to England, where once again he became instrumental in the creation of a new Polish Navy, this time in exile.

Desperate for news of his family, it was some time before he learned that we'd survived the invasion but that the Germans deliberately burned our house.

In 1940, the Royal Navy turned a brand new "N" class destroyer over to the Polish Navy. Following the name change from HMS *Nerissa* to ORP *Piorun*, which in Polish means *Thunderbolt*, my father was appointed as its commanding officer. Over the next year and a half, *Piorun* engaged in endless convoy duties and several submarine attacks, but the most significant action occurred in May 1941 during the hunt and sinking of the German battleship *Bismarck*.

In the early hours of May 24, the *Bismarck*, in company with the cruiser *Prinz Eugen*, in the course of a gun battle west of Iceland, sank HMS *Hood*, the pride of the British fleet, and damaged the new battleship, HMS *Prince of Wales*. To avenge this defeat, the Brits mobilized all available forces to intercept the *Bismarck* before she could reach the protection of the Luftwaffe and find sanctuary in the port of Brest. The *Piorun* became a part of this sea-borne posse when the destroyer squadron of which it was a part was released from convoy duty and ordered to close the fleeing ship. On the violently stormy night of May 25, *Piorun* acquired visual contact with a large ship.

Because the heavy cruiser HMS *Sheffield* was somewhere in the vicinity, and because this ship's nerves were already frayed by an earlier attack by our Swordfish torpedo bombers which mistook it for the *Bismarck*, my father felt it prudent to send a recognition signal. The identity of the ship was unequivocally established when the reply arrived in the form of a salvo. For the next hour, my father maneuvered desperately while drawing the battleship's fire in the hope of presenting the enemy to the other destroyers for a torpedo attack. Though the *Piorun* never had a chance to launch its torpedoes, goaded by the crew to at least fire the guns, my father agreed to this symbolic act, and for reasons of morale, ordered, "Three salvos for the glory of Poland!"

Eighteen 4.5-inch shells thundered impudently into the night, but unfortunately, as daylight later revealed, this cheeky gesture failed to sink his adversary, which had to be dispatched by a concentration of RN capital ships.

Incidentally, at the time of the *Piorun's* engagement, no one knew that the previous evening's torpedo attack by Swordfish aircraft from the carrier *Ark Royal* succeeded in jamming the *Bismarck's* rudders, but as my father unequivocally discovered, her armament was still very much intact.

Under my father's command, the *Piorun* continued escort duties, which included a convoy to Malta and a visit to Halifax. In 1943, he was sent to Stockholm as the Polish naval attaché, following which he commanded the cruiser *Dragon*, and from 1945 until the disbandment of the Polish Navy in 1947, he served as its chief of staff.

Destroyer captain.

From the Frying Pan ...

The "liberation" of Poland from Nazi occupation occurred in our area in January 1945. The usually well-organized German armies had been moving steadily westward for weeks, but as the front came closer, their retreat became progressively chaotic. Abandoned vehicles, canons, ammunition carts, and anything that encumbered their flight marked their passage, leaving the countryside littered with the detritus of a defeated army. As the last wounded and mostly weapon-less stragglers sleep-walked past our houses, their pathetic sight moved some people to offer them warm water to drink or something to eat.

These were the derelicts that the Russian tanks caught that night on the outskirts of our village. After an exchange of gunfire, which we heard from the security of our basement, the shooting faded to the west. In the morning, emotions overwhelmed us as we cheered the sight of passing Russian tanks. Each carried clusters of winter-clad soldiery who feebly returned our expressions of jubilation.

This joy would soon subside, because everyone knew that Poland's occupation by an inimical foreign power was to continue, though administered in another language and clad in different uniforms.

That afternoon, in spite of our mothers' vigorous protest, my pal and I rushed out to inspect the battlefield where several German corpses lay in the tank-furrowed snow. We could see how one of the tanks deliberately adjusted its aim to drive over the head of a wounded soldier, which left a sprawling red stain of crushed helmet and bone. By the time we arrived, the bodies were already bereft of boots and wearable apparel, and gracing the entrance to the tram station lay the carcasses of two horses surgically reduced to skeletons.

1946, My "Great Escape" to Freedom

When the fighting finally ceased, various international charity organizations such as the United Nations Relief and Rehabilitation Administration (UNRRA) and the Red Cross established footholds in the ruins of Warsaw. Luckily, my mother managed to find a job with the Polish Red Cross, which though it provided essential employment, committed her to a torturous, daily, hour-long commute on the jam-packed tram to the city.

The oppressive Communist regime murderously enforced by Russia gave rise to two opposing forces: the population's wishing to escape it, and the authorities' obsessive need to prevent this from happening. As my mother contemplated this dilemma, she knew that even without a wall, Poland remained hermetically sealed against such attempts, which in addition to the perilous consequences of failure was incrementally complicated by the burden of a preteen son.

The hopelessness of this situation preyed on her mind until an entirely unexpected possibility unfolded on her desk. The Danish Red Cross unveiled an offer to accept two hundred Polish boys for two months of rest and recreation in a camp in Jutland. Though my mother immediately forwarded my application, my chances were scant, because all the Communist functionaries insisted on pushing the names of their sons to the top of the list.

The Polish Red Cross rose to the occasion. In great secrecy, the Poles tipped the Danes off; the list of names that reached the Danish medical staff whose job it was to examine and select the candidates came with agreed upon markings identifying the undesirables. When the Danes released their choices, it was too late for the outraged Communist families to register their appeals.

I was one of the lucky ones chosen.

With my mother, who was delegated as one of the chaperones, we boarded a train in Warsaw. Six hours later, a pathetic looking group with distended bellies signifying malnutrition arrived in Gdynia, the town of my birth. Choosing a moment when she wouldn't be seen, my mother approached one of our Danish guardians, and slipping him a letter with the details of her husband's whereabouts in London, she begged him to make contact.

It would be some time before I matured enough to recognize the enormity of my mother's sacrifice. Still in the throes of mourning the loss of her older son, my mother was waving goodbye to her remaining child with no prospect of ever seeing him again. I remain haunted by the thought that I may never have given her enough credit for this selfless and loving act.

Shortly after arriving in Copenhagen, a voyage during which I never stopped retching, I was surprised to be called out by name. A Red Cross representative handed me a phone, one end of which became alive with the unmistakable voice of my father.

Following an emotional exchange, carefully avoiding any hint that he may be coming to steal me away from the camp, he said that he would come for a visit. Like all war-time children, I had the street-smarts to know precisely what he meant and knew to keep my mouth firmly shut.

After a journey that included a ferry ride, we arrived at our campsite in Jutland, which was composed of rows of freshly constructed huts scattered through a pine forest. The staff led us to a building where we received an issue of fresh clothes, new shoes, towels, and plenty of soap, after which we were assigned our quarters. We slept eight to a hut in upper and lower bunks and assumed a scout-camp routine. There were calisthenics before breakfast, sports in the afternoon, and war games or mushroom picking in our spare time. But most unforgettable was the food!

None of us had ever known such abundance. Milk, butter, sausages, eggs, cheese, meats, fish, fowl, and desserts slathered with whipped cream were our daily fare. The freshly baked Danish bread was a revelation. Unlike the wood-chip-filled bricks that we were allowed to buy on points during the German occupation {the offer of which sent my pet rabbit running under the bed where he thumped his legs in disgust,} these crispy-crusted loaves smelled and tasted heavenly.

We were all assigned roles in the camp's organization, and because some-where along the way I must have carelessly bragged that I had taken several lessons in English, I was appointed as the camp interpreter. My mastery of approximately fifty words of this impenetrable language hardly qualified me for the job and regularly brought me to tears.

I lived in constant fear of being summoned, especially by the doctor, who apparently couldn't do his job without my help. Why, I wondered, couldn't they hire a veterinarian? Those guys never have to ask a cow where it hurts.

Attempting to hide was futile; my cruel mates enjoyed my discomfort too much to allow me any respite and mercilessly dragged my protesting body into the light whenever my name was called. This misery came to an end some three weeks later with the arrival of my father.

It took some time to get used to this foreboding though familiar-looking stranger. My stiffness softened considerably when the camp commandant invited me to sit next to my father at the head table for the evening meal, from where sneering openly at the assembled riff-raff gave me enormous satisfaction.

The following morning, after bidding farewell to my jealous chums, the understanding Danes drove us to the train station. We took the ferry to Sealand and spent several days in Copenhagen renewing our interrupted acquaintance. It was the start of a new, and a radically different, existence.

After boarding a ship in Esbjerg, we disembarked at Harwich, which happened to be the final resting place of the demobilized Polish fleet. Still manned by Polish sailors, the remaining submarines and ships lay rafted together, a dozing display of former might. Prominent among them was the destroyer *Piorun*.

I dripped with pride walking behind my father, who was piped ceremoniously on board, and we spent the rest of the day visiting the ship that my father helped to make famous. She could have used a paint job, and though the coquettish rake of her bows and funnel hinted of past dash and glory, the detumescent droop of those guns which once threatened to annihilate the Bismarck undeniably heralded the end of her useful toil. The following day we arrived by train in London, where my father occupied flat number 336 in the White House, a residential hotel opposite the Great Portland Street Station, which exists to this day. (Forty-seven years later I rented the same room during one of our stays in London.)

Until I started school, I would accompany the chief of staff of the Polish Navy to the nearby Polish naval headquarters on Wimpole Street, where he introduced me to many of his officer friends, some of whom I still clearly remember. They were the aristocracy of the Polish Navy: Captains Stoklasa, Kodrębski and Zajączkowski, along with his old friend from the Black Sea days, Hulewicz, who was the godfather of my brother, Witold. Like my father, they were all separated from their families and welcomed my juvenile impressions of life in Poland under the Nazi and Soviet occupations.

To get away from the formality of the headquarters and to satisfy my natural *wanderlust*, I began exploring the local area, and soon became intimately familiar with everything between Regent's Park and Oxford Street.

Post-war London was a drab, gray, and tired looking city suffering from the effects of its wartime experience. Though signs of destruction in the form of uncleared rubble were still in evidence, this was negligible when compared with the deliberate levelling of Warsaw. Rationing was in place for staples such as eggs, butter, sugar, and meat. To obtain these things, Londoners formed conga-line-like queues stretching for blocks. This became my job. Armed with a ration card, I spent hours standing in lines before various shops, which allowed me plenty of time to observe life in this new and enthralling universe. The streets were teeming with uniformed personnel, and by reading their shoulder patches, I could keep a running count of their national origins. Whenever I saw a countryman's uniform, I'd make deliberate contact, which required me to apologize in Polish and never failed to cause raised eyebrows.

I remember being fascinated by the traffic; the streets were jammed with it. It was primarily composed of military vehicles and taxis, while many private cars were still equipped with gasbags on the roofs, but it was the double-decker buses that captured my imagination. How did they remain upright? I quickly caught the fever of exploring London from the front seat of the upper deck.

"Vands vort," or "Le vis ham," I would say to the befuddled conductor, roundly pronouncing the vowels while stepping hard on each consonant as I proffered a handful of coins for him or her to grub through for the right change.

I could have continued this freewheeling life forever, but it was now September, and an unwanted spoiler hung darkly over my future. After a month of scouting, my father settled on the school of his choice. It was a Catholic institution run by the religious Order of Silesians, the austerity of whose compound was more than matched by its surroundings in the slummy working-class borough of Battersea.

With great foreboding, I accompanied my father for the registration. We were welcomed by Father Chadwick, the headmaster whose steely demeanor, as I was later to find out, only changed to a smirk when he was about to deliver the strap. I was soon immersed in an alien ambience dominated by a disciplinarian environment sternly administered by the Fathers in a language I did not understand.

The short-tempered, cassock-clad priests perfected the art of concentrating the pupils' attention by well-practiced deliveries of wooden blackboard erasers, vicious slashes with rulers, and by encouraging the reluctant to rise from their seats with a helpful pull of the sideburns.

It was self-preservation that served to enable my rapid familiarity with English; I was eighth in my class by midterm, and second by Christmas.

The two years I spent in the English school are not crowned with the fondest of memories. Being one of two foreigners in the class, the other a scion of a rich Uruguayan family, it took a while to be accepted. Some competence in soccer along with my eagerness to learn cricket helped, and though I was on cordial terms with my classmates, no lasting friendships ensued. More amicable company existed in the active Polish Scout troupe I joined, which met regularly on the premises of a Polish club on Gloucester Road.

My father steals me away from a Red Cross camp in Denmark.

Though I may not have enjoyed the process of English schooling, the benefit of distance reveals its effectiveness. The discipline made me shape up in significant ways. I came away with a background of Latin and a feeling for history, and being compelled to memorize Pope, Dryden, and Gray had an unanticipated effect: instead of pushing me away, I developed an enduring love of poetry, which remains with me to this day. In sport I learned the value of fair play; I could score a hundred in spelling, and perhaps most significantly, I developed a fear of authority.

The most compelling attraction of my tenure was London itself; the city became a lasting source of wonder, and every weekend I indulged my obsession by methodically exploring every bus route end to end. Since my mother was still stuck in the communist hellhole of Poland, this eccentric yet highly motivated curiosity provided my father with a welcome respite from parenting duties.

1947, My Mother's Harrowing Escape from Poland

To liberate my mother became my father's obsession. Though some secret escape organizations had formed in Poland, these were commercial concerns which, because of the risks involved, charged exorbitant sums of money.

How my father made contact with one of these cells, and how he forwarded the money, remains a mystery. With the arrangements in place, my mother was alerted to be ready to leave the house at minimal notice. The escape across two defended borders would be accomplished in a series of handovers to safe houses. Instructions soon followed: she was to report, plainly dressed and without luggage, to a staging address in Kraków. There she discovered that she would be accompanied by a fellow escapee, the wife of an army officer. This nervous and highly strung woman was in a perpetual state of incapacitating terror and would prove to be a drag for the entire ordeal.

From Kraków, the women were transported to a frontier village from which a road led to nearby Czechoslovakia. Profiting from local knowledge about the sentries' habit of leaving the main road lightly guarded in favor of patrolling the adjoining woods through which escapees were expected to pass, the organizers employed a clever ruse.

The crossing was scheduled for a Sunday morning; it was a day of increased pedestrian traffic between the neighboring villages straddling the border, whose inhabitants routinely visited each others' families and churches. Accordingly, accompanied by a twelve-year-old boy who was assigned to them as their guide, the women were instructed to walk boldly along the road directly at the guard house, and if questioned, to say they were only crossing over to attend mass.

Legitimized by the ingenious distraction of the barefoot lad and bolstered by an absence of luggage, they aroused no suspicion, and the single guard waved them through. The boy then led them to a place from which they were whisked to a nearby town, where they spent the night awaiting the next stage of the journey.

The following morning, a woman who would escort them to the Austrian border led them to a train. Though the three of them would share a compartment, they were to act like strangers, and if anything went wrong, the two women were on their own.

All went well until the train inexplicably stopped in an uninhabited area.

Russian soldiers surrounded the wagons, and starting from the rear, worked their way forward, demanding identification. To everyone's horror, people with their hands in the air began assembling under guard in a field.

As the search came closer, my mother and her companion sat paralyzed with the knowledge that as soon as they were ordered to show papers, which they didn't have, the game was up.

The search soon reached their wagon. With the opening of each compartment door, tension grew to a boiling point. Presently, a young soldier opened the door. After scrutinizing each woman in turn, evidently by now bored by the game, he couldn't be bothered to ask for papers and beckoned his companions to move on. Barely breathing, two petrified heart-attack candidates tried to recover what was left of their wits; for my mother, this would forever remain an accredited miracle.

The following night, their excitement was slated to ratchet up a notch or two, because to enter Austria they were going to have to cross a river.

They hid for a day in a border town, and when darkness fell, a man arrived and led them to his boat, which was concealed in the reeds along the shore. While the women waited in the shadows, he spent some time gauging the rhythm of the passage of the sentries and their dogs on the opposite bank.

All this activity was equally dangerous for the members of the escape organization, who deserved every penny of the considerable fee paid for their services.

When the boatman felt it safe to attempt the crossing, they boarded the skiff and huddled in prayer as he rowed their numbed bodies to the other side. The man stayed just long enough to show them a path through the woods, and as soon as he vanished, they were on their own.

Woods at night inexplicably awaken in me a primordial fear animated by the conviction that every tree conceals a crouching, fiery-eyed monster ready to spring. I can therefore only imagine what my mother felt as she and her panicking companion groped their way from the river through inky thickets, where the lurking danger was not only real … it was lethal.

An eternity later, they arrived at a clearing where moonlight revealed a settlement. From here, a tram would deliver them to Vienna in the morning.

Vienna, like Berlin, was divided into four sectors, each respectively administered by the occupying forces of the USA, France, Russia, and Great Britain. With tickets supplied by the boatman, they boarded the tram, which eventually deposited them at the blessed haven of the British Legation.

My mother spoke English poorly at the time, but fortunately she found a French-speaking agent to whom to explain their presence.

"I need to see your papers," said the woman behind the wicket.

"We have no papers; as I told you, we've just escaped from Poland," explained my exasperated mother.

"If you have no papers, I'm going to have to turn you over to the Soviet authorities."

Coming on the heels of an emotionally exhausting week during which her life was at stake, this was decidedly not the treatment my mother expected from an ally; quite understandably, she threw a hysterical fit. This considerable commotion caught the attention of a passing British major, who luckily understood French. Inviting her into his office, he calmed her down and asked her to explain the situation.

Wondering if the British could be trusted but having no other options, she hesitantly revealed the details of her terrifying ordeal and informed him that she was hoping to join her husband, who was a senior officer in the Polish Navy in London. The major copied the information and asked her to return the following day.

After a sleepless night spent in fear of what may await them, my mother left her worn out companion in the rented room and returned to the major's office in the legation. He was in an expansive mood as he stood brandishing a confirming telegram from my father. In addition, he assured her that while they waited for appropriate documentation, the ladies were to be housed in a British military camp.

Six weeks later, on June 16, 1947, my father and I embraced my mother as she alighted from a military Dakota at Northolt airport to start life anew as a family after eight years of separation.

The meaning of freedom can only be adequately understood by those who nearly lost it.

We moved into a house in Penge, a dreary but affordable blue-collar area in the south-east of London. Its proximity to the Penge East railway station allowed me to be in school in forty-five minutes.

The termination of my father's naval salary came three weeks after my mother's arrival. The official day of demobilization of the Polish armed forces in exile occurred on July 10, 1947. Dressed in his naval blues for the last time,

Captain Plawski presided over a ceremony commemorating the retirement of the naval ensign to the Sikorski Museum in London.

This was a difficult time for Polish ex-servicemen who were becoming, according to foreign secretary Ernest Bevin, "a source of increasing political embarrassment in our relations with the Soviet Union and [communist] Poland."*

Already in 1946, Attlee's Labour government, in concert with the Truman administration, caved in to Stalin's pressure to de-legitimize the Polish government in exile, recognizing instead the puppet government installed by the Soviets in Warsaw. This decision led to the exclusion of the one nation, which was arguably the staunchest of the combatants, from marching in the Allied victory parade in London.

This shameful act was followed up by Bevin who, by repeating Russian propaganda, myopically insisted that it was the Poles' "duty" to return to Poland, and that "as few Poles as possible [should be allowed] to remain in this country."** The Poles would have loved to be able to return to their homes and families like the other demobilized forces could, but the country for the liberation of which they had so gallantly sacrificed everything was under Russian occupation. Fully aware of what awaited them, only some twenty thousand Poles, which was fewer than 10 percent, reluctantly chose this route.

Eager to have all Polish combatants return to Poland where they could be controlled and de-fanged, the Polish Communist government propped up the Brits with a vigorous, lie-laden campaign. Some of this bait landed on my father's desk in the form of an invitation for him to accept a promotion to admiral, and to become the chief of the Polish Navy.

My father chose to ignore this extravagant bribe, and the wisdom of this decision was amply illustrated by the fate of his colleague, Captain Mohuczy, who accepted this offer. Mohuczy was arrested soon after arrival and joined the thousands of returnees whose sin of having been tainted by contact with the West resulted in summary executions, dying in prison like Mohuczy, or at best being condemned to a life of internal exile.

To help in the relocation of the now pension-less and jobless demobilized Polish veterans, my father accepted the post of commandant of a resettlement

* Lynne Olson and Stanley Cloud, *A Question of Honor*, [New York: Alfred Knopf, 2003], 396.

** Olson and Cloud, *A Question of Honor*, 397.

camp. Its purpose was to find countries willing to accept immigrants, which in those days was no less challenging and controversial than it is today.

Having helped to find sanctuary for many, when this job terminated a year later, my father's prospects of making a living as a fifty-three-year-old retiree in charge of a family appeared hopeless. It was then that he received a most unexpected communication from a Canadian naval officer whom he had met when he visited Halifax in the *Piorun* in 1941. This gentleman, now a commodore and flag officer of the Atlantic Coast, was Rollo Mainguy.

Rollo wished to know whether my father might be interested in being sponsored to Canada. The family was invited to live on the Mainguy property near Duncan, BC, free of charge until they found their footing.

As Tennessee Williams would later write in a different context in *A Streetcar Named Desire*: "Sometimes there is God so quickly."

My mother's interpretation anticipated the playwright. She saw it as the third example of a trio of miracles, the second of which was the chance encounter with a British major who happened to be fluent in French.

Free from communist oppression, my mother and me in London.

1948, *Immigration to Canada: Growing up in a New Land*

I had just turned fourteen in July 1948 when we boarded the RMS *Nova Scotia* in Liverpool. The British government was so eager to get rid of its Polish embarrassment that His Majesty treated us to a first class ticket. One way, of course. We disembarked at Pier 21 in Halifax a week later.

After a kaleidoscopic, seven-day-long train journey that introduced us to the breathtaking immensity of our new country, we arrived in Victoria. Waiting for us at the ferry terminal were friends of the Mainguy's, Herb and Winnie Gray, who drove us to Rollo's property close to Maple Bay. The romantic, cherry-tree-lined driveway that led to the fully furnished house assigned for our disposal could easily have served as a location for a Chekhov play.

We explored the property in company with our neighbor. There were 470 acres of it, so it took some time.

"Wow! Look at the size of that partridge," I shouted on seeing a large bird fanning open its tail.

"That's a willow grouse" corrected Mr. Burton. "It's one of the smaller species. Wait until you see a blue grouse."

The season wasn't to start until September 10, but my father had brought his prize Holland and Holland double barreled shotgun, so two months of bird meat was guaranteed. This would go well with the chanterelles and Boletus Mirabilis, which surfaced with unimaginable fecundity and were to be my job to harvest.

Moving in was easy; earning a living was a beast of a different complexion. For my parents, these harsh realities were just beginning to surface. There were no government welcome mats or social assistance; there was no income support, subsidized accommodations, job training schemes, or free English lessons. It became clear that physical work as laborers was their only option.

My father's first job was to act as the leader of a septic tank excavation team on the property of a retired Royal Army major. The other shoveller was Mainguy's newly arrived guest, my father's longtime friend, Captain Konrad Namiesniowski. Though they had to dig a ten-foot hole through clay, the job was finished in a week. My father's next employment came courtesy of Herb Gray, who owned a Dodge dealership in Duncan. It turned out that the garage had been short a janitor all these years, and my father's skills fitted the job description perfectly. Dear Herb even loaned him a car so he could commute the nine kilometers to work.

Soon my full-time berry and mushroom picking chores had to be set aside. Yes, it was school time again. We knew little about the protocols governing Canadian schools, so to make a proper impression, my parents delivered me to the headmaster's office dressed in my English school uniform, complete with jacket, shirt and tie, gray shorts, knee-high socks, school cap, and black shoes. I endured the longest day of my life. However, from the sanctuary of my desk where I tried to make myself invisible, I could see some promising potential: half of the pupils were girls.

Even when attired in less showy garb, giggles followed me everywhere. As the school's only foreigner, my weird, limey-tinged accent, short stature, and unfamiliarity with the boilerplate sports of softball and basketball immediately made me a target of the school bullies. My most fervent protectors from this scurvy lot were the girls. However, I soon proved that I was a scrappy little SOB, and when I took one of those bullies on, though I emerged messed up with scratches on my knees and face, the practice slowed to a crawl, and all of them eventually became my friends.

I recall causing gales of laughter when I asked for the meaning of a frequently used expression, which to me sounded like *asiho*. The explanation, delivered between fits of hilarity, included graphic descriptions of the location of the *ass*, and fitting details of the accompanying *hole*. There was, however, a quantum difference between this school and its English counterpart, evidenced by the refreshing lack of studied nonchalance and condescending formality.

My desperate desire to be accepted by my peers was unexpectedly met during the first sports meet, when I discovered that I was the school's fastest sprinter. Regardless of whether this was caused by growing up in a country where this skill had life-saving attributes, it was an ability that changed everything. From then on, my friendships blossomed; I became active in extracurricular events, insinuated myself as the head bench-warmer of the basketball team, and joined my classmates in making the school the centerpiece of our lives.

Meantime, my father's career as a janitor revealed some distinct disadvantages. In spite of Herb Gray's best intentions, the job could not provide my father with a living wage. This could only be found in industry, which in BC was lumber. Accordingly, Konrad and my father obtained work at the Chemainus lumber mill as sorters on a green chain, a job characterized by its relentless pace. For a fifty-four-year old man unaccustomed to physical work, it was a suicidal decision.

The terms of employment at the mill required all workers to be unionized. This was anathema to my father, whose revulsion with unions stemmed from an experience during the war when the *Piorun* had to be docked for boiler repairs in Greenock. His message to headquarters specifying that he was only going to be out of commission forty-eight hours was met with an unexpected reply: the ship was ordered to refrain from the task until dockyard personnel completed an inspection. Suspecting a misunderstanding, he reiterated that his men were trained to perform this job, and that they were starting forthwith.

An immediate "stop work" order arrived at the ship, along with an invitation for the commanding officer to report, swords and medals, to the admiral.

"This is a job that falls under the jurisdiction of dockyard maintenance staff," the admiral painstakingly explained, "and we risk a strike if I let your men do the job."

Appalled, my father returned to the ship, where everyone had to cool their heels for the five days allotted by union rules for this work. For the Poles, eager to bring an end to the occupation of their country and the enslavement of their families, such an enforced pause was not only incomprehensible—it was treasonous.

Toward the end of November, as I cycled home from school, I heard little mewling noises emanating from a bush. I stopped to investigate, and after parting the branches, I discovered that the source was a half-frozen Labrador puppy. I extricated the animal, wrapped it in my coat, nestled it among my books in the handlebar basket, and brought it home. Revived with warm milk, the little pup recharged overnight, and I was ecstatic to have acquired a pet. But my parents felt honor-bound to find its owners. When they did, I was obliged to return it to the farm, whose inhabitants revealed an unusual story. Their bitch had given birth to thirteen pups. Unable to cope, one by one she dispersed seven of them far around the countryside. Mine was the first to be found alive. Though I was grief stricken to part with this adorable fur-ball, the story had a happy ending.

On Christmas Eve, the farmer and his wife drove to our house and, claiming that the pup never recovered from our rejection, delivered her with a blue ribbon round her neck and pleaded with us to keep her. Rena became an indispensable part of our family for the next eleven years.

Although as a unionized laborer my father was earning a decent salary, it was obvious that the nature of the work made the job unsustainable. Eager to sink their roots in the new land, my parents rushed into a hasty partnership with another Polish family whom they hardly knew. It consisted of a middle aged woman, her powerfully built brother who was working with my father at the mill, and the woman's eighteen year old daughter. There was also the woman's husband, who immediately vanished. On the strength of a loan my father obtained from a bank, the partners made a down payment on a gorgeous thirty-seven-acre property fronting Somenos Lake, planning to open a guest house. It was called *Little Paddocks*.

Unfortunately, decades of neglect had returned the vast gardens, orchards, and numerous farm buildings of this once genteel domicile to their anti-diluvian state. It required a complete overhaul. The ladies could attend to the task all day, but the men could only join them on weekends and evenings after work at the mill. Unfortunately, we soon learned that the woman was mentally unstable, the brother lazy, and her attractive daughter's involvement in the project severely limited by her nocturnal habits, which she needed to sleep off during the day.

After several months of effort, we returned three rooms to an acceptable state, but with no money for advertising and no experience in running a business, the project was doomed to fail. The money earned from the few guests who stayed a night or two was swallowed up by my mother's excessively opulent Polish cuisine, and I remember a distinguished Polish visitor, whose literal interpretation of the name "guest house" resulted in his departing after a week's stay without bothering to remunerate his hosts.

In spite of this workload, my father's patriotism did not permit him to refuse the offer to produce a weekly Polish radio program every Sunday from radio station CHUB in Nanaimo. This required both parents to start preparing the show the night before, a task which often lasted until morning. Because it was cheaper than driving, my father traveled to the radio station by bus, which removed an entire work-day from the schedule.

Predictably, this relentless pace took its toll. In the winter of 1952, concurrent with the collapse of the business, my father's health failed, and exhaustion coupled with a gall-bladder operation landed him in the hospital.

Starved of funds, he cashed in his life insurance, then at a laughable price sold a precious gold chain and his heirloom shotgun, along with my mother's remaining jewelry. Our prospects were hopeless until, in movie-like fashion, the family was saved by the arrival of the proverbial cavalry.

It appeared in the form of the Royal Canadian Mounted Police who wished to know if my father would accept a job as a translator in the special branch of the RCMP in Victoria. Given the timing, I would have been an idiot to dispute my mother's predictable attribution of this event to an act of providence. This miraculous reprieve sent my parents to the capital, where they acquired a fixer-upper while I remained in Duncan as a guest of the Gray family to complete grade twelve.

In 1955, the RCMP moved my father's job to Vancouver, and the now-familiar routine of fixing up an old house and preparing rooms for rent started all over again.

My father's first job in Canada, 1948.

Grade 9 class in Duncan.

Our first car.

School's fastest sprinter.

Heavitree Farm.

Maths, Citizenship, and My Service in the RCAF

Our class graduated in 1952. The warmth with which I remember my school days, a feeling shared by my classmates, can be attributed to our teachers. Apart from their day job, they sacrificed their private time organizing dances, outings, entertainment, and graduations. They applauded our sports teams and appeared to take a personal interest in all aspects of our existence.

Though I scraped through most of my subjects, two gave me particular trouble. Shop was one of them, to which my understanding teacher provided an elegant solution: he agreed to pass me if I promised never to touch his power tools.

The other was maths. The blame for my difficulties with that inscrutable subject can be traced directly to a misunderstanding between my teacher an me. Mr Jickling failed to grasp that my answers were intended to be taken ironically.

Flunking maths meant that I would be ineligible to enter university: a consequence I was too ashamed to reveal to my parents. Thoughtfully, the school board provided an escape route for people like me via an opportunity to write supplemental exams before college registration. All I needed to do was acquire self-study materials and write the test.

I joined my parents in Victoria immediately after graduation and helped to restore two rooms for rent. Soon, a more reliable long-term clientele moved into the house, which included a Mrs. Tompkins, proud ex-mistress of the poet Robert Service.

My father's salary, room rental, and my mother's well-tended vegetable garden and flock of egg-laying chickens laid the foundation of financial solvency.

I was eager to help, but unlike the previous summer when I found a well-paying job at eighty-five cents an hour fighting forest fires (a massive raise from the thirty-five cents I was earning on weekends in a Duncan butcher shop), no summer work appeared available until I saw a recruiting poster inviting graduates like me to enroll in the Air Force Reserve.

Though it was always understood that I would eventually follow my father's footsteps into the Navy, he agreed that with no other alternatives, a stint in an Air Force uniform might do me some good.

Accordingly, I filled out an application, passed a physical exam, and reported to the RCAF station in Comox, where I discovered that our group of aircraftsmen second class was to be enrolled in a course designed to train us as fighter control operators.

Introduction to military discipline was a cinch for an ex-Polish scout.

Meeting new friends, a spanking green uniform, and a demo flight in a Harvard imbued the experience with all the excitement of a holiday camp. When we weren't pounding the parade square, our time was spent in classrooms learning the intricacies of the Ames 11 radar installation, which was housed in a convoy of trucks still sporting the wartime desert-yellow camouflage of its original North African deployment. Of course, I did not neglect to bring study material for the math exams and vowed solemnly to find time to bone up on this subject.

Several weeks after enrollment, I was abruptly called out of class and ordered to report to the commanding officer. I wondered which of my crimes might have come to light as I stood to attention in front of his desk.

"AC2 Plawski, how did you get into the Air Force? You're not a Canadian citizen!" he said sternly as he looked up from some documents.

Were secrets of the Ames 11 in danger of being revealed to the Polish commies?

"I don't know, Sir, I just signed up at the recruiting office."

"Well, you're here on an administrative error. It's not your fault, Plawski, but I'm afraid you'll have to pack your stuff and leave. Just as soon as you get your citizenship, you'll be welcome to sign up again," he added kindly to soften the blow.

"What did you do?" my father inquired dangerously as soon as I got off the bus.

My explanation caught him somewhat off guard; though we still had a year to go before we could become citizens, it didn't occur to anyone that this should be a problem in the Air Force Reserves. After all, my father's job was in a sensitive field of the RCMP, which required a security clearance.

My father decided that this was a formality worth challenging, so he put in a call requesting an interview with Major General Pearkes, VC, Lieutenant Governor of British Columbia. The invitation to his mansion arrived the following day.

After listening to my father's concerns, the two combatants spent some time exchanging war stories, and following a soldierly handshake, the lieutenant governor promised to see what he could do.

We didn't have to wait long.

AC2 Plawski is to report to Comox forthwith, was the theme of the telegram from the Minister of National Defense which arrived on my father's desk. The first person who wished to see me on arrival in Comox was the commanding officer. How the hell did I manage to get back into the Air Force? He wanted to know.

"Well, Sir, my father spoke to the lieutenant governor, who…"

I didn't need to go further.

"Carry on, AC2," he said, dismissing me to parade my newly won status before my suitably impressed classmates.

A month after my reinstatement, I was released to write my supplemental math exam at the Comox High School. The lamentable result left me with one more chance, the aftermath of which was equally predictable. Registration day at Victoria College found my pounding heart vainly attempting to displace my Adam's apple high up in the throat.

"You didn't pass your high school maths," said the registrar as she examined my records.

"I wrote two sups!" I hastened to reassure her, hoping not to be betrayed by my quivering falsetto. "I was sure I'd passed," I lied.

She looked at me quizzically, but for the time being agreed to sign me up for all the required courses, which included Mathematics 100.

Professor Phoebe Noble, a refined and cheerful lady with a gimpy leg, was the teacher of this course. I attended her classes for two sleepless weeks, all the while excreting cruciform building blocks in expectation of being unmasked, but nothing was said. Emboldened by the silence, I approached Mrs. Noble, confided in her that this was not a subject I wished to pursue beyond the abacus stage, and requested her patience.

"Make sure you attend every lecture and do your best," she counseled, which I promised to do.

Though my high school teachers agreed that academically I was a lazy bum, everything changed when I enrolled at Victoria College. Apart from chemistry, which I flunked, and math, which I hated, I became passionately interested in philosophy, history, art, and literature. It wasn't long before I shed religion like an outgrown skin, substituting it with an equally fervent, and likely just as annoying, agnosticism. At least I was able to terminate those pathetic self- betrayals I had been compelled to whisper through latticed porticos to disapproving, clerically garbed strangers secreted in the soulless anonymity of their caliginous confessionals. My apostasy led to a spirited intellectual scrimmage that appeared in the pages of the weekly *Tuesday Noon Review* with my fellow high school grad and future biblical scholar, John Sandys-Wunsch.

Somehow, I found time to play on the college soccer, basketball, badminton, and ping-pong teams; I became a staff writer for the college magazine, *The Martlet*, and filled my idle hours by joining three clubs, one of which, the Catholic Newman Club, inexplicably elected me as president.

My main extracurricular objective at Vic College, however, was to sign up with the University Naval Training Division (UNTDs) as a stepping stone to a naval career. Strangely, citizenship wasn't an issue with the UNTD. Did the lieutenant governor's intervention carry over to the Navy? By the time our citizenship was conferred in 1954, I had become so thoroughly Canadianized, the transition seemed to me like a paper formality.

The depth of this privilege, so profoundly understood by my parents, would elude my grasp until I matured. Though they never forgot their roots and remained continually active as leaders of Polish émigré organizations, being accepted as Canadian citizens was a source of gratitude and pride for the remainder of my parents' lives.

First flight in a Harvard, 1952.

1952, A Cadet in the Royal Canadian Navy

I enrolled in the Navy with boundless enthusiasm. This was rewarded at the end of my first year, when I was chosen as one of two cadets to represent the Victoria Naval Reserve Division, HMCS *Malahat*, at the Queen's coronation in the summer of 1953.

I expected that this would at least include tea at Buckingham Palace, but though it turned out that "Hip! Hip! Hooray!" shouted from the deck of the frigate HMCS *Swansea* during the Queen's sail-past was as close to Her Majesty as I would get, it was still a conspicuous distinction.

Following summer training in Halifax at HMCS *Stadacona*, and before returning to Victoria for the second year of college, I applied to switch to the ROTP, the Regular Officer Training Plan. This meant that the Navy would pay for two years of my tuition in return for my commitment to join the regular force.

To have a son follow in his footsteps on the way to a permanent commission was for my father a source of great satisfaction. For his son, however, the daunting nature of attempting to equal such a distinguished career was still a long way from becoming apparent.

For the second summer of training, we embarked in the cruiser HMCS *Ontario* for an extensive voyage starting in Halifax. The routing took us to Portsmouth and continued to Rosyth, which is close to the St. Andrews Royal and Ancient golf course. Inspired by this hallowed ground, I shattered a hundred for the first time with an impressive ninety-three. The smattering of applause I received from a group of umbrella-toting fanatics watching the action from across the fence in appreciation of my par on the final hole resonates with me to this day.

We next passed through the Kiel Canal, with a stop in Aabenraa befor visiting Copenhagen, Oslo, Glasgow, and Plymouth. After crossing the Atlantic, we put into Kingston, Jamaica, following which we passed through the Panama Canal. After a stop in San Diego, the ship arrived in Esquimalt.

Victoria College in those years only offered a two-year curriculum, which meant having to move to Vancouver to complete my third year at UBC.

After pledging with the ATΩ fraternity, I lodged in the frat house. Although carousing and binge drinking became a daily routine, none of it failed to dampen my expanding fascination with philosophy, history, art, and creative writing. This, however, was slated to be my last year of university.

Whereas ROTP funded students who had chosen technical fields, such as engineering, to complete their degree, for those like me destined for the executive branch, too much knowledge was deemed to be a dangerous thing.

Consequently, at the end of the semester I was to be promoted to the rank of midshipman and to start training in the cruiser HMCS *Quebec*.

Though this prospect was undeniably exciting, having to leave university a year short of a degree began to prey on my mind. This embryonic unease blossomed explicitly during a farewell party held at the home of my parents' closest friends, Michael and Aileen Pulchny.

Michael, the *Paterfamilias* of a brood of nine, had served as a sub-lieutenant in the *Piorun* under my father's command during the war, and was a man for whom I harbored both affection and respect. In the course of an audience in the privacy of his garden, I confided to him that I was engaging in this naval interlude primarily to satisfy my father's expectations, but that my secret ambition was to continue my education.

I distinctly remember articulating my anxiety that this ambition stood in danger of being eclipsed by everyday naval routine, when the uniform becomes an extension of the skin, and inertia makes it easier to stay put. Please, I begged him, don't let me lose track of this aspiration.

Midshipmen at Last

After an eternity in the rank of cadet, those puny black patches that had garnished our lapels for the last three years were finally supplanted by midshipmen's insignia: a seemingly modest change of gilding, yet one which proclaimed that we were now commissioned officers entitled to a salute. Just in case this should turn our heads, we were often reminded that to the fleet, we had merely become "snotties."

I reported on board the cruiser *Quebec* with fellow mids Larry Washbrook, Hugh MacNeil, Scott Moncrieff, and Jacques Petit. The ship was commanded by the redoubtable Captain Desmond Piers, a decorated veteran of WWII. The captain's reputation as an elegant swashbuckler amply preceded him, and his debonair character was reflected in his nickname, Debby.

We knew of his distinguished career during the war as the CO of HMC ships *Restigouche* and *Algonquin*, which were tirelessly employed in anti-submarine warfare in defense of North Atlantic and Arctic convoys, and on several occasions engaged in fire-fights with German warships. It was calculated that of the sixty-eight months of war, our captain had spent sixty-three of them at sea.

After reporting on board and moving into our quarters in the gunroom, we reported to LCdr. Stewart, whose primary job was to navigate the ship, but whose secondary mission was to act as training officer to the embarked midshipmen, a position known as "snotties' nurse."

I strongly suspected that this taciturn, bewhiskered Brit was chosen for this job for his ability to sniff out insubordination through armored bulkheads.

Having evidently pegged me as the principal potential offender, his face would contort into a gorgonian mask of wrath whenever I happened to come into his field of vision. I lived in constant fear of this man, who became known to us as "the bearded kipper."

Captain Piers, on the other hand, interviewed us individually and welcomed us on board like shipmates. During my brief talk in his cabin, he asked me about my father, whom he knew by reputation, and about my favorite sport, which by that time was golf.

We were all looking forward to our first cruise, slated to take us on flag-showing visits to Curacao, Montego Bay, New Orleans, and Nassau. A few days before sailing, I was piped to the navigator's chart room. As I stood nervously to attention, without looking up from his charts, LCdr. Stewart informed me acidly that the captain had appointed me to serve as his "doggy." As such, the navigator explained, my duty would consist of assisting the captain on the bridge for leaving and entering harbor, and to make myself available any time he required my services.

What a unique privilege. I would also be able to observe first hand how the captain ran his ship, and I solemnly vowed not to screw up.

I soon learned that my responsibilities included being the guardian of his Binoculars and the fetcher of his cocoa, and to be always ready to perform tasks for which an ordinary seaman could not be spared.

We enjoyed a pleasant sail through the Caribbean, engaging in training evolutions and drills, such as lowering the sea boats or extinguishing imaginary fires, all of which had to be done on the double.

Debby was particularly fussy about fitness; the officers reported on the quarterdeck each morning before breakfast for some brisk callisthenics, and the men participated in energetic sports on deck, which included stopping the ship to allow the crew to go swimming.

I soon discovered that the captain was a keen and accomplished golfer; he could be seen in his shorts swinging daily at a makeshift practice area on deck, where those so inclined could bring a club and join him in his sport. As a recent convert to the game, I eagerly joined in these sessions, and apparently caught Debby's eye with my enthusiastic if still inept flailings at a ball.

After stopovers in Willemstad and Montego Bay, we headed for New Orleans. I remember spending a magical morning watch on the bridge as we felt our way through an endless fleet of shrimp boats heading out for their fishing grounds, their mast lights making them look like a swarm of fireflies. Debby's wife, Janet, was waiting to join us in this storied city, where no one could show off the Canadian flag with more consummate panache than our rock star of the quarterdeck, Debby Piers.

On the third day of our stay, I was called to the ship's PE instructor's cabin.

"The captain is going golfing; be ready, appropriately attired, on the jetty at one o'clock," he announced, leaving my mind in disarray.

Was the title "caddy" to be appended to my appointment as doggy? Just in case, I brought my clubs.

I don't recall who paid my green fee at the prestigious Pontchartrain Lake Golf and Country Club, but this proved to be the start of a sequence of invitations to golf with Debby whenever he chose to play. This would include Bermuda, Trinidad, Quebec, PEI, and his home course at Ashburn, all culminating with the Country Club of Estoril in Lisbon, which will play a prominent role later in this memoir.

Our extensive winter cruise took us to Trinidad, Tobago, Guadeloupe, St. Lucia, and Cuidad Trujillo in the Dominican Republic, where, in company with *Iroquois*, *Algonquin*, *Athabaskan*, and *Haida* (I believe), we unwittingly legitimized the dictator Trujillo's regime by appearing as the naval centerpiece of his extravagantly expensive and self-serving Caribbean Fair.

One of the highlights of this excess was a soccer match, billed as Canada versus the Dominican Republic, staged at night in the purpose-built auditorium before a paying audience. For the duration of the fair, the Dominican team was buttressed by a selection of South American professionals, who accounted themselves well against such opposition as Argentina, Mexico, and Brazil. They would need all the help they could get, because facing them in the Canadian end, rooted between the goal posts, stood the daunting pillar of impenetrability, the daring defender, George, "The Wall," Plawski.

Thousands of spectators filled the stands as the ship's band played the national anthems; our team captain won the toss, and as the stadium hushed, we kicked off the ball. That was pretty well the last time our team touched the ball that half, except for me at those times when I failed to get out of the way of the screaming white missile.

Within the first minute the opposition had our measure, from which time on they played against us like the Harlem Globetrotters. The score was nine to zero at halftime, though had they wished, the number could have been astronomically higher.

Something unusual happened when we struggled out for the second half: the crowd deserted the Dominican end of the field and, forming a solid ring around my goal, began to cheer for Canada. My saves were greeted with robust applause, and on the single occasion when we managed to maneuver the ball into the opponent's end and their goalkeeper graciously allowed it to roll past him into the net, the crowd went wild.

The game ended amicably with the score thirteen to one, and someone counted that I managed to get in the way of some sixty shots—a fact I could easily confirm by counting the bruises on my body. Up until then, without a shadow of a doubt, this was my finest hour.

Our cruise continued to the American naval base of Guantanamo Bay, followed by visits to Colon, Vera Cruz, St. Thomas, San Juan, Kingston, and, before returning to Halifax, a golfing stop-over in Bermuda, where I "assisted" Debby at Belmont and Mid Ocean.

Soon after our return to Halifax, to the ship's collective sorrow, Captain Piers transferred his flag to the recently renovated HMCS *Algonquin* as the captain of the ship and commanding officer of the First Destroyer squadron.

Our group of midshipmen was also slated for a change to continue our training. We were all assigned to join the *Tribals* or the *Maggie*, but when my orders arrived, I could scarcely believe it: I was to follow Debby to the *Algonquin*. My job as *aide de camp*, as I preferred to call myself, continued unabated. When we sailed up the St. Lawrence, Debby delegated me to assist him when he was the guest of honor at a ceremony in the City Hall at Baie Comeau. During a visit to Dalhousie, he arranged a date for me with the daughter of a friend. As if that wasn't enough, I was obliged to round out his foursome at the Green Gables golf course in Summerside. Thankfully, my midshipman friends, being embarked in other ships, were not in a position to comment on the color of my nose.

Midshipman in command of a Pinnace.

Captain Piers's doggy. Self on left.

A Brush with Royalty

The *Algonquin's* fall cruise began in October; after crossing the Atlantic, we put in at Londonderry and then proceeded to Belfast, where the *Bonaventure* was undergoing final preparations. I sauntered on her cluttered flight deck, blissfully unaware of the pivotal role she was later to play in my life.

Following a visit to Brest on November 6, we tied up in Lisbon. Our arrival was temporarily marred by our jeep driver's over-eager attempt to park too close to the ship, which resulted in his spirited evacuation of the vehicle just before it plunged into the harbor aft of the brow.

Debby, who witnessed the event as he stood waiting to greet local dignitaries who were beginning to convene for a cocktail party on board, took personal charge. With commanding authority he directed the divers, who soon located the jeep, and a crane presently hoisted the dripping but otherwise undamaged car onto the jetty.

It was a masterful demonstration of efficiency performed with inimitable brio, admired not only by the ship's company but also by the gathered guests who, judging by their applause, might have been excused for assuming that it was staged for their benefit.

The capital of Portugal, as we soon discovered, turned out to be a repository of the crowned heads of Europe. From the sumptuous sanctuary of their refuge, the monarchs spent their time plotting the overthrow of their usurper governments while dreaming of their eventual rightful return to power.

Not all were refugees, however, and one of these was presently on board; judging from the relaxed friendliness between him and our captain, their camaraderie was of long standing. He was Juan de Borbon, the corpulent but dashingly courtly father of Juan Carlos, the reigning King of Spain.

Though built like Jackie Gleason, he shared with the actor a highly serviceable two handicap in golf—a fact I was to discover the following day when Debby appointed me to complete a foursome representing the squadron in a friendly match at the exclusive Clube de Golf de Hotel Palacio Estoril. The round was preceded by a banquet in a luxurious private dining room overlooking the course.

Don Juan and Debby presided in effervescent form. The feast was eventually crowned with endless toasts to our respective heads of government, national luminaries, Portuguese navigators, each one of us at the table, and probably every member of the Montreal Canadiens and the Portuguese national football team. Though my memory of the provenance of the remaining three hosts is vague, these gentlemen clearly fitted the image of a highly cultured elite, a status I determinedly aspired to match through the only means at my disposal: an exorbitant excess of alcohol.

On the last day of our visit, a formal ball was to be held in honor of the Canadian Navy. Sometime that afternoon, I was summoned to the captain's cabin. As I stood at attention, Debby informed me that I was being delegated as the escort of a young lady of exalted social standing.

"Her name is Maria Gabriella," he explained, "and her title, Princess of Savoy, stems from being the daughter of King Umberto II, the deposed monarch of Italy. You will call him 'Your Majesty,' and his daughter, 'Princess Maria.'

"I needn't tell you that you are going to be closely watched, Plawski, and I expect you to be on your best behavior," admonished Debby with paternal severity. I departed his presence terrified yet thrilled to the core, and more determined than ever not to screw up.

As the youngest in age and the lowest in rank of all of the ships' officers, this was for me a singular honor, and I spent the rest of the day in a turmoil of pride mixed with apprehension. My only previous experience with proximity to royalty was limited to the distance of the royal yacht HMS *Surprise* to the railing of HMCS *Swansea*, from where, along with the rest of the ship's company, I enthusiastically hailed Her Majesty during her post-coronation Spithead review.

Clearly, all this was about to change, and I began to fantasize of a future surrounded by royals and the cream of the aristocracy. I could imagine myself, though a mere commoner, becoming the toast of this esoteric milieu solely on the basis of my charm, suavité, and of course the binding love of a beautiful princess. After all, history—notably as recorded by Andersen and Disney—is replete with such happenings.

Though I briefly wondered whether my lapsed Catholicism might stand in the way of profiting from this opportunity, I remained comforted by the example set by Henri Quatre of France, who, when confronted with a similar dilemma in 1593, famously accepted his conversion with the pronouncement: *Paris vaut bien une messe* (Paris is well worth a mass).

When evening came, we were collected by a fleet of taxis that delivered us to a majestic, colonnaded neoclassical palace where, after being respectfully ushered inside, a glass of champagne magically found asylum in my hand.

Momentarily, we all paused to absorb the lavishly appointed interior. From an impossibly high frescoed ceiling hung an array of crystalline chandeliers, whose reflections dappled the uniforms of gold-braided, bemedaled glitterati. Accompanied by glamorously coiffed and gowned consorts, the dignitaries created an atmosphere like an extravagant resurrection of the final night of the Congress of Vienna.

Presently, the orchestra sounded a meaningful arpeggio, and all eyes turned to the entrance. A group of distinguished personages had just entered and were being greeted by Debby and the ships' officers. They were accompanied by a small entourage of young ladies, one of whom was a stunner in a blue, floor-length gown.

Debby quickly caught my eye and nodded sharply in my direction.

Nervously, I trotted over and bowed deeply with each introduction, in accordance with how I imagined royalty should be addressed. Their reception of me was formal but distant, entirely unlike the welcome conjured in my imagination, which was to have more closely resembled the return of the prodigal son. Never mind, I mused, there's always the beautiful daughter, the traditional vehicle which catalyzes the inevitable happy end.

It was now the turn of the princess, but as my gaze expectantly shifted to the dazzler in blue, I became aware that a different girl was being ushered toward me. She was a startlingly tall, willowy creature in her early teens, positively radiating discomfort; with a brace on her teeth, eyes of a frightened gazelle, and a handshake like cold cooked spaghetti, she reluctantly identified herself as Maria Gabriella.

"What a pleasure to meet you, Princess Maria," I lied when I finally found my breath.

Our mismatch could not be more graphic. Apart from our vexing difference in height and age, we discovered that neither her English nor my French permitted refuge in banter, and that spending the evening in each other's company under the penetrating scrutiny of both assembled camps would be a source of mutually crippling embarrassment. An introduction to the bevy of ladies in waiting provided a brief and welcoming respite, along with the impress of one azure name: Marina.

Presently, a swarm of liveried footmen presented each of our group with an elaborately garnished crystal goblet of perfectly chilled Perrier, which left me in uncharted waters about the propriety of proposing a toast with a glass topped by a straw, an orange slice, and a miniature umbrella. Just as I began to compose some tension-relieving banality, the crowd hushed and parted, revealing the conductor, his baton raised high, looking expectantly over his shoulder in our direction. The cue was chillingly unmistakeable.

Since no life-saving sinker-hole had formed within running distance, I had no choice but to proffer my arm to the princess and lead her out to the middle of the corrida. The orchestra burst into a waltz, and with the princess towering over me like a gilded giraffe, we stumbled stiffly in the spotlight, our self-consciousness bordering on panic, and it was impossible to discern which one of us felt more thoroughly out of place. Mercifully, we soon became surrounded by a crowd of dancers, which fractionally served to diminish our unease.

Nothing in the lore of fairy-tale mythology prepared me for this turn of events, because this princess, trapped in that awkward age when a girl's voice changes from no to yes—somewhere between puberty and adultery—did not exhibit any of the traditional characteristics.

An eternity dragged by as I stood surrounded by a group of girls resembling aspirants for holy communion. While I vainly attempted to appear enthralled for the sake of satisfying Debby's critically appraising looks, my discomfort could only occasionally be relieved by brief exchanges with the divine Marina. Unexpectedly, the king approached, and with excessive old-world charm requested my permission to dance with his daughter. As I watched them disappear in the swirl of dancers, I suddenly felt a hand slithering into mine. Its owner wore a blue dress.

"Meet me outside!" she whispered and vanished into the crowd.

I stood immobilized with shock. Careful scrutiny of the area revealed that everybody's attention was focused on the dance floor, so I crept to the door and stepped out into the moonlit palace grounds. Apart from a group of chauffeurs smoking next to their limousines, I was alone.

Presently, the door clicked shut behind me, revealing Marina, who with an impish grin handed me a bottle of champagne and two glasses that she had commandeered from the bar, and bid me follow. That was something I'd be willing to do even to my own beheading, a fate not too farfetched to imagine.

Marina approached one of the drivers; after a brief exchange, he bowed respectfully, opened the car door, and handed her the keys. As I hopped in from the other side, she drove briskly away.

This unfolding tale was decidedly outside of the parameters of the Brothers Grimm, and I was still tongue-tied when she meaningfully pointed to the champagne. The pop of the cork shooting out through the window into the night punctuated the start of this improbable adventure.

She drove purposefully up a steep hill to an apparently familiar trysting ground and parked on a high promontory that offered a stellar view of the illuminated city below. Marina was nineteen: precocious, rebellious, and brazenly self-confident. She was raven-haired, ravishing to look at, and altogether mortally infatuating. Thoroughly amused by my entrapment with the princess, she made me recognize its grotesque absurdity.

Steeped in the giddy audacity of this affair, we drank, laughed, and indulged in some inconsequential necking until we knew that this Technicolor interlude must end. When we returned, she released the car to the chauffeur and let me slip back into the hall a few respectable minutes before her.

Awakened by Marina to the farcical aspect of the situation, and moderately buoyed by champagne, I returned to the princess like a captive reprieved, my relaxed state serving to melt some of the frost, and when the time came, I led her confidently in the home waltz.

The parting formalities with the royal family dragged on like a cortège. The situation prevented me from yielding to the agonizing desire to fly to Marina, and my eyes desperately searched for her in the crowd. Did I really, in that distracted state, catch a glimpse of her at the door? Was it she who waved? Who flashed that knowing smile? Did I actually see her stop and blow a farewell kiss? I'll never be sure; she vanished from my impressionable youth an iridescent chimaera, never to materialize again.

Merciless ribbing from my fellow shipmates accompanied me on the drive home, but I was too engrossed to care.

The following day, as I took up my station on the bridge, Keith Lewis and Jack Manore, two ship's lieutenants whom I particularly liked, added their little jabs to the chorus. Has the date for the royal wedding been set? Does the *Gieves* haberdasher have my measurements for elevator shoes?

Debby stayed out of it, but I sensed he was paying close attention. Once clear of the harbor, after sea dutymen secured, I was tidying something up at the back of the bridge when Debby slid over beside me.

In a lowered voice, but with a canny glint in his eye, he spoke these sobering words: "You're damned lucky, Plawski, that you showed up in time for the home waltz!"

I had often speculated about why Captain Piers singled me out for such unique treatment. Could my growing passion for his favorite sport have played a role? Or was it that, though his wife had a daughter, he and Janet had no offspring? Though I will never know, I remain bewildered, yet profoundly privileged to have had the honor of spending a year as my respected mentor Desmond Piers' doggy under his enigmatically paternal command.

Had We Been Cats, We'd have Eight Lives Left

Eighteen months in the rank of midshipman fled like a thief in the night.

All at once, we were sub-lieutenants, and when we thought no one was looking, we could strut in front of mirrors rehearsing Nelsonian poses and admiring the importance of our newly-sewn single gold stripe adorned with that frisky executive curl. Only the subsequent pinning-on of wings would match the feeling of pride that swept us at the time.

Promotion was followed by a month of leave, after which we were booked on the SS *Empress of Britain*, in which we were to sail to England to attend the Royal Naval College at Greenwich, followed by a further nine months of technical courses in several Royal Navy establishments.

Larry and I flew home by catching rides with the Air Force, which eventually delivered us to our saturated-with-pride families in Vancouver. To enshrine the occasion, my father and I dressed in our uniforms, and with my mother between us, we posed for posterity.

Though Larry and I were listed with the RCAF Air Movements Unit for flights to the east, since we couldn't take a chance on being late from leave, we reluctantly reserved backup tickets on Trans Canada Airlines. Hoping we wouldn't have to exercise this option, we made daily calls to the unit, but no seats appeared to be available.

Resigned to having to pay our way back, a final call to AMU on the morning of our scheduled departure revealed a glimmer of hope. A C119 Boxcar was to leave for Trenton that day, but seat availability wouldn't be known until just before flight time. We rushed to the air force base on Sea Island and sat gritting our teeth with anticipation.

Moments before having to drive across to the TCA terminal, to our colossal relief, our names were called. A short time later, strapped into the webbed parachute seating along the sides of the cavernous fuselage, we taxied past the TCA *North Star* just starting the boarding process. Just how lucky we were would not become apparent until the following day.

After huddling for five hours in the unheated, barn-like space, which acted like an echo chamber magnifying the unnerving concussions produced by chunks of ice being flung off the props against the fuselage, we landed in

Trenton. Though frozen and deafened, we disembarked, elated at having saved the air fare.

We heard the news the next morning. TCA flight 810, the aircraft on which we held reservations the previous day, had taken off behind us, and due to ice accretion, had crashed on Mount Slesse in the Cascade Range, killing all sixty-two on board (December 9, 1956).

Subby home on leave, 1956.

Royal Naval College, Greenwich, January 1957–September 1958

Our appetite for Greenwich had been stoked by our predecessors, who had regaled us with tales of ingenious mischief and undetected crimes committed in an atmosphere of elegant permissiveness. In keeping with our recently acquired status, we traveled first class.

The *Empress of Britain* approached Liverpool harbor in a dense fog, but when the visibility lifted, to the harbor master's considerable surprise, the Cunarder entering his port sported a Jolly Roger flag flying from the mainmast.

Our ever alert steward, taking into account the reported extreme displeasure of the captain and deducing from my cabin mate, Charlie's, missing sheet and the shoe polish stains on my and Larry's hands that we may have some knowledge of this event, ensured that the three of us, along with our luggage, were the first off the ship the moment it docked.

After drawing our allotment of duty-free liquor (eight forty ouncers per month for sub-lieutenants), we reported to Greenwich. Greenwich College lived up to its role in becoming the most cultivating stage of our naval careers, and I made the most of it. Its purpose as a finishing school was designed to provide a civilizing veneer to Royal Navy subbies who entered the service without the benefit of graduating from a military college like most of us, or ROTP entries like me with three years of university.

We were lodged in a palatial English Renaissance building originally designed by Sir Christopher Wren at the end of the seventeenth century. Intended to serve as a seamen's hospital, it was a magnificent part of a complex dominated by the baroque Royal Greenwich Observatory.

The academic portion of the curriculum, which included lectures on naval history, physics, maths, and English composition, took place in the morning, while afternoons were devoted to elective subjects whose choices were limitless. We were encouraged to choose any subject we wished, and if this meant engaging Bertrand Russell to teach symbolic logic, or commissioning George Balanchine for a course in classical ballet, so be it. Everyone was assigned a personal tutor, and just to illustrate the caliber of resident instructors, mine happened to be Professor Alan Bullock, a noted scholar of German history and already the acclaimed author of *Hitler: A Study in Tyranny*.

There were no watches to stand, no curfew to abide by, and no duties to perform. Our linen was laundered, uniforms pressed, and shoes shined by a personal batman, who awakened us each morning with a cup of brew. We banqueted daily in one of the finest dining galleries in the Western world, the James Thornhill decorated Painted Hall.

Our slender links with the Navy were limited to wearing a uniform to class and to Sunday divisions, and legitimized by our paychecks, which included a generous foreign allowance in addition to the monthly duty-free liquor ration.

The most precious advantage of all was to be offered the great city as our playground with so few restrictions and so much time to explore. London in the fifties was, like most cities, a calmer and more embracing place than today, and vastly more affordable. There was no problem with drinking round the clock. After the pubs closed at ten, we all met on Denman Street in our beloved den-mother Mary Dowse's White Room, long established as a home by previous classes of Canadian naval brethren, where our portraits decorated the walls, and where our credit was always good until next payday.

When Mary finally shooed us out around 1:30 a.m., we could repair to some blind pig or any hotel that could legally serve drinks in the lobby all night, provided you could convince the barman you were a guest. This was a cinch at the accommodating Regent's Park Hotel off Piccadilly Circus, after which everyone congregated at Covent Garden, where the pubs opened at five o'clock. It was an ideal place to ogle tuxedo-clad revelers and their diaphanously costumed escorts mixing easily with brawny fishwives and bloodied butchers, while con-men and pick-pockets worked the crowd like shadows.

The college closed for Easter and the summer break, which gave me and Charlie a chance to tour France, Italy, and Switzerland in Jacques Petit's new Morris Minor. Many of us took advantage of the galleries and museums and the exploding theater scene. That was where I found my niche. I attended plays and revues, and even forced myself to read the rage of the era, *Waiting for Godot*, the meaning of which eluded me for years. But most significantly, my sojourn served to anchor my fascination with the American musical. Its beginning dates back to soon after we came to Canada, when someone gave us the album of *Oklahoma*. I played it incessantly and memorized all the lyrics, a practice I continued with the launch of every new Broadway production. However, I had never attended a live performance. This soon changed, and you couldn't drag me out of the Coliseum when *The Pajama Game* had its run, or when *Damn Yankees* took its place.

I joined the college's thriving theater group, which produced plays of remarkably high caliber. We wrote the music and lyrics of a variety show in which I appeared in a role similar to the one later immortalized by Joel Gray in *Cabaret*. One scene featured Larry performing pirouettes *en pointe* in a tutu: you simply had to have been there.

However, landing the eponymous role of George in Thornton Wilder's *Our Town* cemented my passion for the medium. Playing opposite me in the juvenile lead of Emily was a girl I'll call Jenny, with whom I had a furtive affair. Jenny lived in mortal fear of being discovered by her live-in lover; consequently, our trysts had to be inelegantly confined to the back seat of the ancient Vauxhall, which Charlie and I had purchased from some wrecking yard for forty pounds.

My single meeting with the source of Jenny's concerns made me an instant convert to her fears, which led to an immediate cessation of intimacies, as her partner turned out to be a mortifyingly intimidating combination of menace and threat shoehorned into a butch embodiment of a female Shrek.

This was also a time of bonding with my friends Larry and Charlie, in whose company I engaged in capers that, in retrospect, appear almost reckless.

The effect of too much time on our hands coupled with a surfeit of disposable tender steered us irrevocably in the direction of mayhem, for which we displayed a natural aptitude. Though we deliberately stopped short of destruction, some of our alcohol and adrenaline saturated pranks kept us mere inches ahead of the authorities.

One such escapade occurred in Cambridge following an evening of wreaking mild havoc in some college dorms. As we drove through the solemn stillness of the sleeping town, we happened to pass a church. I cannot claim that feelings of devotion guided us to stop, but as we circled its ancient girth and admired its star-lit, ivy-mantled spire, a powerful urge convinced us to explore its interior.

An inspection of the entrances disclosed that the building was locked; decidedly not the anticipated state of a house of worship which I assumed should be ready night and day to embrace a penitent in need of immediate spiritual intervention.

A search around the back revealed a basement window which resembled a loading chute. We forced it open, and lowering ourselves into the stygian hole, landed in something that felt like a rubble of rocks. Gripping each other like the blind men in Breughel's painting, we reached a door which opened with a disquieting screech onto what seemed like a stairwell.

The tomb like silence magnified every breath and shuffle, stiffening our neck hairs and honing our alertness to levels of hunted quarry. Are churches haunted, I wondered? Surely the priests must be trained to perform regular excorcistic defumigations. Could one be overdue? We inched our way up the stairs till we emerged in the nave.

When our eyes became adjusted to the stained-glass-filtered light, we saw the bell rope coiled around a fitting. Larry unraveled what was now the tail end of a satanic snake and gave it a vigorous pull. A fearsome, metallic clang shattered the silence. As we took turns on the rope, the night roiled with alarm. The clamor pierced the surroundings and spooked the resident detachment of guardian angels, who in a clatter of pigeons' wings abandoned their post and fled into the night.

When we were done, with eyes of cats we scurried through the church, retraced our steps to the basement, helped each other out, and bolted to the car.

We didn't get far; exhausted by the hilarities, we stopped on the edge of town and fell dead asleep. A polite tap on the window caught our attention. Its cause was standing next to the car. Outfitted in a uniform harnessed in leather, a white helmet, elbow-high gloves, and tall, lace-up boots stood the intimidating embodiment of all the majesty of The Law. We had no choice but to admit to our guilt. Identifying ourselves as subbies from Greenwich, we expected the worst.

We could scarcely believe our ears when his command, "Follow me!" came appended with the word, "gentlemen."

"Follow me, gentlemen!" said the policeman to the perpetrators of the outrage as he mounted his bike and pointed it toward London. Ten miles later, he made a U-turn, and as he passed by, chopped off a smart salute.

It may have been the British class system at work that vaulted naval officers into a category the English bobby considered too dignified to arrest, but this jaw-dropping display of dignity and authority stands in silent rebuke to the knees-on-chest, hands handcuffed behind the back, fingerprinting, fines, jailings, and bribes we were to experience for much more venial transgressions during flight training in Florida and Texas, but that will be covered later.

After the nine stimulating months in Greenwich and three weeks of leave spent touring the continent, returning to the all-but-forgotten attractions of navigation, radar, sonar, anti-submarine warfare, and three months of pounding the parade square of the gunnery school at Whale Island spelled a jolting return to reality.

The technical courses were taught in various naval establishments scattered throughout the south coast of England. Leadership and seamanship were dominant elements of the curriculum, which included a month-long air-familiarization course at HMS Ford, a highlight of which was a low-level demonstration flight in a Royal Navy Vampire, during which my pilot never got over fifty feet while beating up every naval vessel in sight.

Once the courses were over, along with a promotion to the rank of lieutenant came a sobering reminder. We needed to decide on the branch of service in which to perfect our skills to assure the annihilation of the enemy. This was, after all, the sole purpose of our chosen profession.

It was not, for me, a moral issue over which I needed to wring my hands. My childhood had been saturated with this unwholesome human activity, and our enemy was the same cadre of cutthroats who were occupying the country of my birth.

My friends Charlie Poirier, left, and Larry Washbrook with first liquor ration in Greenwich.

I was tempted to request flight training, but being convinced that my age and rank precluded this possibility, I opted for a sure thing: torpedo and anti-submarine specialization (TAS), along with a posting to the West coast.

My orders, exactly as requested, arrived on the same day as Charlie's and Larry's selection for pilot training. The chilling realization that this meant I would be separated from my running mates for the remainder of our careers swept through me like an ice storm. A hastily penned amending message to headquarters informed my career manager that a searing epiphany revealed that I would be vastly more useful to the Navy as a pilot. Without any fuss, my new appointment arrived the following day and changed my life forever.

Playing the role of George in Thornton Wilder's Our Town, opposite "Jenny," Greenwich, 1957.

Flight Training with the US Navy, 1958–1960

Upon returning to Canada, we were informed that flight training with the US Navy (USN) would start in Pensacola, Florida in September, but first we were entitled to a month of leave. I flew to Vancouver to spend the time with my parents. Out of concern for my mother, I prevaricated about the reason for being posted to the US Navy in Florida, but this did not fool my father.

After passing preliminary aptitude tests and medical examinations at an Air Force base in Centralia, we boarded a flight to Florida with a scheduled change in Atlanta, Georgia. What should have been a routine connection turned out to be an exposure to an unexpected new reality. It appeared in the form of two drinking fountains ten feet apart, one labeled *Whites*, and the other *Colored*, and it struck us like a slap in the face.

Welcome to the South, it proclaimed; you might as well get used to it.

When we arrived at the Pensacola Navy Base, we discovered that in addition to Peter Drage, Charlie, Larry, and me, the Canadian contingent was to be swollen by twenty-four graduates from Venture, the officer training school in Esquimalt, class of '66.

Our liaison officer, the affable Bill "Chiefie" Munro, informed us that we were all training to fly Trackers off the *Bonnie*, except for the top scoring four, who were to switch to the jet pipeline in preparation for an appointment to VF 870 Squadron to fly the twin-engine fighter-interceptor, the Banshee. With this incentive in mind, I vowed to apply myself to be one of the four.

After a welcoming speech, the base captain ceded the floor to Navy lawyers, who spent the remainder of the day cautioning the new arrivals about the apparent minefield into which they'd been dropped. They issued warnings against unscrupulous business practitioners, naming names and identifying the known miscreants, but the chief object of their admonitions was the police. This criminal organization targeted naval personnel, who became their main source of income from trumped up charges and illegal practices, which we were about to sample in person.

Larry was the first; he was charged with jay-walking (he wasn't) and had to pay a fine. Charlie and I were taken in a paddy wagon to a police station, where we were fingerprinted and charged with disturbing the peace in a restaurant where, with exaggerated politeness, we tried to help a lone waiter to distribute food to his thoroughly amused customers.

An incident that nearly had me cashiered from the program occurred one Sunday when Charlie and I decided to drive his new Chevy Impala convertible to check out the beaches in Panama City a hundred miles down the coast. We were both in our bathing suits as we headed for home that afternoon with me at the wheel. After pulling out to pass a truck, we became aware of a police car on our tail.

The cop stopped about fifty feet behind us, and since he remained in his seat, it seemed to us a signal that we should approach him. As we got out of our car, he sprang out of his and, pointing a gun at me, hollered, "You, come here!" Then pointing at Charlie, he yelled, "You, get back in the car!"

When I padded over with my hands in the air still covered by his gun, he demanded to see my driver's license. Since my bathing suit was not equipped with a secret compartment for a wallet, I told him our clothes were in the trunk. He followed me until I opened the lid, when he threw me to the ground and, with his knees on my chest, handcuffed my unresisting hands in a trice.

"Get in my car!" he ordered. After telling Charlie that he wasn't to drive, he took me to a jail in the town of Milton. I was arraigned for speeding, drunken driving, and resisting arrest. My request to contact my liaison officer was refused, and I spent the night in conversation with some intriguingly eccentric characters, all of them black, in the drunk tank.

Being tipsy on a Sunday afternoon would have been our normal state; it was therefore ironic that, on this occasion, we had barely enough cash between us to buy a single beer, which we had shared on the beach. Charlie meantime drove back to the base, but he had no idea of my whereabouts.

A Marine shore patrol major released me mid-morning, and without asking any questions, ordered me to pack my gear and head back to Canada. When Chiefie heard our story, he arranged a meeting with the admiral, who dismissed the case, but it was a close run thing.

After the thrill of the first solo in the T34 Mentor, we graduated to the advanced trainer, the T28 Trojan. In this powerful machine we learned aerobatics, formation flying, and aerial gunnery. We were introduced to night flying, and with a hundred hours under our belts, completed our first carrier landings on the USS *Bennington*.

When we finished the basic training syllabus, we drove to Memphis for three weeks of instrument training, but the attractions of the city proved too tempting to leave on schedule, which with skillful malingering I stretched to six.

On the same evening when the four of us chosen to fly the Banshees were in the midst of triumphant celebrations in the officers' club, Chiefie spoiled our revelry by revealing that a message from Ottawa informed that no more jet pilots were needed in the RCN. When we moved to Kingsville, Texas, for advanced training, it would be in the S2F Tracker.

Our last experience with the police occurred during a trip to Houston, where Charlie and I had girlfriends. We were cruising at sixty-six miles per hour, according to the sheriff who stopped us, which considerably exceeded the limit in the village through which we passed. Our choice was to spend the night in jail before paying the $66 fine, or to pay it on the spot, after which we'd be free to go on our way.

Following a prolonged search of our clothing and car, we collected the required sum. To pay, we were obliged to follow the officer to a house, which he said was the home of a justice of the peace. A lady in curlers opened the door, greeted the policeman warmly, and collected the money, which she accepted without tedious formalities like asking who we were or issuing a receipt.

Apart from these inconveniences, the excellence of our training prepared us admirably for our future role as naval aviators. Before graduation, we qualified for deck landings in the Tracker on the Essex class USN *Intrepid*, which is now a naval museum in New York.

Flight training, Pensacola, Florida, 1958.

Flying in the Navy, 1960–1963

On our return to Shearwater, with our newly won wings prominently on display, we joined our training squadron, VU32. From May until August, we learned how to apply our basic skills in the CS2F version of the Tracker before being appointed as co-pilots in the operational VS880 Squadron.

Our three-year tenure in this squadron was composed of four segments: co-pilot ashore, co-pilot at sea, crew commander ashore, and crew commander at sea. Though I hated the right seat with a passion, my saving grace was having drawn Kurt Miller as my crew commander.

Kurt was a USN exchange pilot whose exceptional flying skills were accompanied by an unflappable demeanor. During anti-submarine exercises, the map of the action he had in his head made my clumsy, hand-drawn plot superfluous, and his approaches to the carrier were like on rails.

I received my crew in May of 1962, and completed my tour of duty in 1963 in the discomfiting manner described in the opening chapters.

The as-yet unknown consequences on my career caused by my destruction of good will between two NATO navies, when combined with my job in VU32 which began to feel like treading water, produced an ennui which started to prey on my mind.

Standing L to R: Lt. Kurt Miller, USN, CPO "Moose" Mills, myself and AB Legere.

In whites in Puerto Rico.

THE FEMALE IMPERATIVE

Nourishing the above-stated malaise was the alarming growth of a phenomenon that had already started to manifest itself on our return from flight training with the US Navy in 1960. It pains me to report that the cause of this lemming-like trend was women.

In our early days, though our endless *Cherchez la Femme* reached soaring levels of commitment, it never threatened the nexus of our male comradeship. With my closest friends, Charlie Poirier and Larry Washbrook, we had formed an inseparable alliance from our time as cadets and midshipmen. We became a burlesque trio in which Charlie and I played the roles of instigators, and Larry completed with a compelling portrayal of a willing foil. Charlie's talent for improvised mischief along with his inspired verbal dexterity stood in dramatic contrast to Larry's deceptively oafish presence housed in an unwieldy six-foot-four-and-a-half-inch frame. Though subjected to endless provocations, Larry took it all with good-natured equanimity made possible by the understanding of our roles and by our mutual affection.

Surrounded by a cadre of like-minded un-attached friends, we breezed through these rambunctious, devil may care years, which left me filled with the expectation that this condition was destined to continue forever.

The fatal flaw of this status quo was its dependence on the boys remaining single. Apparently, nature had other ideas. An abrupt mass awakening of the biological imperatives of our formerly acquiescent female companions began driving them to deprive us of our bachelorhood. This mating instinct, to which for unknown reasons I remained immune, day by day deprived me of my running mates.

As I watched my buddies surrender to the malicious pheromones adrift in the maritime air, I wondered if we were programmed like cicadas to metamorphose at a pre-ordained time, but that some anomalous genetic malfunction was causing an inordinate number of my friends, instead of soaring out on their freedom-loving wings, to emerge instead with the halting crawl of humpbacked caterpillars.

One by one, dedicated rakes like Matheson, Montgomery, and MacIntosh, devoted libertines like Turner, Robinson, and Schroeder, confirmed bachelors like Nash, Gibbon, and Curleigh, and fun seeking free spirits like Eliason and

Brown, Brygadyr and Jardine, Miller and Thoms and Stevenson and Ford, all grimly followed each other into wedlock. Most cruelly, this soon included my confidantes, Charlie and Larry.

Deaf to Cole Porter's anthem that "raising an heir could never compare to raising a bit of hell," they abandoned me to a solo rendition of his lonely lament, which asked: "Where is the life that late I led? Where is it gone? Totally dead." *

How could my closest colleagues willingly renounce their liberty to join the very group we so recently derided as *those married pukes?*

Being happy for my friends' contentment with their loving and alluring wives failed to remove the hint of betrayal tainting the air, which sabotaged the quality of excitement that had permeated our lives as bachelors—a condition I unequivocally began to miss.

In case the reader is inclined to interpret the preceding as a flagrant example of misogyny, please believe that, *au contraire*, I have always been, and continue to be, a dedicated, card-carrying feminist. I am irrevocably in love with the female sex, which has not only been an object of a lifelong fascination, but also of enduring respect.

---

* Cole Porter, *Kiss Me Kate.*

THE "NANCY" RESOLUTION

While the turmoil mentioned above churned in my mind, I wasn't exactly standing on the sidelines. This is exemplified by two ladies, both by a curious coincidence living in New York and, implausibly, both of them named Nancy. I hasten to stress that the Nancys were, and remain to this day, entirely oblivious of their contribution to the upcoming and most transformative decision of my life.

The first Nancy entered my orbit in 1958 during initial flight training in Pensacola, when I decided to spend the Christmas break in New York. This was Nancy Wooliver Rigsby, a Princeton graduate and devastatingly alluring model whose credentials, listed on her McClelland Libby Agency brochure on which she appeared with her equally attractive mother, were: "Height 5'6, bust 34, waist 23, hips 34 1/2, eyes gray-green, and glove 7."

The agency was owned by the mother; the family belonged to the highest pillars of society, and I was instantly overcome with an overpowering infatuation.

It soon became evident that my potential as a future naval aviator lacked the necessary gravitas for Nancy to reciprocate my feelings with matching ardor, but presumably my panting puppy-love amused her sufficiently to introduce me to some of her family.

Prominent among these was an uncle, whose Portuguese name I still remember as Solito de Solis. He lived in a suite on West Fifty-Ninth Street overlooking Central Park, and he invited us for cocktails. When we arrived, I noticed that a painting, instantly recognizable as a Rembrandt self-portrait, occupied a couch in the sitting room. I assumed it was a copy until I was casually informed that, *au contraire*, it was an original being prepared for the arrival of a restorer.

Ah so! Well, that certainly solidified the family pedigree.

Nancy also introduced me to her mother, with whom I found myself to be an instant hit, but as is often the case in circumstances like these, it proved to be the kiss of death to my relationship with the precocious daughter, who rejected on principle anything approved of by an adult.

Had this been France, I would have possessed the maturity, probably from about the age of fourteen, to take full advantage of such an opportunity. The scandal of the mother usurping her daughter's boyfriend would be trumpeted by *Figaro*, lampooned by *Canard Enchaîné*, and immortalized by Vadim or Truffaut in a film-noir with Belmondo playing me, Simone Signoret in the role of the philandering middle-aged sexpot, and Brigitte Bardot in character as a pouty tease unsuccessfully spurning my advances.

Sadly, my inexperience and naiveté did not permit such a Gallic finale; it terminated instead with an unfulfilled mother, a wounded suitor, and a daughter pursuing greener pastures at Stanford University after delivering a discouraging note with a tersely phrased: "Forget Me!"

The second Nancy materialized in the spring of 1963 when I was serving in 880 Squadron embarked in the *Bonaventure*. While idly flipping through the pages of the *Halifax Chronicle Herald*, my attention froze on a photo in the society columns. It was taken on the tarmac of the Halifax Airport and depicted the return from Oxford University of a member of the local gentry newly minted with a Doctor's degree. It pictured Dr. Nancy Lane performing a triumphal descent down a TCA ramp into the waiting arms of a welcoming committee.

Whoa! Doctor Nancy Lane? Surely some mistake! This smashing, long-haired beauty in the clinging dress, stiletto heels, and the Miss America chest was Playmate of the Year material, not an Oxford PhD.

The caption stated that Dr Nancy Lane was visiting her mother, address conveniently provided, while on her way to the Albert Einstein College of Medicine in New York for further studies. I let this information macerate for a day or two and then sprang into action.

"A very good afternoon to you, Mrs. Lane," I murmured in my most mellifluously modulated pear-shaped tones.

After introducing myself as an old pal of Nancy, I congratulated Madame on the brilliant success of her daughter and her iridescent future, innocently adding that since I soon planned to be in New York, might Madame be kind enough to furnish me with Nancy's phone number?

As soon as I secured an aircraft for a weekend instrument training flight, destination Navy New York, I placed a call to Nancy. Audibly surprised, she hesitantly agreed to a date.

Gobsmacked, I was; she was utterly gorgeous! I'd always thought that intellectual women had to look desiccated and forbidding, like Virginia Woolf, and I would have been the first to raise my hand in answer to Albee's question.

This intellectual, however, in addition to looks, was cultured, refined, and highly motivated by her academic future in her chosen branch of life sciences, cytology, which she explained was the study of the anatomy and function of cells. Since my familiarity with these was restricted exclusively to their incarcerative purposes, this topic emphatically discouraged consequential discourse.

I recall that as the evening progressed, I began to sense that I was not exactly making an electrifying impression; there was an undeniable culture gap between us, but I chose to believe that it was not unbridgeable when exposed to an athletic dose of my masculine charms.

As we said good night at the door of her temporary quarters in the college dormitory when Nancy consented to a future rendezvous, I felt capable of winging home with no assistance whatsoever from Mr. Grumman.

Accordingly, we kept in touch until my request for another instrument training flight—you can never have enough IFR—was approved. (Instrument Flight Rules [IFR] are regulations for flying in weather conditions when the cloud ceiling is less than 1,000 feet above ground level and/or the visibility is less than three miles.)

I prepared for a full-court press: tickets to the Met (Cavalleria Rusticana and Pagliacci), drinks at Sardi's, dinner at some eatery way beyond my means ... the whole catastrophe. I was trying too hard, and the effort was showing. There was an unarticulated distance between us, which began to tamper with my self-esteem.

The simple explanation that some people are temperamentally unsuited to one another was something my pricked ego could not accept. This required a more complex scapegoat, and I soon settled on a question of educational inequality. Nancy, I decided, partly because of her thoroughbred lineage, but chiefly owing to her education, was markedly above my station. Plainly speaking, when combined with the previous Nancy's "Forget me," which I hadn't been able to do, I was wallowing in a feeling of inferiority.

What could I do to make myself worthy of people like these?

The solution that occurred to me was simplicity itself: elevate my status by requesting that the Navy send me back to school to finish my degree.

DEMONSTRATING DISSENT

Finishing my degree could serve double-duty in preparing me for civilian life; it was an option I was seriously beginning to consider, because though I loved flying and felt bonded to my friends, my most passionate interests had little to do with the military.

Progress through the echelons of command, setting aside other determining factors like favoritism, the right connections and knowledge of French, requires a commitment to the cause and the willingness and ability to lead. Lacking both the skill and the ambition to fulfill these requirements disposed me instead to follow Oscar Wilde's dictum that "life is too important ever to take seriously."

I was also drawn to the radicalizing philosophies of writers such as Kerouac, Orwell, and the brilliant Polish rebel, Hłasko, whose nonconformist lifestyles, so divergent from mine, exerted a strangely hypnotic attraction.

These writers nurtured my romanticized obsession with individuality and personal freedom, already formulated as a child when I imagined that all one needed for eternal happiness was to own a gun, a dog, and a bicycle.

Such convictions were hardly encouraged in the armed forces, and although the Navy was the least stultifying of the services, uniformity of thought and behavior was necessarily a part of the culture.

Opportunities in the Navy to express dissident attitudes were limited, but when one presented itself, I was quick to exploit it. Such a moment occurred during Sunday Divisions, when the ship's company assembled to parade on the flight deck. Prayers ritually followed the formal ceremonies, but lessons learned from the distant past about unpleasantries, such as the Saint Bartholomew's Massacre and the Thirty Years War, supported the sensible rule that Catholics and Protestants should separate for the duration of these devotions.

Accordingly, on the command, "Roman Catholics fall out," those committed to this faith stepped smartly out of the ranks and marched to join the chaplain, who waited sequestered on the bows, leaving the remainder to the ministrations of their Protestant counterpart.

This left me in a quandary, because no suitable segregation had been assigned for folks like me, whose religion was officially listed as "none." Since neither available category conformed to my disbeliefs, I chose what I deemed to be a suitable alternative. I fell out with the RCs, but instead of following them to the bows, I made a deliberate left turn, and with each step defiantly proclaiming my dissidence, paraded ram-rod-straight past the entire assembly to the quarterdeck ladder, which I descended with a purposeful gait to my cabin.

I admit to being disappointed that this clearly provocative act, carried out with all the trappings of a crusade, failed to arouse the anticipated reaction, because after two of these melodramatic departures, only Dicky Quirt, the current squadron Ops officer, accosted me on this subject, but limited his objections to formalities rather than context.

Oh well … heresy simply isn't what it used to be.

Anecdote: Bertrand Russell

When Bertrand Russell was being processed into Brixton Prison in 1917 on grounds of pacifism, in the space on his in-routine marked "Religion," Russell wrote: "Atheist."

On perusing the document, the Warden paused, clearly stumped, but after shaking his head, he good-naturedly allowed that, although there are many religions, we all believe in the same God.

Russell reported that this remark kept him amused for the remainder of his incarceration.

THE NAVY'S CHANCE TO FIX A FAULT

It was clear that the frolicsome part of being in the Navy was behind me, and my squadron mates who had joined intending to make it a career were now preparing to gird their loins in its pursuit. Though inwardly I knew that the right decision was to resign my commission and leave the service, I was not yet prepared for such a drastic move. The first step, I decided, was to go for the degree.

Since I was convinced that this shortcoming was entirely the Navy's fault, it was, therefore, the Navy's responsibility to fix. Infused with righteous indignation, I wrote to Ottawa, offering headquarters an opportunity to redress this injustice by sending me back to university to complete my studies.

A politely phrased reply indicating that a degree was not required to foster my naval career was soon in my possession. Maybe not, but in this case, it wasn't just a career that was at stake: this was about personal advancement, and possibly about salvaging a foundering relationship. After all, didn't headquarters realize that a Navy pilot buttressed by a Bachelor of Arts degree rose immeasurably in eligibility?

Accordingly, within a few days a considerably amplified petition winged its way to Ottawa. This time the reply was less ambiguous—nothing doing, no dice, forget it. The stage was set for a showdown.

My next letter to headquarters was equally unequivocal. It declared: You guys want to play hardball? OK, I resign!

Ottawa's reply was correspondingly explicit: Have it your way, dimwit; your resignation is accepted.

The new reality set in with an unsettling thud. Where was that outpouring of relief? The unshackling feeling of freedom? The joy of a new adventure? They were being muffled by the screeching sounds of the drawbridge being hauled up behind me.

Offsetting this paralyzing blur of events, my career managers in Ottawa handled my file with a remarkable level of patience and understanding. It was the end of March. Knowing that university courses didn't start until the fall, they considerately inquired when it might be convenient for me to finalize my release? Sometime early in August was fine, they agreed. In the meantime, I was to continue my duties in VU32, and the operation on my wonky knee, which needed to be completed before I could be released, was scheduled for June.

THE AIRLINE ALTERNATIVE

The winter of 1964 had, particularly for the Navy, become a time of profound discontent caused by the looming prospect of unification. This dystopian process, rammed self-servingly past an imperceptive Prime Minister Lester Pearson and around an astigmatic parliament by the megalomaniac ex-army lance corporal and now Minister of National Defense, Paul Hellyer, threatened to abolish the Navy as a separate service and to consign naval aviation to the anals of history.

Keenly aware of this situation, the airline industry, which was concurrently experiencing rapid expansion, began besieging pilots at military establishments with offers of obscene wages, cushy working conditions, and the promise of two compliant stewardii in every bed, which caused a hemorrhaging of qualified pilots from the services.

Momentarily losing sight of my objectives, I joined the stampede but curbed it with strict conditions. I resolved that if I were to switch to another uniform, it had to be for an airline with an international route structure, and the only company hiring that met this restriction was Pan American.

To qualify as a candidate, I needed a civilian commercial license and instrument rating. I passed the ride in Moncton in a Tracker that Charlie and I signed out for a cross-country training exercise.

The closest US city where potential hires were being screened was New York. Applicants needed to fulfill three requirements: a Stanine test (aptitude and general knowledge), a medical that, once passed, was good for all airlines, and an interview with the potential employer.

Since United Airlines boasted the loudest barkers, even though I had no intention of flying for this company, I cheerfully accepted their offer of a return ticket, because I knew that their offices were close to Pan Am. Accordingly, having satisfied the above requirements with United, I discretely crossed the street and introduced myself to the competition. My arrival had a startling effect; I was greeted like a long-lost son and made to feel not only welcome, but practically indispensable. I was trotted from office to office, presented as a celebrity, and it wouldn't surprise me to learn that in that whirl I shook hands with the company CEO, Juan Trippe, in person.

This experience was repeated at United Airlines, resulting in two job offers and two starting dates. The script was unfolding like a well-made play, but now the rules of the genre required the obligatory complication. It arrived on cue in the unwelcome guise of the United States Immigration Service. I soon discovered that being a Canadian citizen was not an automatic passport to a job in the US of A. It was all about where you were born, and *Polaks* apparently fell into a group that required careful filtering, since there was a two-year wait list before my request could be considered. Both airlines sympathized, but unable to help, advised me that the job offers were open until I managed to get myself into the country.

The congressman from northern New York State, whom I planned to petition for a private bill, might have been able to provide the solution, but he was on holidays, and Bobby Kennedy was too busy with his ongoing pissing match with FBI Tsar Hoover to respond in person to my meticulously composed three-page epistle.

My last option was to accept the offer of a brief marriage-of-convenience from a stewardess friend working in Atlanta for Eastern Airlines. Given that this lady was a German landed immigrant introduced intriguing levels of paradox: a member of a nation that had been a wartime enemy of both Poland and the US stood to facilitate the admission of an offspring of an ally!

Though this generous offer touched me deeply, it became inadmissible as a manifest transmogrification of irony. With the airline option shelved, I was free to concentrate on winding down my naval career.

LEAVING THE NAVY

It was now time to inform my friends that serving in the Navy had run its course, and I was preparing for an amicable divorce. None of my squadron mates gave me a ghost of a chance. At your age? Going back to school? Face the facts, Plawski—it's hopeless. How can you expect to adjust to a lifestyle requiring self-discipline, asceticism, restraint, heaven only knows—maybe even abstinence—not to mention abstemiousness, which by itself rules out any hope of success. You're chucking away a Navy career full of excitement, travel, fabulous flying, limitless skirt chasing, nightly pissups, a regular paycheck, and the bonhomie of your squadron colleagues, who are your closest family. You haven't a clue about what you're going to study, or where you're going to get the money.

Chilling words, these, especially the part about abstinence. I had to admit that all these arguments were stingingly accurate, but the decision was now carved into stone.

As I sleepwalked through the out-routine firmly in the grip of myopia, I thrust aside all advice to the contrary and cashed in my pension to cover my debts.

The most sobering moment arrived when I realized that this was to be the last time I was entitled to wear my uniform. The golden rings topped off by those coveted wings defined me as a member of a uniquely welded family and were the symbols of my identity; I cherished their impact, and seeing them on my sleeve this final time made me bawl like a baby.

The hardest part was bidding farewell to my squadron friends— venerated confidants of an epoch of joy, danger, occasional sadness, and unparalleled adventure.

Was this truly what I wished?

It had better be.

1964, RETURN TO UBC

The drive west provided a chance for reflection; though I was torn with anxiety about the future, something about the unknown always held a thrill.

I drove all the way in three days.

It was a joy to see my parents again, but now I needed to justify my decision in person. I was particularly concerned about not having sought my father's blessing to leave the Navy, a career that had been the purpose of his life.

I made the case that this decision was mine alone to make and that it rested on an undeniable fact: my recognition that I was not senior officer material. Promotions to my rank of lieutenant were automatic, but I had seen my share of passed over lieutenants and unpromoted lieutenant commanders having their mail sent to the wardroom bar and had no intention of joining their ranks.

I emphasized that I had no interest in competing with my friends for promotions, and that the prospect of continuing in a job for which I lacked passion spelled boredom, stagnation, and was destined to lead to pro-found dissatisfaction.

"I'm thirty years old; I quit at my peak and can look back at my naval experi-ence with unqualified satisfaction, but it was now or never."

Admittedly, where this might eventually lead was a mystery, but my immedi-ate goal was simple: put on the blinkers and complete my degree.

Having gained a measure of my parents' understanding, I settled into my upstairs room, secured a student loan, enrolled at UBC in fourth year Arts, and resigned myself to the ill-fitting role of a scholastic hermit. The subjects I chose were a selection I deemed to be the least challenging for someone return-ing to academe after eleven years of revelry.

"You can't eat philosophy," my father remarked when he saw one of my choices.

He didn't share my hope that epistemological analysis or medieval English poetry might someday enjoy a useful measure of revival; I padded these with seminars in ancient philosophy and history of modern art, rounding out my curriculum with a course on Restoration comedy, drama from 1660 to 1710, which promised some counterbalance of levity.

Adopting a routine designed to minimize distractions, I chose to spend all day on campus in the sanctuary of library stacks, taking breaks to eat my mother's packed lunch in the student union building and suppers in the Ponderosa cafeteria. The punishment was self-inflicted, so I had no right to complain.

I studied at home on Sundays, where after supper my father and I occasionally exchanged that knowing look, which meant driving to the Blue Boy Hotel on Marine Drive for a game of billiards. As a young man, my father used to make a second salary at this game, and his skill was still evident. He introduced me to the sport in Duncan when I was sixteen.

Anecdote: The Billiard Lesson

The Duncan pool hall was bootleg central; typical of this genre, it was a smoke-saturated sanctuary where the town's most disreputable riff-raff conceived their petty crimes. I was ashamed to admit I even knew of this place when my father decided it was time for me to learn the game.

Everyone in the pool hall froze when the threatening figure of my father, attired in a jacket and tie, descended into the dungeon and approached the dumbstruck owner, who stared at him with undisguised suspicion.

"May we get a table?" he inquired, shattering the hush that enveloped the room.

Since my presence seemed to legitimize this request, with relief palpably reflected by the clientele, the proprietor unceremoniously dismissed the players from the center table and started racking the balls for eight-ball.

"Thank you, but we'd like to play billiards," said my father.

Regretfully, the gentleman allowed that billiard balls were not available. Could we settle for snooker? Indeed we would, and in the uneasy silence shrouding the locale, I received my first lesson on how to choose, chalk, and hold a cue, and the basics of the stroke. In keeping with tradition, when we finished, my father left a tip and announced we'd be back in a few days for lesson number two.

On our return, the occupiers of the center table voluntarily terminated their game while the proprietor proudly produced a box of new billiard balls, and for a couple of hours, the pool hall assumed an unconvincing air of respectability.

By the time I graduated I had developed a strong taste for this game, along with a modest measure of skill.

What the Blue Boy lacked in refreshing disreputability, it made up for with good quality, billiard-sized tables. I treasure the memory of those evenings, and chalk them up as some of the happiest moments of camaraderie between father and son.

A HOLY REPRIEVE

As the term progressed, keeping up with the crippling routine of my assignments left little time to savor their content, except for the Restoration Theatre course taught by Dr. Pincus. The period covered started in 1660 when the monarchy, in the person of Charles Stuart, was restored to the English throne.

One of the most revolutionary acts accompanying this event occurred in theater. When these reopened after eighteen years of Puritanical embolus, audiences were startled by an audacious innovation: women's roles were being played by women!

To the prigs, this served to expose the long-suspected radicalizing nature of the medium, while the misogynists among them added an intriguing twist by claiming that it removed the vital aspect of imagination expected of audiences before 1642.

Until it happened, I didn't know that a mini-restoration awaited me as well during the Xmas break. All along I was living at home, contributing $12 per week for my keep. Though the affordability and familial comfort were convenient, these were more than offset by the lack of freedom and the resultant shackling effect on a raging libido.

The pressure of the upcoming exams combined with the prospect of a celibate holiday, a state so ominously predicted by my squadron mates, fused into a mounting mood of depression. Just as I was ready to resign myself to this stultifying outlook, the overcast parted to reveal a Dionysian figure with a familiar face. This improbable vision materialized in the form of John Truran, a fellow student and ex-naval aviator friend, who after flying Banshee jets in VF 870 squadron, enrolled at UBC to study for a commerce degree. Though we shared the same uncertainties about our present pursuits, John's endeavors were considerably assuaged by being accomplished from the welcoming confines of a cozy suite in Kitsilano.

John's holiness may not have been, contrary to my perception, a state capable of surviving a determined scrutiny, but as far as I was concerned, his act was divinely inspired. It consisted of an offer to let me use his apartment for two weeks while he visited his mother in Montreal.

Christ! I was ready to extend my student loan to pay his way to his Scottish *birthplace* if that's what it took to use this pad. I will be forever grateful to John for enhancing my colorless existence with a cartouche of memory, which I will always recall in vivid Technicolor.

My filial duties, however, demanded that I take time out to assist my parents in observing the festive traditions of a Polish Christmas. The sacred part included the sharing of a holy wafer before dining on fish on Christmas Eve, and attending Mass on Christmas Day, while the secular component included the annual matinée performance of *The Nutcracker* on New Year's Eve.

Anecdote: Crashing the National Ballet's New Year's Eve party

This reminded me of when I flew to Vancouver on leave in 1961 to spend Christmas with my parents. The National Ballet of Canada presented the show that year, after which we returned to dinner at home. Though I would never admit that secretly I might have enjoyed greeting the New Year in rowdier company, my understanding folks agreed that since they had no intention of staying up, I was free to seek a livelier venue. For the lack of a better idea, I decided on the Georgia Hotel pub.

It wasn't long before the anonymity of this basement warren lost it inspiration, which motivated me to see if I could find a party. Accordingly, I started on the top floor and began to work my way down, traipsing the corridors and listening for sounds of action. Several levels lower, I walked past a door behind which there appeared to be a promising shindig. Noting the number, I descended to the lobby, picked up the house phone, and dialed the room in question. A lady answered, her voice nearly drowned out by the din.

"I'm terribly sorry to bother you," I apologized, "but I happen to occupy the room below yours, and of course with your party above me, I won't be able to get an ounce of sleep."

I could sense the eyes rolling and the hand over the mouthpiece.

"Since this is New Year's Eve," I continued, "I don't want to be a spoil-sport, so I wondered if you might agree to an elegant solution. Would you consider inviting me to join you?"

With relief audible in her voice, she cheerfully agreed to my proposal.

In answer to my knock, the door was opened by none other than Celia Franca, the founder and artistic director of the National Ballet of Canada. I needn't have worried that the overcoat over my arm might raise suspicions about the truthfulness of my complaint; I was welcomed with great cordiality, and planting a mickey on the piano cemented my right to participate. Being fresh from the performance, I knew the names of the principals, and as the evening progressed, I fell madly in love with one of the ballerinas; however, I found it discomfiting that this feeling was warmly reciprocated not by my intended, but by the company's lead male dancer.

A SIFTING OF PROSPECTS

On January 2, I turned the keys over to John and reluctantly re-entered the pumpkin world again, but I never forgot his kindness and was later able to reward his generosity by tirelessly proffering his candidacy for employment to the management of Skyway Air Services.

As spring approached, I needed to start pondering how to exploit that vaunted BA, should I be successful in its quest.

The end of March heralded the annual cattle call on campus, an event during which a variety of companies trolling for candidates established their presence in the student union building. I still hadn't a clue what to do next, but thankfully the representatives of Beaver Lumber and IBM Computers, with which I applied for jobs, recognized that my talents might be more usefully employed somewhere else.

A more realistic option emerged with the civil service, which was actively fishing for applicants. Though I found the prospect profoundly repelling, desperate times compel desperate agendas. The only department that held any appeal to me was the foreign service, a choice my interviewer supported because of my time in the Navy.

To qualify, candidates needed to submit an essay illustrating Canada's role in world affairs. Because the upcoming finals gave me no time to produce an original document, I sequestered myself in the Canadian History section of the library, where I found a book by James M. Minifie, providentially entitled: *Canada: Peacemaker or Powder Monkey.*

Profiting from an observation attributed to Picasso that "good artists copy and great artists steal," I dipped into both options by shamelessly plagiarizing the entire preface and submitted it under my name. The results were not expected until May, so I forgot about this initiative and concentrated on cramming for the exams.

Coincidentally, a fellow student and ex-naval aviator, Lou Reimer, mentioned that he was soon to report back to Skyway Air Services for his recurrency training on the TBM *Avenger* for the budworm spray season in New Brunswick. He'd been telling me about the obscene amounts of money, like three hundred bucks before breakfast, that you could make on this job. This left me strangely unmoved, because for mysterious reasons that to date I cannot explain, I had entirely discounted seeking work in aviation.

The subject cropped up again in conversation during a layover visit by Christine Chojnowski, a TCA stewardess friend from Montreal whom my mother unequivocally decided I should marry for no other reason than her Polish descent. That's precisely the attribute that initially attracted me to her as well, when I saw her name on a TCA crew list pinned to a board in the radio room at the airport in Sydney, Nova Scotia, where I landed in 1963 in the course of fleet exercises.

Since "stewardii" constituted a rich source of dating material, I memorized her name, and on my next visit to her city, called the number I'd obtained from information. When a female picked up, I brazenly sallied forth in Polish. Though her familiarity with the language was cursory, it sufficed for her to grasp that I was angling for a *rendezvous*, and the result was an amicable relationship that was still ongoing that spring.

Christine's encouragement for me to explore Skyway served to melt my mother's misgivings about flying, and as soon as my exams were over, I proceeded to Abbotsford where this company was based.

ALMOST THE END OF A FIREBOMBING CAREER

The familiar noise of a large piston engine undergoing a run up was the sound that met me as I stepped out of my car in the Skyway parking lot that sunny April day in 1965. Entering the hangar, I was greeted by the familiar shapes and smells of airplanes, which I thought I had left behind forever when I departed from Shearwater that distant year ago. A mix of Cessnas, a Harvard, and several imposing TBM Avengers were being serviced by men in white coveralls.

(The Avenger is a single engine WWII carrier-borne torpedo bomber. Initially designed by Grumman, it bore the designation TBF; the TB identified its function as a torpedo bomber, while the letter designator F stood for Grumman. When General Motors began manufacturing this type following an order from the US government to change its assembly lines from cars to aircraft, the company designator F was changed to M. Because TBMs started entering the fleet soon after the attack on Pearl Harbor, they were named Avengers. Pilots endearingly re-named them "Turkeys.")

I entered a room marked "Office" and introduced myself to the operations manager, Peter Deck.

"So you flew Trackers off the aircraft carrier?" remarked Peter, scanning my log book. "Any mountain flying experience?"

Well, there was that infamous beat up of the Wentworth ski resort in Nova Scotia so inconveniently witnessed by that humorless admiral, but I chose to skip it.

"It's something we look for in this firebombing business, you know."

Firebombing? Hell, I was just hoping for that budworm.

"But you do have some heavy piston time we might be able to use; there's a TBM out there needing a run-up. Al McDonell will give you a hand. Why don't you have a go and see me when you're done?"

Dazed by this unexpected turn of events, I located Al, who to my surprise and joy turned out to be a retired RCN chief petty officer whose jocular disposition instantly established him as an ally.

TBMs had already been phased out of the Navy when I joined the squadron directly out of USN flight training in 1960, so I'd never even peeked into a cockpit. As I approached this machine, I was struck by the immensity of its heft and girth. It dwarfed the T 28 Trojan, which we all thought was such a monster in comparison to our initial trainer, the T34 Mentor. But unlike all of the airplanes I had flown, which had tricycle gear, this was a tail-dragger.

Al showed me the foot-holds and hand-grips for climbing aboard, helped me into the cockpit, then handed me a checklist and started his checkout.

"The throttle and mixture controls are conventional, but believe it or not, this crazy vernier screw jack is the prop control. Here are the mags, the starter and primer, down there is the parking brake, and before you taxi, be sure to unlock the tail wheel."

He monitored the procedures as I fumbled the unfamiliar engine into life, then after climbing down and listening carefully to its sound, performed a little dance. I would become intimately familiar with this routine over the next dozen years, and never ceased to marvel at the unerring way Mac's ear told him practically everything about an engine's performance and condition.

The sprightly foot shuffle was his thumbs up.

The way this behemoth squatted on its tail, which reared up the engine nacelle with its elephantine cowl flaps and blocked the view precisely where you needed to look, made taxiing a challenge.

After reaching the run-up area, I set the parking brake, and my field of vision narrowed to the checklist and instrument panel. Religiously completing each item, I reached the procedure to perform the magneto check. This required an increase of power up to thirty inches of manifold pressure, which is over half of the power available. Glued to the gauges, I gingerly advanced the throttle, when through the roar of the engine and all the shaking and shuddering, my senses perceived an attitude change.

Looking up, I realized to my horror that this cantankerous ogre had reared up its tail, and bent on some fiendishly suicidal mission, appeared intent on excavating a hole with its prop to bury itself, along with its unsuspecting neophyte, right there under the tarmac. In a desperate reflex, I chopped the throttle. The mammoth momentarily teetered on its wheels then crashed clumsily back down on its tail-wheel.

What the hell? Some kind of microburst?

I checked the windsock; it hung like a wet rope. Utterly befuddled, I discontinued this kamikaze mission and taxied back to the ramp.

"How did it go?" asked Mac as he climbed up on the wing.

Still visibly shaken, I stammered out what had happened.

"You didn't have the stick back?"

Feverishly, I scanned the checklist.

"It's *not* on the checklist! Everybody knows you have to have the stick back in a tail- dragger."

Oh, sure, everybody knows … bloody obvious now, but this cowboy had hardly even *seen* a flipping tail-dragger. Such a thing never even crossed the threshold...

"Never mind," consoled Mac, "we'll get a mule, pick up the elevators, and I'll have them bolted back on in no time."

How could this recent ally be so insensitive to someone just back from a near-death experience?

"How did it go?" asked Peter as I entered his office.

Sheepishly I started to tell him. He stared at me with incredulity.

"You didn't have the stick back?"

No, goddammit! I didn't have the bloody stick back! Nobody told me to have the goddamn stick back! In fact, you can have your fucking stick back, and you know what you can do with it!

That was what my guts were screaming to say, but instead, I blurted out some incoherent apology.

He shook his head in disbelief.

"Let's go have a look," he said as I followed him out to the aircraft.

Mac was perched on a ladder, filing the end of a prop blade.

"Took a quarter of an inch off each blade nice and even," Mac said with a grin. "I'd been having trouble getting the RPM up on this engine; maybe that'll do the trick."

I broke out in a cold sweat. In the Navy, touching the propeller to anything meant an automatic prop or even engine change.

"Come back to my office; we'll talk about it."

Yeah, I know what we'll talk about. They're probably going to make me cough up for the damage, and I might as well say sayonara to the job, to post-graduate studies, and to all the dreams of a lucrative and thrilling career.

"Sit down, son; that was a hell of a close call. It's not all your fault, though. I should have given you a more thorough briefing."

"But what about the prop, Sir? In the Navy …"

"Not to worry, Mac will take care of that; but as far as employment is concerned, with your lack of tail-dragger experience, I'll have to have a hard think about it. I'll give you a call tomorrow."

I still remember the torment of emotion on that interminable drive home.

What an opportunity squandered! A passport to the future ripped to shreds. Of course, it could have been a helluva lot worse … on the other hand, what about Skyway's apparently cavalier attitude to safety? Did I really want to fly in civilian aviation?

I didn't dare tell my parents what had happened; I just said I expected a call tomorrow and shut myself in my room.

After that Polar night, the dreaded call came through.

"This is Peter. Get your butt over here, we've got some training to do. We'll start you off in the Harvard."

At that exalted moment, I could readily have embraced a faith, but for the time being, my mother would have to do. My log book shows two dual trips with Peter in the Harvard followed by one solo, after which I was deemed to be qualified for the TBM.

To prepare for this historic flight, I studied the aircraft manual and familiarized myself with the cockpit and with emergency procedures. Peter briefed me on the behavior and flying characteristics of this admittedly daunting machine, and as soon as the butterflies settled in my gut, I was ready to roll.

Skyway had a resident *goofer* group that gathered outside the hangar on such occasions, and they were out in full strength. If they expected a nose over, they were to be disappointed, since I had boldly inscribed, as the first item above the "Engine Run-up" section of the checklist:

STICK BACK! AS EVERYBODYKNOWS.

The 1950 horsepower Wright Cyclone engine responded with a thunderous roar to my measured advance of the throttle, which rattled and shook everything in the vicinity. With the wind on the nose, and the tail-wheel locked, the airplane maintained a straight line. Following Peter's instructions, when the airspeed reached fifty knots, I eased the stick forward to raise the tail off the ground then gently pulled back to lift us into the air. With the gear and flaps up, climb power set and the cowl flaps in trail, I could shift my concentration to the enjoyment of the experience.

What a feeling!

Just a scant week ago I had no inkling that I would ever fly again, and here I am in the cockpit of a WWII torpedo bomber the likes of which, operating from aircraft carriers, helped to turn the tide of the war.

I took the airplane up to altitude, where I tested it in slow flight and performed stalls in various attitudes and configurations. As expected, it was heavy on the controls but held no nasty surprises. If the engine should stop, bailing out without hitting the horizontal stabilizer might be a squeeze, but with its double row of cylinders and the three-bladed prop to bulldoze saplings away from in front of the cockpit, it could make a crash-landing a viable option.

Had the kibitzers remained in place for my third flight, they would have been treated to the sight of a substantial trail of smoke belching out immediately after takeoff caused by a fried battery that produced a total electrical failure. I made an abbreviated circuit, and with the hatches wide open plunked down on the runway, somewhat excessively thrilled by the experience.

The next stage of the check-out was to get a feel of the aircraft at maximum gross weight. Before taking up a load of water, Peter explained the drop mechanism. The TBM tank consists of two hydraulically operated compartments with a total capacity of five hundred imperial gallons. The pilot can drop the doors singly or a salvo of both. There was also an emergency method of tripping the doors manually in case of hydraulic or electrical failure.

After a takeoff run, which was twice as long as when empty, I climbed to a safe height, where I repeated the above maneuvers and learned that a stall in such a condition was categorically inadvisable. On returning to the field, I was cleared to make two single door drops near the hangar, followed by two salvo drops to get used to the pitch-up accompanying load release, which at the normal speed of 120 kts was easily controllable.

Exciting as it was, this training was all for naught, as there were no TBM seats available that season. Nevertheless, I was ecstatic to get a foot in the door with a contract to fly the birddog. I was to fly the Harvard and a Cessna 180 starting in July for a thousand bucks a month plus per-diem and hourly flight pay. A few typewritten pages described the birddog pilot's job.

I was to fly the air attack officer (AAO) to the target, where he formulated a plan of attack. I was then required to fly the tanker's proposed flight path, noting the altitude, direction, visibility, air conditions, any notable impediments en route, and any useful geographic markers the tanker pilot could use for his lineup. After the AAO described his drop requirements to the arriving aircraft, I was to demonstrate the desired flight path to the tanker while maintaining a stream of color commentary, including the above information.

Once the tanker was established on the approach, my job was to slip in above and behind the tanker's left side to permit last minute verbal corrections. When the load left the aircraft, I was to make a sharp right turn over the drop area to enable the AAO to make his assessment.

That was an enormous amount for a beginning pilot to learn, and as I was soon to discover, an experienced birddog pilot was crucial to the efficiency of the entire operation. Given all this responsibility, I still wonder how the companies had the conscience to determinedly keep the birddog pilots' pay well below the tanker pilots' for decades.

What unbelievable luck that the firebombing season dovetailed so neatly with the academic year. Could this be the unexpected breakthrough that might permit me to consider post-graduate education? The start of a new career? A thousand bucks a month won't go far, but if sometime in the future a TBM seat becomes available, who knows?

The main thing was that there was hope, but in keeping with a Polish proverb, it was still "a proposition written with a stick on water."

As a knee-jerk reaction to this freshly opened option, I rushed over to the Faculty of Law. Yes, they told me, I had the requisite qualifications and was welcome to enrol. Unfortunately, a visit to the law library and a brief perusal of the legal texts I was required to assimilate provoked a decidedly detumescent effect on my recent enthusiasm for this profession, and I walked out resigned to the fact that my entry into courts of law would have to continue in the role of defendant.

For guidance about my academic future, I turned to my Restoration Theatre professor, Dr. Pincus, who was also my counsellor. I did well in his course, and at his bidding recounted my acting experiences in the Navy and my long infatuation with theatre.

Why don't I apply to the Theatre Department? he suggested.

I should have thought of it on my own.

Accordingly, I presented myself to the head of the department, Dr. John Brockington, or "JB" as he was popularly known, and informed him that I wished to enroll in the MA program. JB looked up over the rim of his glasses, and with a significant shake of his pendulous jowls, allowed in his characteristically mincing voice that this would be possible only after completing an undergraduate year in theatre.

That suited me fine. I jumped on this suggestion and left the office buoyed with purpose and dizzy with that intoxicating feeling that I was on the brink of a new and exhilarating adventure.

SELLING ENCYCLOPAEDIAS IN MONTREAL

Toward the end of May, Peter Deck told me that a TBM slated for the budworm project in New Brunswick needed to be delivered to one of the pilots living in St. Jovite, Quebec. If I was interested, the job was mine, and someone would give me a lift back to Abbotsford once spraying was completed a month or so later.

There was no pay involved, of course: no, no, no, heaven forbid, out of the question! This was just an opportunity for me to build some time.

I called Christine in Montreal, and with her agreement to put up with me for a month, volunteered to do the flight.

Around this time, a letter arrived from Ottawa. Its respectful tone informed me that, on the grounds of my perceptively penetrating essay, I was welcome to commence work in the Department of Foreign Affairs forthwith, with an instant promotion to level 2 in recognition of my naval service. Though highly flattered by the offer, I forwarded my regrets on the same grounds as Groucho Marx when he said that he'd never join an organization that would have him as a member.

On May 25, Avenger pilot Plawski, with six and a half hours of experience on type, reported for duty in Abbotsford. With Peter Deck's help, we plotted the stages of my journey. It would be strictly a map reading, visual flight rules (VFR) crossing aided by non-directional beacon (NDB) navigation.

Without getting overly technical, the only navigation instrument available on the Skyway Avengers was a radio magnetic indicator (RMI) composed of a needle superimposed on a magnetic compass card that points in the direction of the beacon, whose radio frequency was selected by the pilot.

With Tanker 4 loaded to the cowl gills with spare parts, and with stacks of aviation charts cluttering the cockpit, I started out on my solo adventure.

Following overnight stops in Regina, two nights in Winnipeg, and one in Sault Ste. Marie, I delivered the craft to St. Jovite on May 30, *virgo intacta*.

After moving in with Christine and being chronically short of cash, I started a job hunt. It was quite an eye-opener to discover what a thankless task this must be for someone trying to scratch out a living. Eventually, I succumbed to the promise of easy money from an ad about selling Colliers' Encyclopedias door-to-door. This was to involve a two-day course spent memorizing a sales pitch, followed by a demonstration of how to apply it during a field trip with an instructor.

The course, a fascinating study in the psychology of persuasion, included specific instructions of how to wipe one's feet before entering a client's premises.

With my script committed to memory, and dressed like Seventh Day Adventists, my instructor and I ventured into the field, where he was to demonstrate its application.

We knocked on numerous doors all morning but never got past the threshold. The afternoon was no better, but reacting to my visible discouragement, my leader assured me that he had an ace in the hole. Producing an address book, he announced that at three o'clock he had an appointment to make a presentation.

Dutifully arriving on time, and mindful of the rules of engagement regarding the wiping of feet, we trod the mat mechanically like a couple of dogs after a squat in the park. We then followed the young couple into their sitting room, where they raptly monitored every word of my instructor's masterful presentation.

Of course! They eagerly agreed; an encyclopedia was precisely what they needed all along, and for just the price of a few cigarettes per day (part of the pitch), they would be silly not to subscribe to those essential supplements contained in the annual yearbooks as well.

When out of sight of the contented customers' house, the instructor's triumphant gesture, signifying *voila!* did nothing to dissuade me from believing that I had just witnessed an elaborately rehearsed set up.

For our first unsupervised day on the job we were driven to Sherbrooke, where after receiving maps of our assigned areas, which included the address for the five o'clock pick-up, we were on our own. I found myself in a seemingly well-to-do blue-collar neighbourhood amid rows of welcoming homes and pleasant gardens. The dwellers, however, failed to reflect their environs.

After a dozen rebuffs, I dropped the tight-assed formality of my rehearsed address in favor of a friendly, everyday greeting, which—voila!— resulted in an invitation. A fuss was made over my thankless profession by a friendly, middle-aged couple, and coffee and biscuits were served, but somehow the subject of encyclopedias failed to come up.

Mildly disheartened by my lack of success, I ate my pre-packed lunch on a park bench and with renewed resolve strode in the direction of a more promisingly opulent neighborhood.

I approached a handsome, tree-shaded mansion and rang the bell. A gentleman attired in a bathing suit whose bonhomie suggested a trace of insobriety opened the door.

"Come right in," he said exuberantly. Ignoring my momentary reluctance, he steered me into his foyer. Waving off my anemic attempt to start a presentation, he led me to a swimming pool, where a lavishly stocked roll-away bar awaited under a vast umbrella. Something about this gent's demeanor relaxed my initial suspicions regarding carnal motives, and never the shrinking violet in the face of proffered liquor, I accepted a drink.

It turned out to be an afternoon brimful of hilarity in the company of an urbane French radio station talk-show host who was happy to have found a compliant drinking buddy. When it was time for my rendezvous, my host, still in his bathing suit, insisted on delivering me to my pick-up point, where I poured myself into the waiting van to the amazement of my fellow students and disgust of my instructor.

I didn't bother to show up for work the following morning, devoting myself instead to a more rewarding task of helping Christine paint her new apartment.

1965, FIRST SUMMER OF FIREBOMBING

When the time came to return to the West Coast, it was Peter Deck himself who arrived in a TBM. To my amazement, after waving me into the pilot's seat, he crawled into the back where not only was he trapped in a cramped and noisy compartment, but he was entirely at the mercy of the fledgling up front. I was to develop great respect for Peter Deck; he tirelessly introduced me to the requirements of the job, mentored my progress, and never tired of reminding me that the trees, which look so soft from the air, are made of wood. Without hesitation, I credit him for my air tanker career.

On July 1, my mother drove me to Abbotsford, where I was to pick up a Cessna 180 and fly it to Prince George to birddog a pair of Cansos operated by a company called Flying Firemen. Known also as PBY Catalinas, these versatile, twin-engine amphibious flying boats served in the air forces and navies of numerous nations during WWII, escorting convoys and providing anti-submarine reconnaissance as well as air-sea rescue.

These two old RCAF retirees were flown by a pair of highly experienced pilots, Alex Davidson and Sheldon Luck. As I was soon to find out, Sheldon was one of Canada's most famous aviators. He soloed in 1930 at the age of nineteen and did most of his early flying as a bush pilot in the north, where he lived up to his name. Among his many achievements were the inauguration of a Vancouver-to-Whitehorse mail and passenger service, while during the war, as a volunteer ferry pilot, he delivered B17s, Liberators, and Marauders to England. With a pencil-thin Errol Flynn moustache, he was a smooth talking, easy walking, crooked-smile-but-straight-teeth prototype of a swashbuckling professional pilot.

Sheldon continued to fly fire bombers, including the A26, well into his seventies. His achievements can be examined in the Ottawa Aviation Museum, where he is inducted into the Aviation Hall of Fame.

After stints in Fort Nelson and Prince George, I was sent to Smithers to birddog a pair of company TBM's where, to my delight, I discovered that Mac was the chief engineer.

One of the tanker pilots was Don Hill, an ex-RCAF search and rescue pilot, while the other was the lanky young Tommy Wilson, colloquially known as

Willow, a highly experienced flyer for his age who obtained his commercial license at the age of eighteen.

Smithers was a friendly little backwater town picturesquely situated in the Bulkley River valley in the shadow of the imposing Hudson Bay Mountain.

Not long ago, this mountain was crowned with a glacier. Now, a jagged remnant of ice overhanging a moraine is all that's left of this once magnificent monument of nature.

A further attraction was a nine-hole golf course that, as was customary with many northern clubs, came equipped with sand "greens."

A WWII style wooden hangar housed the tanker base, which we shared with flocks of resident swallows, along with unmistakable signs of nocturnal habitation by more resourceful dwellers with whom we fought a daily battle over anything comestible. The crews were billeted at the Hilltop Hotel, from where we commuted to the base in a company van.

In response to the growing fire hazard, Peter Deck flew in with an extra Avenger a few days after my arrival to beef up our team.

On July 16, which is my birthday, Peter presented me with a gift in the form of a trip in a TBM, which he authorized as a test flight. Can anyone imagine such a gesture in today's tight-assed and regulation-strangled world? Perhaps Peter was already planning ahead, because a few days later when the fire-horn went off, he intercepted me as I sprinted toward my Cessna.

"I'll birddog this fire; you get into tanker 7 and see what you can do."

Oh my God! Just like that?

I chased after Don and Tom to the fire and tried to imitate everything they did. Two full days of multiple targets with Peter's forensic debriefings was my baptism of fire.

What a feeling! I was now a tanker pilot!

Well, not quite.

I soon discovered that learning to firebomb requires a prolonged process of apprenticeship. Simply put, the objective in firebombing is to determine the correct trigger point to release the load at the right altitude and airspeed—piece of cake on flat ground with good visibility in no wind conditions. However, variables like a howling gale, precipitous slope, severe downdrafts, or visibility curtailed by smoke and widow-makers poking up through the forest canopy complicate the issue considerably, while a combination of these can make it as demanding as a night landing on the pitching deck of a carrier in an Atlantic blizzard. Both require acute situational awareness, good hand-eye coordination, calmness under pressure, the gift of feel, and a willingness to accept a calculated risk—skills that are only acquired through practice and experience.

For a beginner, just getting some of the parameters right while keeping the airplane flying and the engine within limits is a definite challenge, and this jockey had a long way to go.

Luc's photo of me in Tanker 12.

Anecdote: Neil Armstrong, Navy Pilot

A few years ago, I had the unique privilege of being a guest of Bob Fish, the trustee of the Museum of Apollo 11, the orbital mission whose crew made the first landing on the moon. This museum is situated aboard the Essex class carrier USS *Hornet*, which is tied up to a jetty in Alameda, California.

In his book, *Hornet Plus Three*, Bob describes the role of the *Hornet*, which in 1969 deployed to the Pacific to retrieve the returning astronauts. While writing the book, he became a personal friend of Neil Armstrong, who was a Navy pilot before becoming an astronaut.

On learning that I had also flown in the Navy, Bob recounted the following story: he'd asked Neil to isolate some particularly notable incident or experience during his remarkable career. Expecting something associated with the space program, he was amazed to hear Neil state, without a trace of hesitation: "My first night carrier landing."

I know this revelation will make all my Navy-pilot friends join me in feeling warm and runny inside, particularly when considering that our landings took place on a carrier that displaced a modest 20,000 tons compared to our American contemporaries who flew off ships much larger than ours.

HYDER, ALASKA, AND HOW *NOT* TO STAGE A FLY-PAST

Peter left our group early in July, and with a new birddog pilot in his place, we were sent to operate out of a temporary base in Stewart, a small mining town on the Canadian side of the Alaska border that abuts Hyder, Alaska.

Hyder boasted a hotel, the Sealaska Inn, where the bar never closed as long as a single customer remained on the premises, which is of course where we all checked in. To reach it we had to pass the customs officer, the erstwhile counterpart of today's Homeland Security, who after five o'clock closed up shop, leaving the frontier between the two nations undefended until morning.

Fires were plentiful in the area, and to attack them we carried a product long since abandoned called "Gelguard." This was a pink powder that when added to water turned it into jelly.

Since water leaves no mark on the forest canopy, and on a hot day suffers from massive evaporation during descent, Gelguard attempted to address both problems. The dye left a visible stain at the drop site, and the jellification marginally inhibited evaporation.

A glacier-fed creek, which conveniently meandered next to the runway, served as our water source and kept the beer supply for Mac and the loading crew at an appropriate temperature all day.

Flying out of Stewart was a haphazard operation, because every takeoff from the dirt strip produced a blizzard of dust, which acts like sandpaper when mixed with engine oil. Arriving aircraft needed to circle the field, and planes on the ground couldn't start their engines until it settled. In spite of this handicap, we flew steadily for three days before being recalled to Smithers.

On takeoff from Stewart, I experienced a condition about which Peter had cautioned me, which also appeared in the aircraft manual in the form of a warning. When making a right-hand climbing turn, it was vital in this airplane to maintain balanced flight by keeping the ball in the middle;* otherwise, there was a risk of slipping to the right, which could cause rudder reversal.

Sure as hell, there I was in a tight, right climbing turn, waving farewell to the adoring public below and paying no attention whatsoever to the job at hand when … *Wham!* The rudder locked hard to the left.

Observers on the ground watching an airplane that shortly after liftoff starts crabbing sideways in a slow, nose-high descent while maintaining takeoff power could be excused for presuming they were being treated to an artfully crafted stunt performed by a pilot possessed of superior skills.

The situation in the cockpit looked somewhat different.

I was bloody well stumped.

To start with, no human strength could center that rudder. I remember frantically shoving the stick forward as far as it would go while desperately fighting to get that wing up. After an eternity, the forgiving airplane somehow flew itself out of this pickle, but thankfully my passenger never knew how close we were to returning to *terra* altogether too *firma*.

After returning to Smithers, Willow quit Skyway to fly De Havilland Otters in Guyana, and Peter departed for Abbotsford, which left me, Don Hill, and the new birddog pilot in Smithers as sole protectors of the Prince Rupert District.

Don Hill and me in Hyder, Alaska, 1965.

TRANSPORT CANADA AND STUDENT PILOTS
MUST *NOT* READ THIS SEGMENT

Unseasonable cold put a damper on our flying, which allowed me to spend time on the golf course getting used to putting on sand greens.

The weather soon changed to downpours, which resulted in Forestry releasing the tanker crews and standing the base down. Since it was too wet to play golf, Don and I picked up a couple of crocks and repaired to our rooms in the hotel, where after a few hours we were thoroughly blitzed.

Then the phone rang. It was the dispatcher.

"There's a fire in Terrace," she announced sweetly, "so would you kindly get your butts to the airport forthwith."

It was obvious what we needed to do, but these were pioneering days when everyone was always looking over their shoulder, afraid of losing their job. Immersed in this culture of fear, unprotected by unions and definitely out of touch with our brains, we were convinced that turning the flight down meant a direct line to that dreaded bus ticket home.

Strangely, the details of this flight remain eerily etched in my memory. We agreed to be extra cautious and to act as each other's guardians, triple checking our checklists and scanning each other's airplanes for any visible oversight. After a crawl in marginal VFR up to the Telkwa Pass south-west of Smithers, to our amazement, we broke out into a sunny day on the other side of the mountain range, where we found the birddog orbiting a fire on a steep slope.

Brimful of boundless bravado, we each scored a bullseye.*

After a reload in Terrace, we confidently repeated the performance, after which we were released to home base. Throughout the flight, I had the illusion of total control and remember an overwhelming feeling of ecstasy, which I expressed by belting out Broadway songs at plexiglass-shattering pitch.

---

* The air attack officer assesses each drop for accuracy and effectiveness, which is a comparison between intent and result. Because experience allows us to imagine the elongated footprint of an average single door drop, assessments are given related to this datum. Calls such as "Half a load short" or "One load right" are easily understood and contain all the information the pilot requires to adjust his trigger-point or the track of the next delivery. Occasionally, even if the load is misplaced, it may still be judged as effective.

Sobered by this experience, on the drive home we agreed that we got away with something monstrously idiotic.

As the 1965 season drew to a close, we were introduced to a Smithers tradition that dictated that at least one practice per year was to be a public event. This always took place over the empty field adjoining the tanker base. Accordingly, the local radio station disseminated the information, which attracted about a hundred spectators who gathered around the perimeter. Since Don and I had been military pilots, we decided to fly the demonstration in formation. We took off with me in echelon starboard, and following a low pass over the field, performed a formation drop.

Absurd? You bet! But a little frivolity works wonders for morale, and our heroics were appropriately acknowledged that evening at the Hudson Hotel, which marked the end of an unforgettable debut.

1965, THEATRE DEPARTMENT, UBC

On return to Vancouver, I enrolled in the Frederick Wood Department of Theatre, where in consultation with JB, we assembled my curriculum. He suggested a mix of academic courses devoted to theatre history along with an introduction to acting, directing, and production.

While Doctors Klaus Strassmann, Don Soule, and JB handled theatre classes, the production aspect, such as lighting, scenery construction, and stagecraft, was the domain of Norman Young.

I was by far the oldest student in the department, but I doubt if anyone could match me for keenness and enthusiasm.

We were well into the course-work when three weeks after the fire season officially ended a fire broke out on Mount Washington, the ski resort west of Courtenay. Skyway frantically put out a call for pilots—not an easy task, since most had returned to their real jobs and were scattered all over the country, but eventually a workable number congregated on base and waited for instructions.

Comox was the closest airport to the fire where temporary loading arrangements could be installed, but this was an operational air force base, and these were the days when our government refused to confirm or deny whether Canada harbored nuclear weapons. In spite of this, Skyway obtained the necessary clearances, and the above question may have been answered by the way our personnel were rigorously escorted by tight-lipped guards to and from our airplanes.

Our group of TBMs created a bizarre sight next to the Voodoos, CF 100s, F5s, and other pedigreed stock whose pilots observed our activities with condescending bemusement, but I would not have swapped places with a single one of them. (We learned much later that the resident CF 101 Voodoo squadron was equipped with Genie air-to-air nuclear-tipped guided missiles.)

Two days later, happily enriched, I was back in school. The program called for all students to take part in every aspect of production, including stage managing and acting in a play. When my turn came, JB cast me as Lord Dumaine in his production of *Love's Labours Lost*, for which he obliged me to grow a beard. I still cringe at the memory when, hopelessly dried, I wandered around the stage in a daze, senselessly repeating: "I'm so in love! I'm so in love."

It was an intensely productive year at the end of which I was ready to start the MA program. However, now that spring was in the air, it was time to switch sights to the other chapter of my existence by preparing for the flying season, a ritual due to be repeated for the next thirty-four years.

Love's Labours Lost, UBC, 1967. Me holding the wench, Pat Rose center, Dermot Hennelly on right, and Lionel Lukin-Johnson under the hat.

1966: MEETING LINC, AND THE AERIAL CIRCUS OF BUDWORM SPRAYING IN NEW BRUNSWICK.

I looked forward with great anticipation to the start of the flying season, because I was about to take part in the experience of a lifetime. It was the budworm spray program in New Brunswick.

I found the Skyway hangar a hive of activity. Spring preparations were in full swing with radiomen, electricians, and engineers briskly performing their preparatory tasks.

The main greeting area was outside the administrator's office, where Percy Lotzer was busy signing in the returning pilots. There was a palpable excitement animating the air, full of hearty backslaps and manly handshakes, as well as introductions of freshmen like me. It felt awesome to be joining this team of kindred spirits, a civilian counterpart of a Navy squadron to which I profoundly desired to earn the right to belong.

Anchoring the activity was a blond, sturdily built fellow brandishing a hefty stack of papers.

"I'm Al Linkewich,"* he greeted me as he crushed my hand while proffering a sheaf of stapled, office-length pages with the title: *Pilots Notes for Firebombing.*

Since nearly everything I'd learned the previous year came via word of mouth, I was indeed pleased to receive something in writing from a person I assumed was a Skyway instructor.

"That is not official Skyway literature!" Percy's stentorian voice boomed from his office.

In confusion, I turned back to Linc, noting his subtle gesture of dismissal. Uncertain of what lurked behind this exchange, I was about to walk away when he took my arm.

"That'll be ten bucks," he said, unwittingly revealing a dominant trait of his complex character with which I was to become intimately familiar over the next forty-six years of unbroken friendship.

---

* Al wrote his first two books on firebombing using his original name, Alexander Linkewich. Sometime later, he officially changed it to Linc Alexander, and all future reference to him in this narrative will use the name Linc.

As I was soon to discover, from the day Linc dropped his first load of water out of a Stearman in 1960, his naturally analytical mind began to concentrate on synthesizing what he was learning into a structured form. The stacks of paper that he was handing out were to lead to the publication of his first book on the subject, a hard-cover volume published in 1966 that bore the same title, *Pilots Notes for Firebombing.*

The TBM in which I completed my re-familiarization bore the number "12" on the tail and carried the arresting civil registration: "MUD." This was the airplane I was now eagerly loading for the transcontinental trip, mindful not to forget my golf clubs, which accompanied me wherever I went. After careful experimentation, I learned to fit the bag within the tangle of the rudder, elevator, and tail-wheel control cables in the rear section of the plane.

Firmly in the grip of euphoria, I roared for takeoff to start this grand adventure. I was part of a thundering formation of fourteen Avengers, our white fuselages and yellow-tipped silver wings glistening against the backdrop of the snow-capped Coastal Range. We spent the first night in Cranbrook, each stop offering new opportunities to get to know the members of the team.

We had a dentist, a ski-hill operator, an airline pilot, a geography professor, a farmer, a lawyer, and me—a theatre student—all of us military retirees. The remainder was of ambiguous provenance, but no matter what our background, we all shared a relentless passion for flying.

In addition to a staggering array of spare parts, we carried an electrician, a radio-man, and half-a-dozen wizards of the wrench, without whom this expedition may as well have stayed home. After stopovers in Winnipeg, Duluth, and Ottawa, on the sixth day we landed in Juniper, one of the many clearways hacked out of the boonies specifically for the spray program in New Brunswick.

During the general briefing, we were shown maps of the blocks to be sprayed, and I learned that the pay scale varied with the distance of the target from the airport.

We were assigned to teams with strange names like "Jughead," "Whisky," or "Ping Pong," while the name of my threesome was "Donkey."

Spraying was done in three-plane echelons at 150 knots, 125 feet above the tree-tops and 450 feet apart, which was the ideal separation to permit the swaths to descend with a slight overlap to the ground.

The lead Avenger pilot's job was to align his team with two pointer aircraft, which controlled our track from a thousand feet and flew at half of our speed.

They ordered "booms on" and "booms off" at each end of the block, as well as over any bodies of water. The reason for this caution was that DDT suspended in diesel oil, which we were using at that time, though a proven killer of insects and larvae, was also lethal to fish.

Had we read Rachel Carson's *Silent Spring*, published in 1962, we would have learned that long-term properties of persistent pesticides like DDT were unknown, that they were suspected of being carcinogens, and that they caused fatal thinning of birds' eggshells. However, along with the majority of the population, we were not aware of these dangers, and restrictions against the indiscriminate application of DDT were not implemented in North America until its ban ten years later.

Until then, we blithely carried this mixture in our belly tanks from where it was pumped into over-wing booms fitted with spray nozzles calibrated to a predetermined flow rate, and the pilots' only control was an on-off switch. At the end of each block we would stop spraying, and in a balletic maneuver, which was a joy to behold, we reversed course to parallel our previous direction. If done correctly, this reversal saved precious time, which might result in an extra flight.

Spraying could not start until the *bugologists* determined the *instar*, a term that described the maturity of the larvae and the stage at which they became vulnerable to the poison.

Several teams remained in Juniper, while the rest of us flew to Dunphy, a strip attractively located along the south-west Miramichi River near the village of Upper Blackville, where the distinctive white steeple of a church acted as a welcoming beacon. We parked alongside several American TBMs and a swarm of antediluvian, open-cockpit Stearman biplanes, which would have made Billy Bishop feel right at home.

Whereas Juniper accommodations consisted of four-person cottages with upper and lower bunks, Dunphy offered lodgings more closely resembling classic German *Stalag Luft* designs, with rows of beds along each wall and an entry at both ends.

The absence of refinements such as lockers forced us to store all of our possessions in suitcases under our beds, and the atmosphere inside was thick with the smell of dirty socks, soiled linen, and pilot braggadocio, while the snoring at night produced a cacophony no sea lion colony could rival.

We shared these accommodations with a colorful assortment of American professional spray pilots, the majority of whom flew Stearmans. For these nomads, the New Brunswick budworm program constituted the spring segment of a circuit that started in Central America, progressed northward through Florida where they sprayed army-ants, and continued through the cotton fields of Louisiana.

One of the Yankees, who billed himself as Colonel Patterson of the Confederate Air Force, swaggered to his TBM splendidly attired in a peacock-ish, custom-made flying suit topped off by a rococo bandana, while another arrived with a single possession: a toothbrush, which he carried wherever he went, its handle defiantly protruding out of his shirt pocket.

This man never undressed for bed—not even, thankfully, his cowboy boots.

We may have lacked privacy, but no one could complain about the round-the-clock, logging-camp style cuisine, which included an annual all-you-can-eat lobster blowout.

Since spraying could only be effective when the wind was slack, which usually meant just after dawn and again late in the afternoon, our daily routine was dominated by the weather. We were called to breakfast when it was still dark, and if conditions weren't right at daybreak, everyone trampled back to bed. If the wind was calm, the sound of the air horn caused a frenzied stampede. It was all about getting that extra load before the wind picked up.

Stearman drivers were particularly aggressive during this Le Mans-style start, sprinting to their machines and then racing each other to the loading pits. Though collisions were rare, spirited disputes were frequent, which occasion-ally led to fist fights on the tarmac. To have witnessed the daily anarchy of the budworm flying circus was to have participated in an unforgettable experience.

I recall one particularly unorthodox display of piloting skills when a Stearman turned on short final just as a TBM began its takeoff roll. Unable to fit in behind the rolling aircraft and unwilling to perform a go around, the Stearman pilot added power, flew over the top of the departing aircraft, and landing nimbly ahead of it, graciously cleared the runway in time to permit the TBM to continue the takeoff. It was hard to decide if the chutzpah award should go to the Stearman driver or to the Avenger pilot who coolly continued his run.

Ralph Langemann recalled an incident involving Stearman pilots who repeatedly used the superior maneuverability of their machines to sneak into the pits out of turn ahead of the TBMs. In spite of being warned by TBM pilot Jimmy Fewell that if they pulled this stunt again he just might fail to see the Stearman ahead of him, one rashly repeated this trick.

Ralph described it as follows: "Jim just kept moving slowly ahead; the Stearman driver frantically waved his arms, but Jim just kept coming. The TBM took about three slices out of the rudder of the Stearman before it made its escape at full throttle across the infield with ribbons of rudder waving in the slipstream. Never had that problem again."

Linc also used to recount a hilarious incident he had observed at Juniper.

To start a Stearman engine, the pilot had to swing the prop. Since most Stearmans had no functioning parking brakes, their pilots dug little pits for the wheels, which offered a degree of stability. After switching on the magnetos and fuel, the pilot set the throttle for approximately 1200 RPM, and after swinging the prop until the engine started, he trotted around the wing and climbed into the cockpit. On cold mornings, however, a higher throttle setting produced a better chance of a quick start. On this particular day, the pilot had set it too high, because when the engine caught, the aircraft leapt out of its depressions, nearly decapitating the hapless aviator, and rolled merrily away.

The machine started off charging like a demented bull toward the row of TBMs parked on the other side of the runway, but just in time, the tail wheel locked to one side, causing the runaway beast to start turning in circles.

For a while everyone stared helplessly at this dizzying sight, then all pilots sprinted to their planes and, like a herd of spooked buffalo, scattered to the far end of the field. This perilous pirouette lasted some fifteen minutes until a courageous Navy mechanic slipped inside the turn, dragged himself onto a wing, and chopped the throttle.

We completed block spraying in three weeks, leaving the river blocks to be treated with a different chemical called Fenitrothion. Two pilots were required to stay behind, who in the interest of fairness were traditionally those with the lowest earnings from the contract. I happened to be one of the two, while the other was Kenny Owen, an American flying for Skyway.

Spraying the river blocks was fun to fly, because the tight turns of the creeks and streams required us occasionally to stand our airplanes up on a wing, which was far more thrilling than flying straight lines in formation. The main hazard of the operation was the chemical itself. Mac brought this emphatically to my attention when, after a spray run, he showed me his glove with which he'd wiped the paint off to bare metal from inside the flap where the slipstream sucked in the goop. In subsequent seasons, pilots spraying this stuff were required to wear pressurized helmets, but pioneering ventures are often remarkably free of such cumbersome and costly refinements.

We returned across Canada as a twosome, which I, though junior to Kenny, was unexpectedly designated to lead. It wasn't long before I discovered why. Because Kenny had been a navigator in the USAF, it was hard to explain his pious aversion to map reading. His other eccentricities, such as his habit of unplugging his radios shortly after takeoff, were also a mystery; it did, however, make for refreshingly silent flying until his squeaky voice announced his presence shortly before landing. I accepted these aberrations, and my only instruction to him was to keep me in sight.

We arrived in Ottawa without incident, where we spent the night. The next morning, with a steady stream of chatter, the Ottawa tower controller exhibited an unusual amount of interest in my airplane, which prompted me to ask if he would like to see it up close on departure.

This, it seemed, was what he was angling for. With his blessing, I took full advantage of his invitation, circled the field to build up a good head of steam, then grass-high took dead aim at his glass palace. After nearly removing the structure's whip antennas, I pulled up into a vertical chandelle, which had to have rivalled my champion low pass in the Navy. For once, I became the fighter pilot that fate had denied me but which I'd always imagined should have been my destiny.

With Kenny behind me, I set a course for Kapuskasing, about five hundred miles to the north-west. This stretch of the Canadian Shield is a flat tapestry of intertwined lakes bereft of identifying features, which requires staying on course, because at low altitude the middle segment was outside the range of radio navigational beacons.

Paradoxically, such an abundance of water is a source of comfort for pilots of single-engine, retractable-gear aircraft, since in case of engine failure, it's by far the safest surface on which to alight. Our Avengers were particularly adept at ditching, because the retardant tank tucked into the bomb bay provided sufficient buoyancy for the aircraft to float for some time.

Anecdote: How to Ditch a TBM

John Truran discovered this virtue while spraying in Quebec in 1971 aboard MUD, the very aircraft I was presently flying, when his engine started to back-fire, belched smoke, and lost power. Realizing there was no way he could nurse it to the airport, John wisely decided to ditch, which he accomplished using all the skills he had acquired flying seaplanes.

Setting up a gentle descent, he watched in amazement as on touching the water, the prop separated from the engine and improbably thrashed itself sideways on the surface until it sank some fifty yards away, while the rest of the airplane glided smoothly to a stop. John waited patiently in his seat until a helicopter perched a skid on the canopy, which allowed him to pull himself aboard without getting his feet wet. After being hauled out of the water, the airplane was flying within weeks.

Similarly, my cabin mate in the *Bonaventure*, Dave Matheson, used to recall how in 1959, on his way back to Shearwater, he was forced to ditch a TBM in the sea near Chebucto Head. He and his crew were likewise rescued by choppers as they waited patiently on the floating machine. Dave was doubly lucky, as the aircraft subsequently sank in deep water, which made it impossible to prove that the most probable cause of the engine failure was fuel starvation.

About halfway to Kapuskasing, I was startled by the unmistakable high-pitched voice of my flying mate.

"Where are you?" he inquired.

Assuming he was making a position check, I started searching my map. It was hopeless. With my automatic direction finding (ADF) needle aimlessly circling around, having lost the Ottawa beacon, I was dead-reckoning still out of range from KAP.

"Damned if I know, Kenny. Where do you put us?"

"I don't know," he answered.

A quick check of the sector where he should have been revealed that Kenny had vanished. A cryptic exchange followed.

"Have you got me in sight?"

"No."

"When did you last see me?"

"I don't know."

"What does your ADF show?"

"It isn't working."

"Tell me what you see below."

"I'm over a lake."

Oh bully … there's a million of them.

Eventually, he described some features of a large lake, which seemed to correspond with something on my chart about twenty miles to the south. I told him to orbit where he was, and I'd come to get him. It was not the right lake. They all look alike. I tried another and finally spotted him. I ordered him to get on my wing and from now on to keep his radio on.

"OK," he replied in his childlike, unaffected way. Christ! How can you even get angry at someone like that?

CLOSE CALL NEAR REGINA

After fueling in Kapuskasing, we proceeded to our next stop in Winnipeg, from where the weather, except for isolated thunderstorms, was forecast to be clear all the way to the Rockies. When we finally saw one, *isolating* might have been a more accurate description. This mammoth stretched across our entire arc of vision from the ground up. Regina radio reported that the storm had already passed to the east of the airport, leaving strong winds but good visibility behind it, which in our area was deteriorating rapidly. Since there appeared to be no way around this monstrosity, I did what any prudent pilot would do under these circumstances: descend to the Trans Canada highway and let it guide us to our destination.

Presently, day changed to night, and I had to push right down to the deck not to lose the visual flight path created by the lights of the traffic below. We were now embedded in vicious turbulence flying into a headwind that barely allowed us to pass the cars going in the same direction. I took a quick peek to my right; Kenny was bouncing wildly fifty yards away, managing to stay in position. The curtain of rain made a continuous din like tearing burlap, and little streams of water started leaking into the cockpit. While my right arm churned the stick in spastic arcs attempting to maintain a semblance of control, I peered desperately through the prop arc to maintain visual contact.

I have no idea how, in that visibility, I caught a glimpse of that radio tower just to the left of my nose.

"Break right!" I hollered, as in an instant, knee-jerk reaction, with both hands on the stick I hauled the airplane up and to the right, somehow missing both Kenny and the steel guy-wires that radiate outward to the ground from the top of these structures.

As is common with prairie storms, we were in the clear two minutes later and landed in carefree sunshine. I remember remaining very still in the cockpit for some time after shutting down, the sudden silence broken only by the soothing litany of little metallic pings that large piston engines make as they begin to cool—a rosary of sounds that a soul might make as it slinks away on tip-toe from a close encounter with eternity. It was thanks to the headwind, of course:

only the drastically reduced ground speed gave me a chance to spot that tower in time. Even though most pilots are loath to discuss them, we all remember our close calls; with me, this one certainly holds its place near the apogee.

1966, FIREBOMBING, SMITHERS

Back in British Columbia, with my new flying partner, Ralph Langemann, we arrived at our assigned tanker base of Smithers on June 13 and took up residence at the Hilltop Hotel.

Ralph had learned to fly with the Air Force, and I soon discovered numerous similarities in our career paths that had led us to firebombing. Ralph could have stayed in the military, but when at the end of his tour he was asked whether he might consider making it his career, he dispelled all ambiguity with a grease-penciled comment across the questionnaire, stating: "Not fucking likely!"

On July 3, intense fire activity in the vicinity of Terrace caused us to reposition to this spectacularly scenic area, where we were joined by Linc and his team from Kamloops. Because cheaper accommodations usually assigned to wandering tanker groups were conveniently unavailable, for nearly three weeks we stayed at the plush Skogland Resort near Kitimat. Flying almost every day, we spent our evenings toasting our luck while luxuriating by the lodge's swimming pool.

"Guess where I'm supposed to be tomorrow," challenged Ralph one evening as we settled in for a nightcap. "Starting training with Canadian Pacific Airlines."

A story eerily parallel to mine soon began to emerge. In addition to CP, Ralph had also applied with United Airlines and received a job offer from both. On sober reflection, he concluded that there was nothing that airline flying could offer that came close to rivalling what we were engaged in right now. Moreover, this meant he could return to university, where like me, he briefly considered becoming a lawyer. Shrugging off this repugnant option, he enrolled instead in post-graduate studies in geography at the University of Calgary.

While reminiscing about our respective times in the services, Ralph mentioned an intriguing fact about the Air Force's singular attitude to religion.

Though Ralph had formally declared that he was an atheist, when he received his dog tags (we didn't have these in the Navy), he found himself baptized as UCC (The United Church of Canada). To redress this error, he requested new tags; when they arrived, Ralph was again officially credited with a conversion. Further research revealed the unexpected fact that, in the RCAF, atheists came under the authority of the UCC—surely a most commendable Canadian expression of Christian inclusiveness.

With Ralph Langemann in Smithers, 1966.

HOW TO LAND AN AIRPLANE WITH A PUTTER

Lightning strikes at Lava and Tetachuk Lakes provided two days of action in some of British Columbia's most scenic terrain before rains finally washed the season out. Not all was over, however, because since I won the President's cup at the Smithers golf course for the second year in a row, I was asked to represent the club in a tournament in Terrace.

Luckily, Rick, the pilot who held the fire patrol contract, was an avid golfer, and his Piper *Cub* became our mode of transportation. Since there was no room for golf bags in his airplane, he just stuffed some clubs loosely around me in the rear seat. Feeling like I was in a cage, we arrived at our destination.

The Thornhill golf club that hosted the two-day event also had sand greens, but unlike in Smithers, these greens were coated with tar. I learned their secret sufficiently well, because on the last day, with one par-five hole to go, I was carrying a four-shot lead.

Unbeknownst to me, the same golf gods whose mischievous ways have followed me on the links all my life were already honing their skills in Terrace.

The spiteful sons of bitches steered my ball into a series of unplayable lies until victory was safely out of reach, then allowed me to hole-out from fifty yards for an eleven.

I lost the tournament by a stroke, and in retrospect, I must confess to having reacted poorly to this outcome by downing the same number of drinks at the club as my score on the last hole. On account of this, before boarding the *Cub*, Rick sensibly removed the control column from the back cockpit, which left an empty receptacle on the control rod.

I was restless on the way home, but observing the little stump with a hole in it as it moved about between my feet gave me an idea. After some experimentation, I discovered that the handle of my putter, once I removed the rubber tip, fitted perfectly into the empty slot.

"Rick!" I shouted, rotating the club in circles to show him I had perfect control of the airplane. "Would you let me land this thing in Smithers?"

I can only imagine his anguished eyes as they rolled back in their sockets, but though I'm sure he was ready to take over at the first sign of trouble, he let me carry on.

I am willing to bet that there isn't a soul on this continent who can match my achievement of having landed an aircraft, while palpably drunk, with a putter.

1966, NIGEL TURNER AND THE MUSICAL APARTMENTS

To help me move my furniture from my parents' house to my apartment in a new high-rise on Pacific Boulevard, I engaged the services of my school-chum, Nigel Turner. Since Nigel is slated to appear in several supporting roles in this narrative, I'll introduce him now.

Nigel was an accredited eccentric with an enormous, two directional appetite: for knowledge and for food. After graduating from Cowichan High, we attended Victoria College, after which he obtained a science degree. He next studied medicine, but barely months before receiving his MD, his healthy disdain for worldly achievement caused him to chuck that for a lark and instead study art at Emily Carr.

Nigel was infectiously cheerful, and his workload at the art school seemingly never prevented him from being available for other activities. I therefore invited him to assist me each time I moved, which to my knowledge was his only source of income. Though he appreciated the money, it was the extravagant amount of food my mother fed him at lunch, and the suppers I invited him to share, which made him so eager to help.

I look back fondly on the fourth-floor apartment in Pacific Towers with its view of the sea, because it was there that I began my Master's program in directing, and because of what is about to be described in the following chapter.

Nigel Turner and me, Frosh Day, Victoria College, 1952.

MEETING RITA

Saturday, September 3, 1966, was to be the most important day of my life. It occurred when my Navy buddy Kenny Stephens, who was at that time a pilot with Pacific Western Airlines, invited me to a party in the sex-and-drop in center he shared with some fellow pilots in West Vancouver. I looked forward to this event with great anticipation, because many of my naval aviator friends were now flying with the airlines, which should ensure the presence of air-goddesses, our favorite source of playmates.

Presently, Keith Stirling, an ex-squadron mate now employed by Air Canada, amply fulfilled this expectation when he made his inimitable entrance in the company of two charming candidates.

You lucky swine, I thought as I scrutinized the new arrivals.

Suddenly, my gaze froze on the blonde.

As my eyes devoured this petite, sweetly feline natural beauty with the impossibly lovely face, my pulse quickened, and I realized that I'd forgotten how to breathe. Before I could formulate some stratagem, however, the two girls disengaged from the group and settled in a room far from the action, their body-language radiating *n'approche pas*!

It took a while, but after circling the pair from a safe distance, I summoned enough confidence to risk an overture. I don't exactly remember what she said, but from the moment those adorably accented words flowed from these alluring lips, all I wished to do was to cradle that angelic face in my hands and listen to her whisper them forever into my mouth. (Never underestimate the power of hyperbole.)

Somehow, I managed to convince her to join me by the pool, where she reluctantly allowed that she was German, living in Paris, and her name was Rita. Christ … that's even less information than the Geneva Convention allows prisoners of war to divulge to their captors.

"Is there any chance of getting together sometime?" I hazarded anemically.

I don't date outside my species might serve as an approximation of her reply. It was apparent I was rapidly liquefying my social capital.

"Well, could I at least have your phone number?"

To get rid of me, I suppose, she rattled off some numbers and sauntered away. Phoney, I assumed. But just in case, I wrote them down.

What was the cause of this bulletproof aloofness? I wondered as I observed her from a distance.

She left the party early, but the memory of this captivating being smoldered within me for a day or two, after which I decided to dial that suspect number. I could hardly believe it! It was her voice on the phone.

"Hello, Rita. I'm so glad to catch you at home. I've been thinking about you …"

"Zis is not Rita," Rita interrupted. "I am zi roommate."

Well, that stuck a sock in my mouth.

Challenging this fib could be fatal, so I muttered something about calling some other time and hung up.

The little bitch! The scheming, clever little bitch!

I was stumped on what to do next. I waited a day to cool off and tried again when, with the same hormone-titillating Parisian inflexion, she delivered the same maddening evasion.

"When do you expect Rita to be home?" I asked evenly with faked politeness while seething inside.

"Maybe two days," she offered.

A hope? A faint promise of a lifeline?

I put the call through on schedule. The same voice answered, but magically, this time Rita was Rita. She felt safe because she was about to leave for a three-day layover in London.

Picking up on this revelation, I brightly suggested that she should take this opportunity to catch a play, Peter Shaffer's *Royal Hunt of the Sun*, which was getting rave reviews.

Pause.

"You're interested in theatre?"

"That's what I'm studying at UBC; I'm starting my post-graduate degree in directing."

Silence.

Something akin to a transformation appeared to be brewing on the other end of the line. Switching smoothly to a more casual tone, I decided to press my advantage.

"Maybe you can tell me about it when I collect you at the airport on your return?"

That's when Providence finally jabbed her in the butt with a sharp stick.

"OK," she agreed, and three days later I watched as this entrancing little blonde in the dark green Air Canada uniform and the cheeky bowler hat stepped off the airplane onto the tarmac at the south terminal of the Vancouver airport and changed our lives forever.

Well, not just yet.

The introductory phase started with our first date in my apartment.

Rita....Ritusia.... I began toying with declensions of her name in Polish while I sat sketching her hand as it gracefully cradled a glass of gin tonic.

Rita.... Ritunia....

A most useful characteristic of the Polish language is its capacity to alter the connotation of nouns, adverbs, and adjectives by modifying their endings. Apart from number and gender, a name can be made to express a rainbow of nuances, including tense, voice, or mood, ranging from threatening or hateful to lovable and adorable without, like in English, the addition of adjectives.

Rita.... Ricia.... I continued, Ricia.... Kicia...

Kicia! A cuddly Polish diminutive of "kitten." It was a perfect fit, and the nickname stuck. From then on, the formal "Rita" remained reserved for more censorious addresses, such as: "Rita! Where did you ever hear language like that?"

Our relationship began to unfold like a fairy tale. Until meeting Rita, I had never nurtured notions of permanence in my relationships, but it wasn't long before my feelings began to undergo a mentalmorphosis. This infinitely intriguing creature who had unexpectedly burrowed into my existence was a person with whom I could broach the possibility of spending a serious chunk of a lifetime.

I quickly recognized that beneath the beguiling flower-child exterior lurked an unexpected sophistication nurtured by classical French schooling, which had infused her with considerable knowledge and appreciation of history, art, and literature. She was a little bookworm stuffed with novels by French writers like Stendhal, Balzac, and Flaubert, and she was an avid reader of biographies of such as Pushkin, Lermontov, and Mayakovsky.

Additionally, I discovered that she possessed a formidable strength of character, which for me had always been a powerful aphrodisiac; her self-assurance, married to her beguiling Europeanness, rendered the package irresistible.

We soon adopted a workable routine; after finishing my studies, I picked her up at her Cardero Street apartment and we walked to my pad on Pacific

Boulevard. I felt like the co-star of a Harlequin Romance that unfolded bliss-fully, page by page, fully expecting the next chapter to follow in seamless suc-cession when Rita blindsided me with a bombshell!

All along there was this boyfriend in New York, you see, whom she was planning to meet on her upcoming layover in Toronto. Since her conscience recoiled against seeing two admirers concurrently, his seniority prevailed, com-pelling me to take a graceful bow.

Rita behind veils of mystery (Cibachrome print through silk scarf).

My sketch of Rita's hand on our first date.

A KICK IN THE *COJONES*

This was an eventuality for which I was singularly unprepared. How could anyone suspect such a celestial creature of being capable of concealing such satanic traits?

When jilted, women seek consolation in extravagant shopping sprees for jewelry and fancy trousseaus. Men are simpler creatures who sublimate being dumped with alcohol and cars. Though schoolwork dampened the former, I nevertheless lived up to the stereotype by acquiring a racy little red Triumph Spitfire, which isolated me and my misery in its sleek confinement.

I still felt wounded, betrayed, and thoroughly sorry for myself, though mercifully this torment could be blunted by a daily entombment in my schoolwork.

One of the ways theatre students earned spending money was to act as extras in films and TV productions. I was lucky to have had several walk-ons in the *Littlest Hobo* series filmed at the Hollyburn Studios, as well as roles in numerous commercials. Sometime during the Christmas break, I auditioned for the lead in a CBC Festival historical series whose theme was "The Bad Men of BC." The script, written by George Ryga, was called *How to Break a Quarter Horse*. It was to be directed by Don Ecclstone and filmed that spring in Penticton. Considering the experienced actors reading for the role, some of them Playhouse leads, I assessed my chances at zero. It was, therefore, most surprising to receive a call from Don later that evening, during which he asked me whether, judging from the script, the central character in the play was guilty of the crime with which he was charged.

I answered that I didn't know, but something prompted me to suggest that I'd play it as if he was. Such acting sophistication was entirely outside of my capabilities, but my reply sounded convincing to Don, and for the first and last time in my life, I heard those coveted words: "You've got the part."

This vaulted my bragging rights in the theatre department to ethereal heights, and added the considerable sum of $800, plus residuals, to my coffers.

RITA RETURNS!

Throughout this time, Rita was hardly forgotten, and painful memories boiled to the surface when I passed her walking arm-in-arm with her roommate, Anna, on the sea-wall. I believe it was sometime in February when I could stew no longer and gave her a call.

As unexpected as her departure was, her apparent willingness to see me again re-affirmed Oscar Wilde's assertion that women are meant to be loved, not understood. It seemed that Dame Destiny had merely hiccoughed, which hardly surprised me, as I'd had her already tabbed as an unpredictable harpy whom I'd always suspected of tippling.

Rita had split from her friend, and the reason, she told me, resulted from a disagreement on a matter of principle. Oh yes, beneath this aura of cuddlesome femininity thrived a volcano of passionately held convictions, which I continue to discover to this day.

After we'd happily resumed our relationship, I decided to ask Rita if she would care to supply a context to her attitude at Kenny's party.

"Pilots," she replied.

"Pilots? What about them?" I asked.

"They're cheap and only have one thing on their minds."

Jesus, she's talking about my friends; well, maybe some of them, but she'd only been flying for five months. How could she have arrived at such an opinion?

"All of them?" I asked apprehensively.

"All the ones I met."

"But you knew *I* was a pilot. What made me different?"

"*The Royal Hunt of the Sun*," she replied.

"But you said you never went to see it!"

"It didn't matter," she said, a seraphic smile creasing her lips.

Is that what separated me from the herd? Was it all because of theatre?

Well, if that is the case, then thank you Aristophanes, Sophocles, and Euripides; thank you Marlowe, or Bacon, or the Earl of Oxford, or whoever wrote those fabulous works attributed to Shakespeare. Thank you, you splendid playwrights of the Restoration; thank you, Oscar, Noel and GBS, Pinter, Stoppard and Mrożek, Simon, Mamet and Albee, and even the unattended Peter Schaffer.

Thank you all for contributing to this priceless gift. And to the galaxy of gods above who oversee all that transpires, I send a single prayer: Please gods—*please*—don't let me fuck up!

New Year's Eve, 1967.

My sketch of Rita.

1966–1967, FIRST YEAR OF MASTER'S PROGRAM; DIRECTING MROŻEK'S *STRIP TEASE*

The most important assignment of the spring semester involved directing a one-act play. The search for material led me to the Polish literary publication *Dialog*, where I discovered a script with an English title, *Strip Tease*, written by Sławomir Mrożek.

The theatricality of this surrealist black comedy and political satire resonated with me on every level and prompted me to find an English translation. There was only one, by Nicholas Bethell, whose version entirely failed to capture the nuances and humor of the original and sounded pathetically like the work of an English schoolboy. I had no choice but to attempt something I'd never done before: translate the piece myself.

Strip Tease was to be staged in April at the old Freddy Wood Theatre, a structure composed of two army huts joined together in a T, nestling in a row of similar shacks that served as classrooms on the western side of East Mall.

The play, like much of Mrożek's work, is an allegorical lampoon of the political and social climate of the Eastern Bloc. It was a two-hander in two intriguing ways: it was written for two characters and required the construction of two enormous, menacing, and entirely articulate hands.

To help to build these, and to operate them in the play, I was fortunate to engage the ever-eager Nigel Turner. His access to the art school's workshops was as indispensable as his technical expertise. To build the hands, we first constructed a wooden skeleton with articulated joints. Fish lines attached to the fingertips were threaded through fittings on each joint and emerged through the wrist attached to individual handles. Rita made a huge canvas glove into which to fit the entire assembly, which after being stuffed with Styrofoam was mounted on a dolly. This permitted Nigel to wheel it on and off stage while manipulating the lines to make appropriate gestures. It could point, beckon, signal "gimme," grasp articles of clothing, or rise up in a fist.

I was fortunate to engage two of the department's most talented actors, Dermot Hennelly and Jace van der Veen, to portray the two characters.

The play opens with two well-dressed businessmen who find themselves inexplicably locked in a room. One of them, a man of reason, counsels that they should wait for a rational explanation, while the other is outraged and makes a loud fuss trying to get out. The ruckus causes a door to fly open, through which the audience sees the electrifying appearance of an enormous hand. With its index finger, the hand beckons the agitator to approach and, poking his chest, makes it clear that it wants his jacket. His hesitation causes the hand to rise, its fingers curled into a fist. Succumbing to the gesture, the character offers up his jacket, which the hand accepts and disappears.

During the ensuing argument in which the analytical man accuses his companion of unnecessarily provoking hostilities, the hand re-appears and in identical fashion demands *his* jacket as well. This disrobement continues until both men are down to socks and underwear, at which time another hand appears from an opposite door and leads our heroes, shackled and hooded, out to an unspecified but clearly unpalatable fate. Philosophical bickering between the two men continues to the end to hilarious effect.

Such symbols of totalitarianism were not lost on the Polish Communist authorities, who eventually banned Mrożek's work, forced him to leave his country, and revoked his passport.

The introduction of Mrożek was an eye-opener to Canadian audiences and would play a pivotal role in my brief career in theatre, while *Strip Tease* was the first play under my direction seen by Rita and my parents and proved to be a grand finale to a year saturated with academic subjects as well as directing assignments.

Though concentrating on the exams was complicated by the thrilling prospect of flying again, to drop the ball at this stage was unthinkable. A last-minute burst of energy resulted in a pass, which set the stage for my second year of the Master's program and for the summer's flying.

1967, REGRETTABLE EVENT IN NEW BRUNSWICK

Glowing with enthusiasm, I reported to Skyway, re-familiarized myself with the TBM, and after a forty-minute solo was ready to go.

It was to be another combination of budworm spraying in New Brunswick followed by a season of firebombing. My low seniority landed me in Smithers again, but with Ralph Langemann as my flying partner, Al McDonell as the chief engineer, and my resolve never to have a bad time, it promised to be another summer of frolics and fun.

The cross-country odyssey began on May 24, when our "squadron" of nine spray planes, plus Skyway chief pilot Les Kerr who was bringing a spare, took off for Calgary. After stopovers in Regina, Winnipeg, Duluth, Sault Ste. Marie and Ottawa, we arrived in Juniper, New Brunswick, on June 5. When Don Hill and I moved into one of the four-man cabins, we discovered that we'd be sharing it with the boss himself, Les Kerr, and a new hire, Bruce Lebans.

Since the bugs weren't ready for spraying, we resigned ourselves to the familiar period of waiting. One morning following a night thunderstorm, I was awakened by activity in the cabin and saw Les and Bruce suiting up to fly. I leapt briskly out of bed, only to have Les quietly motion me back into the sack.

"It's OK," he whispered as they slipped out of the shack, "there's a fire somewhere, but only two airplanes are required."

As we listened to the roar of the departing Avengers, Don and I agreed that there was something fishy about this scenario. If this was a revenue flight, why did the boss take the flying away from his pilots, who should have been sent in order of seniority? Moreover, why did he take Bruce? Bruce was the most junior pilot on the team; he'd been hired the previous year to fly the birddog (at a salary we discovered was $200 per month higher than other first-year birddog pilots). He was new to the TBM and had no previous bombing experience.

While they were gone, our team convened for a discussion about this blatant act of favoritism and decided that if this were to happen again, we would confront Les to seek an explanation. To our surprise, a similar scenario unfolded the next morning. Since Les was in our cabin, it fell to Don and me to do the confronting.

For a moment, Les and I were nose-to-nose, an awkward arrangement when facing an adversary towering a foot above you, but it was all in vain. Les had his

way, but the unfairness of his act sowed a seed of distrust in the group, which
in my case was to play a role in an important future decision.

*Budworm spray group, NB. (L to R: Ralph Langemann, Gary Lumsden, myself, Don Hill, Bruce
Lebans, Slim Knights, Zahorsky, Linc Alexander; front row; Moe Green, Boyd Cooper, nk, nk.*

LINC'S CAREER MISS AT KANAKA BAR

The spray season ended lucratively at the end of June, and on July 3, Ralph and I landed in Smithers. The fire season started dismally in the northern part of the province. Periods of yellow alert* interspersed with weekly practices became our routine, while all that time we were aware that our buddies in the south were flying their butts off. (A system of alerts established by Forestry determined our standby status. Red alert meant all pilots on base ready to fly. Yellow allowed 30 minutes to get airborne, while Blue One and Blue Two increased this time to one and two hours respectively. Green was a general stand down issued in days.) This begged a logical question: Why not release the inactive groups from Smithers and Prince George to help the situation in the south?

This was an awkward question to ask, because Forestry personnel were equally aware of this anomaly. It stemmed from two sources: the division of the province into regions, and the proprietary attitude regional managers developed for their tankers. Having a fire break out in the region while the resident tankers are engaged elsewhere risked looking unprofessional, and besides, it's always been done that way. It was this power of inertia which allowed me to become a permanent fixture on the golf course.

Unexpectedly, twelve days later my ten-pound Forestry radio came alive, informing me to get my ass to the airport for a base change to Kamloops. On landing, we found ourselves in a cauldron of activity; fires were raging in the Fraser Canyon, urgently requiring backup.

The complex geography of this river as it cuts and meanders through the Cascade Mountains produces torrents of swirling winds, which wreak havoc with retardant. Because loads blown to shreds before they reach the ground necessitate multiple re-loads, the fire-bombing community fondly christened this sector as "Happy Valley."

Immediately upon arrival I was dispatched to Kanaka Bar, a sprinkling of houses surrounding a gas station on the east side of the river south of Lytton where a blaze driven by the wind was threatening the community. Luckily, I was behind Linc, which would allow me to observe how an experienced pilot handled such conditions. The wind was howling from the north, and only a small hill stood between the fire and the settlement.

The objective was to build a chemical guard on the north slope of this hill between the buildings and the fire. I observed Linc carefully as he flew into the wind, over the structures, over the hill, and past the flames before pulling the trigger. *Perfect!* I thought as the load left the airplane, but then something unexpected unfolded before my eyes. The retardant seemed to hover in place, and then driven backward, it overflew the fire, continued past the hill, and eventually scored a bullseye on the settlement itself.

Having deliberately flown so far past the target, Linc couldn't believe the birddog officer's assessment, who had called him two loads short. It was a sobering demonstration of load behavior in a gale. Several days later, rains extended their reach southward and wiped out our parade.

When the Forest Service announced that three pilots could take three days off, Linc and I jumped on this opportunity to drive to Vancouver. It would be natural, en route, to examine our handiwork in Kanaka Bar.

As we approached, we saw that enough retardant eventually got piled up on the rise between the fire and the settlement to allow ground crews to build a fire break. However, we weren't ready for what we saw in Kanaka Bar. Linc's drop covered everything in sight. Pink retardant colored the sidewalk, the gas pumps, the open framework of a new construction site, roofs, walls, and unbelievably even splattered the inside of an English-style telephone booth.

With an air of innocence, I approached the corpulent, babushka-clad lady who was gassing Linc's car.

"Why is everything so pink here?" I inquired.

"You no beleeeef!" she burst out, interrupting the fueling. "Vee haff heer beeeeeg fire," she continued, propping up her Ukrainian accent with expansive, fly scattering gestures, "and brave pilot, he come and trow zis red stuff and safe our lifes!"

"He safe our lifes!" she repeated for emphasis.

Our hero could now be unmasked.

"This is the pilot who did it," I said, dragging Linc over by his sleeve.

For a moment she stood rooted with disbelief; then in a few strides of rediscovered vigor, she disappeared into the house. When she emerged, she was shepherding generations of her family, who surrounded Linc and took turns lavishing him with a tumult of undiluted Slavic emotion, replete with backslaps and embraces, all seasoned with copious tears, and I could swear that, through the crowd, I even saw someone kissing his hands. We drove away through a gauntlet of adulation, but not before they reminded us to settle the bill. We were to recall this incident, which stood unrivalled as the best miss of Linc's career, with great affection for many years to come.

Because Rita was in Paris enjoying her first leave from Air Canada, we accepted my parents' invitation to spend the time in their home. A reminder that I was still an employee came in the form of a call from Percy Lotzer: since I was in Vancouver, he wanted me to ferry a TBM (IMK, Tanker 2) with Gil Findlay as a passenger from Abbotsford to Kamloops. This signified the end of our idyll, and the following day, Ralph and I returned to the cooler climes of home base.

Inseparably wedded to the Forestry radio, I settled into my career-spanning routine of standing by on golf courses and dropped my handicap to plus one— easy to do on sand greens where one-putting is the norm.

A LITTLE BLOWN JUG

Safely nestled in Smithers, I decided to challenge the well-established law that stipulates that inviting an out-of-towner to visit invariably provokes a base change. Accordingly, I threw caution to the wolves and invited Rita to join me for a few days following her return from Paris. I reserved a room at the Tyee Motel, the most elegant lodging in town.

The Vancouver-to-Smithers journey was composed of two segments: a Pacific Western DC-6 flight to Prince George, followed by a transfer to a Central Mountain Air DC-3 for the final leg. Though this was admittedly an awkward arrangement for someone in the throes of jet lag, what won't we do in the cause of love?

Since we had not flown for a week, on the eve of Rita's arrival, Forestry scheduled a practice. It was not Ralph's lucky day; somewhere along the way, his engine blew a jug (better known as a piston), causing him to limp back to the base with his airplane covered in oil.

On the day of Rita's planned arrival, while I spent my time pacing off the dimensions of the terminal building, the PA system crackled into life: "CMA regrets that, due to mechanical problems, the flight from Prince George is delayed."

"What's going on?" I asked, rushing into the radio room.

"They blew a jug out of Prince George just like your buddy yesterday, and they're bringing in another airplane; that's all I know."

Oh dandy, I thought, and that's when my Forestry radio woke up: I was urgently required at the tanker base.

The place was in a state of fervid activity; I didn't need to ask.

"It's your doing, George; you activated the base-change-law. We're transferring to Castlegar."

"When?"

"First thing in the morning; we load up at daylight."

How very flipping loverly! Now what? I supposed that CMA could deliver a message to Rita to return to Vancouver, except if …

I hurried over to Al Kydd, our birddog pilot. Al was a person whose integrity rendered the notion of a bribe out of the question, so my appeal needed to be on humanitarian grounds. It must have touched a sensitive nerve, because Al agreed to smuggle Rita in his plane.

Transporting unauthorized personnel was risky business, as I was to discover later in my career, but this time there were no Forestry *quislings* ready to blow the whistle. There was one serious complication, however—Al needed to stop for fuel in Kamloops, where it was imperative that Rita's presence remain undetected.

I also had to stop in Kamloops for gas, as well as to drop off Ralph, who flew with me as a passenger to pick up a spare machine, since his was still grounded. With these tricky arrangements in place, while the rest of the crew repaired to the bar, I took up a vigil at the terminal.

Rita's airplane landed at midnight. After embracing my exhausted little blonde, I had to tell her the plan, the cruelest part of which was to have to get up at dawn.

When we dressed and stepped out of the motel room, we found a world immersed in a blanket of fog. We would have to wait at the base until it lifted.

When the sun eventually peeked out, I led Rita to the Cessna, where we discovered that Al had another passenger. This was our engineer, Gord Nielsen, and it's no secret that members of this profession live shackled to their toolkits, which weigh about the same as a Volkswagen.

How Al and Gord managed to wedge Rita and her luggage into the back seat remains a mystery. When I landed in Kamloops and walked past the birddog parked on the tarmac, I knew that under the heap of Gord's coveralls lay a sweltering and highly discomfited young lady.

Kamloops was a beehive; the entire south end of the province seemed to be on fire, and even Kelowna, where there was no permanent tanker base, was activated as a reload facility. Mercifully, Al departed for Castlegar within the hour.

After refueling I took off, loaded with retardant to action a target en route somewhere east of Kelowna, after which the birddog released me to Castlegar.

Rita had already taken a taxi to a motel. The six-hour journey left her parched and exhausted, but the adventure was something she'd never forget, and our gratitude to Al for risking his neck, an act which deserves equal billing with the tale of Androcles and the Lion, will live with us forever.

Meanwhile, Ralph was having a most adventurous day. To begin with, nobody warned him that his hurriedly assigned tanker had a skittish carburetor.

He took off sometime after me with instructions to action the same target and then follow me to Castlegar, when somewhere along the way his electrical system packed up, which included his radios.

Since it was starting to get dark and this was Ralph's second mishap in two days, given the well-worn adage that such incidents happen in threes, he might have considered a more prudent course of action by heading straight for Castlegar. Ralph was not programmed to believe in superstitions: gamely, he diverted to his assigned target, where he made the birddog understand that he was nordo (no radio), for which we had a published procedure.

After demonstrating the run, the birddog took up his customary station behind Ralph, who, armed for a salvo, followed the indicated flight path and pressed the drop button.

Nothing happened.

Executing a go-around, Ralph prepared to use the emergency system on his next pass when the birddog pilot, assuming Ralph misunderstood his intent, descended to repeat the run over again. Somewhat miffed about the waste of time, Ralph set up a long final, and flying the same route again activated the emergency dump.

Same result.

Because Ralph had never been to Castlegar, and picking his way through unfamiliar mountains in the dark was not to his liking, he wisely chose to spend the night in nearby Kelowna. Relying on the tower to follow his unlit airplane on radar, he executed the drill for a VFR nordo approach, and maintaining a respectable speed commensurate with his airplane's heavy condition, set up for landing.

A curious thing happened when his wheels touched the ground; whatever it was that impeded the operation of the emergency bombing mechanism suddenly released, and while his load scored an impressive bullseye on the center-line, his now empty machine leapt nimbly into the air. Ralph tried to salvage the landing with a purposeful burst of power, but his balky carb was not up to the task, and as he would later be fond of recounting, he found himself floating fifty feet in the air with a scant sixty knots on the clock.

Gravity now took over. In a test of the limits of its deck-landing capabilities, the aircraft slammed to the ground, which effectively shook loose any remaining retardant.

As searchlight-equipped fire trucks hosed pools of pink goop off the runway, Skyway and Forestry brass barnstormed about what to do with Ralph. It so happened that a company Cherokee was in Kelowna to fly an engineer to Kamloops where there was a spare TBM. Ralph was instructed to load his gear aboard, and with Grant McGarrigle at the controls and Gord Parley in the front seat, they shaped a course for home base.

Ralph's adventure was not over yet. Partway through the trip, the overwing entrance door of the Cherokee sprung open, causing a whirlwind of maps, hats, coats, and clearances to disappear into the night. Gord spent the rest of the trip grimly pulling on the door in an effort to diminish the frigid gale coursing through the cabin, while Ralph considered strapping on his chute and leaving this chaos behind. He finally joined us in Castlegar the following morning.

We bombed our butts off for the next three days. I logged 10.6 hours and made seventeen drops on the second day, followed with sixteen loads on the third, and Rita was able to observe all the airport activity from poolside of the motel just across the Columbia River.

With targets galore, we expected an extended and profitable stay. That was until, after a satisfying morning action with five drops already delivered, the dispatcher called Ralph and me into the office. We were required to return to Smithers.

A little blown jug, 1967.

CASTLEGAR: EXAMPLE OF A MANAGERIAL DECISION

We surmised that they must be having a fire-bust, but a check of the Smithers weather left us baffled. It was marginal VFR in cloud and rain. I had no personal interest in staying, because Rita had gone back to Vancouver that morning, but what a shame to be leaving such an active area.

Everyone was busy as we overflew Kamloops, and the boys took turns slinging barbs at us regarding our mission. We checked in with the Fire Center to verify that we were needed in Smithers, but all they could tell us was that the orders came from Victoria, presumably at the region's request. We had no choice but to press on. By the time we passed Quesnel, all we could see was a dark cloud bank spreading across the horizon.

A steady rain started in Vanderhoof, and by Francois Lake we were down to five hundred feet. From Houston on, we were on the deck following highway sixteen all the way to Smithers. As we taxied in through pools of water, the base appeared abandoned. Moments later, someone bundled in a yellow slicker popped sleepily out of the building. I'll never forget his words: "What the fuck are you guys doing here?"

We passed the question on to Percy Lotzer. That same evening we received instructions to return to Kamloops on the morrow. After checking into some motel with just wallets and a toothbrush, we were back at the airport the next morning. The weather was atrocious, but legalities ordaining VFR minimums had all the relevance of a hydrant in Hades.

As soon as we lifted our wheels, we ducked down to the highway and engaged once more in the now familiar practice of following car lights, eventually attaining the luxury of marginal VFR. There was an undeniable hazard to this undertaking, but had one of us crashed, the cause would unequivocally point to pilot error without anyone fingering the abject stupidity of the managerial decision that contributed to the event. We started work immediately after arrival in Kamloops, and my log book shows an uninterrupted stretch of flying from August 5 until September 5.

Sadly, my original flying partner, Don Hill, was killed on August 8. Inexplicably, he'd descended into trees in controlled flight, and the best guess for the reason of the crash was medical incapacitation.

Anecdote: Believe It or Not

Strange operational decisions like the one described in the previous chapter were uncommon, but when a poem I had written describing such an event appeared to foreshadow its happening, that caught everyone's attention.

It occurred in 1979 when I was flying A26s in Prince George, where I wrote a poem called *Flexibility* which satirized the misuse of tankers by using them as a weapon of last resort instead of as Initial Attack.

I invented a situation where upon receiving a smoke report, in the interest of economy, the duty officer (DO) first sends out a patrol plane, the slowest—but most importantly, the least expensive tool to verify the sighting.

When this pilot reports a fire in slash, the DO sends out a birddog to confirm the observation. By the time the birddog arrives, the blaze is raging in timber, and since his estimate of load requirement exceeds the resources, no tankers are dispatched.

The following event happened on June 29.

We weren't on alert until noon, so with my poem in hand, I drove to the downtown Forestry office early in the morning, where I managed to solicit one of the secretaries to type up my manuscript. Then I dropped in for a chat with the duty officer just as his telephone rang.

It was a smoke report, and as I watched him plot it near the familiar-to-me grouse hunting areas close to Baldy Hughes, I knew we would have an early dispatch. Without waiting for an official announcement, I sprinted to my car and arrived at the base, expecting the usual pre-launch activities.

The smoke report? Oh, yes, it was all in hand.

The dispatcher had been ordered by the duty officer to send out a patrol plane, which was already on its way, and no, she had no instructions to contact the pilots for an early dispatch. I performed my pre-flight inspection and sat in on the developments.

Presently, I overheard the patrol plane confirm the fire, and the dispatcher was told to get the birddog on base. There were still no instructions to alert the tanker pilots.

Now wait a minute … is somebody pulling my leg? Has the DO been looking over the typist's shoulder at my poem?

The air attack officer and his pilot arrived together half an hour later and took off at 11:30 a.m. The scenario began to unfold in an alarmingly eerie re-enactment of my poem. The only departure from my script was that our team of three tankers *did* get launched sometime after twelve, but by that time the fire had grown sufficiently to need the Williams Lake group for backup. At the end of the action, what might have been accomplished with one round of retardant required six tankers to drop six loads each.

When I faxed my poem to all the bases the following morning with my sworn testimony that I'd written it *before* the previous day's action, it unsurprisingly was dismissed as the usual Plawski BS. This coincidence of life imitating art (forgive me for elevating my doggerel to such heights, but I need it to make the metaphor stick) with such precision defies rational explanation.

LINC GETS FIRED

When the season ended, Linc came to spend a few days in Vancouver. We happened to be visiting my parents when the phone rang. Percy Lotzer was pleased to have found me, because fires had broken out in Kamloops, and Forestry wanted some tankers. Might I like some extra work?

I had already registered at UBC, but who cared if I started a few days late?

"You bet I do, Percy. I'll be there first thing in the morning."

He couldn't find any other pilots, he added. Did I have any idea how he could get a hold of Linc?

"It's your lucky day, Percy; he's standing right next to me."

I was taken aback to hear Linc say that he agreed to fly on condition that the hourly rate was raised from $35 to $50 per hour.

"Way to go, Linc. That's a gutsy move!"

Linc made the case that, since we knew that Skyway's remuneration for post-season flying was considerably higher, this should be passed on to the pilots.

"Brilliant! Press home the advantage while you've got him by the balls!"

By the tone of the conversation, this argument was not gaining much traction.

"The choice is yours, Percy. Fifty bucks an hour, or I'm not coming."

A moment later his face went ashen.

"I've just been fired," he said as he handed me the phone.

"The pay stays at $35 an hour, George; you said you'd be available. Can I count on you tomorrow?"

Who had who by the balls? I knew I'd have to cave in.

"OK, Percy, since I agreed, I'll be there. But I'll expect you to honor the higher rate," I added fatuously, trying to save face.

We stood for a while in silence. Indignation was soon to follow. How could the company unceremoniously terminate its most experienced and knowledgeable employee over a pittance? Loyalty and respect could vanish over fifteen bucks an hour?

Linc had seven years of experience, so his options were good. With a mere three years under my belt, I felt exposed and vulnerable, and I just couldn't afford to lose my job.

"You had no choice, George; you did the right thing," Linc offered to diffuse my anger.

The atmosphere was toxic when I arrived in Abbotsford the following morning. I reminded Percy that, though I agreed to fly, I still expected the higher rate. It was then that he delivered a line that still stings in my ear:

"Forestry would never allow it."

Forestry would never allow it? What preposterous bullshit! I decided to stipulate one condition: if he found another pilot, I wished to be replaced.

When I arrived in Kamloops, Forestry expressed deep disappointment to be served with just a single tanker. When calculating effectiveness, two machines represent a factor considerably higher than a simple multiple. I kept my mouth shut and flew three loads on each of the first two days, but the intervals between drops were unacceptable. On the third-day, Forestry released me. As expected, Skyway paid me at the seasonal rate.

Though it had been a fabulous summer, I found the company's conduct in New Brunswick, as well as the handling of post-season flight pay, sadly unbecoming, while their treatment of Linc was inexcusable. For the time being, however, there were more pressing concerns.

1967–1968, SECOND YEAR OF MASTER'S PROGRAM

Since Rita and I were merging our lives, our first objective was to find suitable accommodations, and my well-padded bank account permitted a measure of extravagance. A suite on the fifteenth floor of Laurier House on Beach Avenue overlooking English Bay fitted the bill nicely, and Nigel, rewarded as usual by ample meals at both ends, obliged by helping with the move.

When JB spotted my address on my enrollment form, his eyebrows hoisted the considerable scaffolding of his face to lofty heights as he proclaimed that no student of his had ever been able to afford such luxury. It was indeed a fabulous location, capped by a nightly spectacle of bewitching sunsets and the promise of a first-row view of the Polar Bear Swim. In other words, it was an ideal snuggery in which besotted new lovers could become acquainted, although, to allay Air Canada's concerns about its employees' morality, Rita was obliged to keep her digs on Cardero Street.

Mountains of assignments, essays, and practical exercises, along with more translations of Mrożek filled each passing day, but within this overwhelming workload, and very much under Rita's supervision, I found the time to try a new experience: marijuana.

ACACIA LEAVES, GATEWAY TO MARIJUANA

Although I'd been fascinated by mind-altering drugs ever since I'd read Kerouac, Huxley, Alpert, and Leary, this was all theory, because in the Navy we achieved similar results with daily consumption of a paralyzing excess of alcohol.

I approached this experiment without apprehension, because we were aware that everything the government published about the killer weed's addictive properties was false. Besides, I knew that I didn't have an addictive personality; otherwise, I would have left the Navy as a hopeless alcoholic.

Although I was often exposed to dope smoking at university parties, in spite of the provocatively enticing allure of its illegality, I was never tempted to dabble, because my lungs were intolerant of smoke. It was a discovery twice revealed. The first time was in Poland during the war in the adult-proof sanctuary of a laboriously scooped out sand cave, where my pal and I decided to act like grownups by trying out this *verboten* activity. In the absence of tobacco, we turned to the readily available alternative of dehydrated acacia leaves, which we lit after crushing and rolling them in a page of German propaganda.

Except to suggest it as a cheaper alternative, I am not in a position to recommend this product as a substitute for tobacco or marijuana, because desperately ill shortly after ingestion, I was compelled to surrender to the therapeutic care of my discomfited mother.

My second excursion into smoking occurred in Duncan when I was about fifteen. Two years after arriving in Canada, my father underwent a gall bladder operation, following which his doctor insisted that he stop smoking. This was a tall order for a man habituated since his late teens, who freely confessed that when standing continuously on the bridge of his destroyer during the war, he was capable of smoking seven packs a day.

Such an assignment might have seemed impossible for a weaker mortal, but my father accepted it as a challenge to his character and went cold-turkey overnight. His only concession was to smoke, without inhaling, half a cigar on Sundays.

One such afternoon, after my father had snubbed out his stub, my parents drove away on some errand. Left alone, with traces of the aroma still perfuming the air, the devil found easy access to my unformed brain and persuaded me to have a try. When my parents returned, they were greeted by the mute remains of their beloved lying immobilized on the bed, his face a death mask oozing a calamity of icy sweat, evidently a mere pace from eternity. No words of reprimand needed to be spoken.

Rita's introduction to tobacco followed a more familiar path. Inductees to the Sorbonne, of which she was one, after surviving the crushing demands of two successive baccalaureates, arrive as ready-made rebels. The French, already genetically predisposed with an *ésprit des barricades*, on entering university express their adolescent furies by immediately starting to smoke. Like some of their exemplars, such as Sartre, Camus, or Gide, they wouldn't dream of being seen on the terrace of a café without a *Gauloise* or a *Gitane* artfully displayed as a natural extension of the hand.

Rita proved not to be immune to this allure, which on arrival in Canada became a logical stepping stone to an occasional joint. I was, therefore, able to study its effects at first hand, and the results appeared sufficiently intriguing to give it a try. That's when the problem began.

At the merest hint of the ingress of the alien substance, my virgin lungs exploded with expulsive vigor. Repeated attempts produced identical results.

What to do? The stuff can be effective when eaten, we were told. I swallowed a pinch of dope wrapped in a red lettuce leaf with a spoonful of mayo and sat back to await the effect, but the expected epiphany remained obstinately out of reach. Brewed like tea likewise failed to have any impact. Nevertheless, once begun, the quest continued with dogged determination.

I recall vividly how the breakthrough occurred. It happened one Sunday when, after the coughing stopped, I took Rita's hand and led her to the window to gaze over English Bay at a particularly painterly sunset. A vestige of THC must have sneaked into the bloodstream, because I found myself enraptured by the recognition that I had never experienced the feeling of a hand with such sensuous intensity. This clasp transcended mere touch; it seemed as if I was connected to a conduit that opened into Rita's very soul: a sensation strangely accompanied by a simultaneous understanding of the metaphysical process involved.

I've got it! By George, I've got it!

This inauguration eventually expanded into a more profound penetration of this multilayered aphrodisiac of the senses, which by enhancing perception, transmogrifying reality and making a mockery of time, spawned experiences spanning a gamut from the ambrosial to paroxysms of hilarity.

Cannabis was a substance which Linc, my fellow practitioner, named the perfect drug, and it was appropriate that my resident flower-child was the one to induct me into this defining ethos of the culture of the sixties.

LINC FINDS WORK IN CALIFORNIA

These diversions were short-lived, because I needed to devote my attention to translating Mrożek's play *Karol* (*Charlie* in English), which I planned to direct that semester.

The previous year's presentation of *Strip Tease* served to raise sufficient interest in the work of this previously unfamiliar playwright to convince Norman Young, Freddy Wood's technical instructor, to reverse his resolve never to act in student productions by taking one of the roles. He joined the cast of Val Romilly and Wayne Robson, and the show proved popular enough for JB to permit an extension.

Meanwhile, after being fired by Skyway, Linc wasted no time in looking for a job in the States. He approached Rosenbalm Aviation in Oregon and Aero Union in Chico, California, but because these companies were only hiring applicants with multi-engine experience, they steered him to Sis-Q Flying Service in Montague, California, which serviced Northern California with a fleet of air tankers, including TBMs.

Bud Davis, the owner of the company, was highly impressed that Linc had published a tactical manual about this relatively new profession, and he informed him that if he obtained a US Federal Aviation Agency (FAA) commercial license and instrument rating, the company would clear his way through American immigration and qualify him to be hired.

Bud also intimated that a second TBM seat might be available. When Linc relayed this news to me on his return, it presented me with an unexpected dilemma: how to follow Yogi Berra's advice when confronted by a fork in the road. Should I follow in Linc's footsteps and explore this enticing new option?

Though Skyway hadn't fired me, the scars of resentment for the company's treatment of my friend remained unhealed, and I couldn't help wondering if I hadn't been fatally tainted by this unpalatable affair. More importantly, sniping at the peripheries of my conscience was a thorny question: Could I manage the additional workload of preparing for FAA exams while coping with the crushing demands of my coursework and my year-end finals?

It all meant a colossal change of lifestyle, weighted by the sobering thought of having to sever my affiliation with Skyway. A gnawing sense of *déjà vu* associated with the resignation of my naval commission began to infuse the air. Still, the notion of flying in California wove the spell of a seductress, and temptation happened to be the one thing in life I've never been able to resist. I would have to give it a go.

On the first day of the Christmas break, I hugged Rita, strapped on my Triumph Spitfire, and lit out for Montague.

FOLLOWING LINC'S EXAMPLE

Montague was a minuscule settlement in Siskiyou County in the northernmost part of California. I drove to the airport and parked near a hangar that housed several Avengers, but what principally caught my attention was a group of sleek twin-engine fighters, which I recognized as rare Grumman F7F Tigercats.

I found Bill Davis every bit as courteous and affable as Linc had described him; we enjoyed a friendly chat, after which he examined my credentials and bluntly offered me a job. There was an opening in Santa Rosa, and the fire season started sometime in June.

I learned that my monthly paycheck would exceed Skyway's, that flying pay for the TBM was fifty bucks an hour after the first twenty-five hours each month, and that a generous per-diem covered the expenses. Additionally, I'd be reaping a built-in bonus, because the Canadian dollar was 7 percent lower than the greenback, and to top it all, Bud assured me that I would not need to linger on a Polish wait list, because Sis-Q would process my application with the appropriate government departments.

Just before I departed, Bud surprised me by asking if I knew a mechanic who might be interested in a job. I promised to see what I could do, immediately thinking of Al McDonell.

Dizzy with joy, I decided to continue south to visit my Navy friend Bill Park, a Banshee pilot who was now flying for United Airlines and living the good life in Redondo Beach. I was humming along a freeway somewhere south of San Francisco when I perceived a loss of power. What the hell? I had lots of fuel, but the engine was quitting and the car gradually slowed down. Selecting neutral and turning off the ignition seemed like a sensible emergency procedure, which left me just enough kinetic energy to coast to an off-ramp and glide to a spot short of an intersection that looked promising for hitch-hiking.

Feeling lucky not to have had to park the vehicle on the highway, I picked up my suitcase, locked the car, and walked to the road. There was nothing to the left, but a modern building sporting a prominent sign stood about a hundred yards to the right. The sign read: "BRITISH LEYLAND."

I am not making this up!

It was a showroom and service center for Triumph automobiles, and as I later discovered, the only one south of the Bay area. They towed my car to the garage and ascertained that the repairs would take five days.

How do I get to LA from here? I wanted to know.

Luck served me again. The San Jose airport was a few miles up the road; the Leyland people were happy to drive me there and pick me up when I returned for the car. Nothing beats American hospitality.

Bill Park picked me up in LA in his white Chevy Impala convertible, his six-month-old German shepherd, Venture, posing like a Pasha in the front seat. Bill hardly needed a dog for bait, but with this irresistible pup, trolling for chicks must have been like fishing with depth charges. After a night of revelry, with palpable relief for us both, Bill departed for a three-day layover, which left me his house, his car, and the daunting responsibility of babysitting his pet.

I soon discovered that Venture proved to be equally well known on Manhattan, Hermosa, and Redondo Beaches, where he introduced me to amaranthine coveys of breathlessly adoring *Baywatch* admirers, which greatly relieved the burden of my obligation.

I was hoping to be asked if Venture was a good watchdog, to which I had a prepared reply: "Yes, but he doesn't tell." But sadly, I never got the chance to use it.

Bill's return revived the Saturnalia, but the following day, after abandoning the several plots I'd been hatching on how to abduct this endearing animal, I bid *au revoir*, flew back to San Jose, and after collecting my car, rushed home to Rita, brandishing my job offer like a trophy.

The following day I called Al McDonell to tell him about the possible mechanic's job in California. Al hadn't had a raise in years and was also ready for a change. He called me back a day later, happily announcing he'd received an offer he couldn't refuse and would be joining us in the spring.

Sis-Q scored an undeniable coup by inheriting three Canadians who would prove to be an asset to the company, and for whom this was to become an unforgettable experience.

Me and a real fighter pilot, Bill Park.

1968, MEETING ROD LANGLEY, BUDDING PLAYWRIGHT

At the beginning of January, my directing class received a major assignment. We were each to choose a play from a selection submitted by students of the Creative Writing Department and direct it on the main stage of the Frederick Wood Theatre.

I took a stack of scripts home and began the laborious task of winnowing for intelligible substance.

As my out-basket filled, I imagined magazine editors swamped with submissions, wielding the "REJECT!" stamp like a hammer, and understood why the only thing I'd ever sent to a periodical that was accepted was a subscription.

When a play entitled *The Station* ascended to the top of the pile, I thought it was there by mistake. It was a two-hander saturated with intriguing ambiguities whose language and structure read like an unfamiliar-to-me work by either Pinter or Orton. On checking the last page, however, the name Rod Langley appeared, along with a phone number. A laconic Australian-accented voice answered my call, and when it admitted to authorship, we arranged to meet.

Rod was in his early twenties, tall, angular, and somewhat loose-jointed, with a cheerful, no-worries-mate disposition. He lived with his Canadian wife, Coleen, in a basement suite redolent of the settings of the then-prevalent English kitchen-sink dramas, which after some tidying might have served as a set for *Look Back in Anger*. We sized each other up, and for want of someone better, agreed to join forces.

This enforced collaboration soon revealed a mouthful of teething problems, which began to dissolve after we agreed to revert to our assigned roles: when I stopped rewriting his dialogue and Rod refrained from directing my actors.

Our effort earned us a solid pass in our respective disciplines, and for Rod, *The Station* would become his all-time most produced play. Notably, this initiation was for us the beginning of a productive theatrical collaboration as well as a lifelong friendship.

Unlike our smoothly running play on the Freddy Wood stage, not all was well with the continually malfunctioning engine of my Spitfire. Rather than pursue repairs, I chose a more impulsive solution: I drove it to Thomas Motors, the Triumph dealer on Kingsway, and drove out with a new TR250.

It was a snazzy, yellow number, a TR4A body with the characteristic bubble on the hood, but now equipped with a sporty six-cylinder engine: pictures with Rita posing beside it were cover material for *Motor Trend* magazine. Unfortunately, the maiden voyage would have to wait, since the already obscenely heavy academic workload became further augmented by the need to start assimilating tons of information from aviation manuals.

To get away from the chaos, Rita and her room-mate, Anna, chose a sensible solution: at the end of March, they flew off to Mexico for a two week holiday.

Her absence allowed me to focus my undivided attention on cramming for the finals, at the end of which Shakespeare and Co. had to make room for the stern presence of the Federal Aviation Agency.

HOW TO CHOOSE AN IFR EXAMINER

I hadn't practiced instrument flying since leaving the Navy in 1964, and as all pilots know, skills in this department require to be continually honed. Moreover, the navigation aids in Navy aircraft were limited to Tacan, ADF, and Range, but we had no VOR or ILS, on which the entire airway and approach system was based. These I needed to learn from scratch.

In May, I booked flying lessons in Bellingham, where Rita occasionally accompanied me on training flights. After obtaining an American commercial license, I started a syllabus of instrument training. Predictably, I didn't exactly ace the program. My instructor did his best, and after four days of intensive workouts, I decided to risk a check ride, which if I flunked might cost me my job.

On June 7, with Rita in company to prop up my courage, we drove to Bellingham, where I rented a Cessna 172 and flew to Payne field, where the check rides took place. Terrified of drawing one of the disgruntled washouts from more lucrative flying jobs that this position sometimes attracted, I was much relieved to be met by an affable gent by the name of Ron Smith.

Ron eagerly inquired about my experience, and his attention peaked when I told him that I was an ex-RCN carrier pilot and a graduate of the US Navy training program.

"Go do your walk-around while I finish the paperwork," he said, leaving me with Rita, who hugged me for luck.

Presently, Ron emerged with maps and instrument approach charts along with an intimidatingly fat notebook, and we taxied out to the tarmac. He chatted non-stop as I performed my checks, which he briefly stopped to allow me to copy my clearance and deliver the pre-takeoff briefing, then returned again to what turned out to be his favorite subject: naval aviation.

After I lined up on the runway, Ron propped up the screen before the windshield to simulate instrument conditions, but as soon as we were airborne, his commentary continued.

Is this some test to see if I can operate under this barrage of distractions? I wondered.

I believe we made one ILS approach to minimums, after which I received clearance to the beacon for a hold. I hated holding, because except for direct entry, the other two methods required timed tracks on specific headings, which I invariably screwed up. (ILS stands for Instrument Landing System: elements of approach procedures too cumbersome to explain in detail.)

This task became further complicated by the need simultaneously to pontificate on the delicate business of centering the meatball during night carrier landings.

On reaching the beacon, I started a left turn when I felt Ron's hand on the controls.

"No, no, no, this is a right turn, I've got it," he said as he returned the aircraft to its proper course.

A dose of cold sweat impregnated my already soaking attire. An error like that should be an automatic down.

I continued the ride in a daze when Ron took down the screen for the approach back to the field. His chitchat stopped long enough for me to talk to the tower but breezily went on until I shut down in front of the hangar.

Rita looked at me quizzically when we walked into the briefing room, to which I could only reply with a shrug. After a few more minutes of banter, I couldn't hold back any longer and somewhat waspishly asked if I'd passed.

Ron paused momentarily, and then as if fishing for an afterthought, delivered this unforgettable quote: "Oh yeah, you had it on the walk-around."

I had reason to believe that Rita felt immeasurably safer when we flew back to Bellingham, knowing that an FAA certified instrument pilot was at the controls.

The following day was a blur of activity devoted to bidding adieu to our beautiful Laurier House apartment, which Rita and I remember with such fondness.

The ubiquitous Nigel Turner helped with the transfer, and when I delivered him back to his lodging, he was as usual happily overstuffed with my mother's Polish hospitality.

Linc arrived from Red Deer that day to join me for the trip to California.

We spent the evening musing about last year's experiences, which shaped this new direction. Linc had been fired, so he had no choice, but for me, quitting Skyway was a risky undertaking and was entirely voluntary. So why was I leaving?

Solidarity with Linc and disgruntlement about his dismissal were the precipitating factors, while lack of job security and a climate of favoritism at

Skyway played a supporting role. But the clinching reason was undoubtedly the clarion-call of the unknown and the intoxicating whiff of adventure. To accomplish this, however, I was breaking a bond forged with a group of great new friends: pilots, engineers, and Forestry personnel, and I was severing allegiance with a company to which I owed my start in this thrilling and demanding profession.

Was this truly what I wished?

It had better be.

1968, GOODBYE SKYWAY, HELLO SIS-Q FLYING SERVICE

On the gloriously sunny morning of June 9, 1968, after loading some of my bulkier stuff into Linc's red Buick, I bid *au revoir* to my parents, embraced Kicia, and followed him in my TR to commence an unforgettable period of our lives.

We arrived in Montague late in the afternoon. At our motel, we met another new hire, Ed Real, a veteran of the Second World War, during which he flew P38 Lightnings in the USAF. Ed, whose boyish appearance entirely belied his age, was slated to fly the envy of all tanker pilots: the powerful, twin-engine, F7F Tigercat.

The following morning, Bud introduced us to May, his recent bride, and to Bill Benedict, the chief pilot. Bill was a retired USAF colonel and a WWII pilot with extensive experience in fighters, which included captured German machines. He gave the impression of being a stern, no-nonsense kind of guy, and as we would soon discover to our chagrin, he was a dedicated abstainer.

I also met the chief mechanic, Harry Chafee, whom Linc described perfectly in his book as "a stocky, intimidating man with a crushing handshake, a tight brush cut, cherubic face and dark piercing eyes which scanned me like a laser". *

Harry showed his hand when he told Linc that if he wanted to fly for Sis-Q, he'd better get a haircut; accordingly, we were both dutifully shorn on arrival.

Bud chose me to start our checkout the following day. I remember how satisfying it was to be in a solid, muscular machine again, with tons of power and that throaty roar after all those piddly little Cessnas in training. My task was to demonstrate a low pass over the field at eighty-five knots. Slow flight is fundamental to developing a feel for an airplane, a condition pilots routinely practice in various configurations.

After takeoff, I made a long, lazy turn, lined up on the runway, and lowering full flap began reducing speed to eighty-five knots. The Avenger is perfectly capable of flying at that speed, which is a full ten knots above the stall, but as I neared that figure, I found that I needed to carry a great deal more power than expected, and the aircraft was extremely sluggish to control. I staggered over the observers on the ground in an inelegantly wobbly fashion, then joined the circuit and landed.

---

* Linc W. Alexander, *Firebomber Into Hell*, USA, BookLocker.com, Inc. 150.

Seriously puzzled by this performance, I asked Harry if perchance the airspeed indicator needed calibration; he brushed this off, ascribing my problem to clumsy piloting. Nevertheless, I warned Linc during lunch about this unexpected characteristic before it was his turn to fly. It was then that someone approached our group to announce that the airspeed indicator was now fixed, as it had been indicating ten knots high! No bloody wonder I'd had problems with control. I'd been balanced on the cusp of a stall for the duration of the pass.

"Close call," reads my log book.

Since our assigned bases weren't ready to accept us, we checked out in the company Cessna 210 as well as in Bud's private twin-engine Cessna 310, but mostly we just hung around, oblivious of the devil's close watch on our idle hands. Who sneaked that forty-ouncer of over-proof vodka into our room that afternoon is still a mystery. The high octane was not apparent until we had done justice to the contents, after which we repaired to the local eatery and occupied a table.

Since this was a somewhat unprepossessing cowboy joint, one might have expected some tolerance toward a degree of exuberance of the clientele, but for some reason, none of the staff exhibited much enthusiasm to serve us. As we waited, Linc and Ed became aware of my absence, and the mystery of my disappearance wasn't solved until someone noticed a pair of bare feet sticking out from under the table.

With their Samaritan instincts aroused, my friends came to the aid of their fallen comrade by grabbing a foot each and, giggling uproariously at the sight of my head bouncing down the entrance steps, dragged my limp body past the startled patrons to the door. Unfortunately, the hilarity of the spectacle failed to arouse a similar reaction from Bill Benedict, who happened upon the scene.

This subject flared up the following morning at a briefing in Bud's office when Bill stomped in, and in a voice convincingly tinged with outrage, unequivocally recommended that Bud should fire us all on the spot. He then capped his performance by storming out of the room. Since such an act would have placed the company in the embarrassing position of failing to fill three Forestry contracts, Bud chose to defuse the situation by soliciting our agreement to more temperate behavior.

Several days later, Bud asked us to drive our cars to our respective bases and wait for him to collect us in his Cessna 310, in which he would fly us back to Montague to pick up our airplanes. He was already waiting for me when I drove into the Sonoma Air Attack Base. After perfunctory introductions, we flew to Ukiah to pick up Linc and then proceeded to Ed Real's summer home of Willows.

Architecturally, Willows was a well-preserved example of mid-depression chic, while Ed's standby-base at the airport consisted of a single trailer perched forlornly on an un-mown slope, whose austerity brought to mind the art of Andrew Wyeth. This combination instantly diffused any remnants of jealousy we may have harbored about Ed's flying the Tigercat, even though this beauty was undeniably the leading star of the apogee of the piston era.

Back in Montague, when I phoned Rita to update her on my plans, she bowled me over with the news that a friend of hers was driving to San Francisco and could drop her off in Santa Rosa on the twenty-second, the day after my arrival and my first day of standby. What a way to consecrate the opening of the season in California.

My heart was singing, to borrow a stale cliché, as I examined my assigned Turkey for the flight to Santa Rosa. It bore the SIS-Q color scheme: a silver fuselage with red cowlings and wing-tips. It sported the number "24" on the tail and came equipped with a zero-time engine. As I performed my inspection, I paused for an affectionate pat of her cowlings and promised to be super-gentle with each of her fourteen cylinders, but I warned that should the need suddenly arise, I expected every one of those 1,950 horses to spring instantly into a gallop and to keep up the pace until the panic subsided.

With this understanding, we arrived safely in Santa Rosa, where I was met by an assembly of company and Forestry personnel. I was deeply touched by the warmth and conviviality of these people who stood ready to welcome me as one of their own, two of whom immediately gained my trust: my flying partner, Orrin Carr, and the base foreman, Ron Thomas.

Orrin was a handsome man of medium build with wavy, graying hair, gracefully approaching his fifties. Dominating his features were his squinting, azure eyes, which in concert with a subdued tone of voice conspired to convey the hint that the listener was about to be entrusted with something not only confidential, but unmistakably scenting of scandal.

On the other hand, Ron, known to his friends as Mouse, was short and wiry; he had dark wavy hair, a smooth olive complexion, and his smiling eyes radiated enthusiasm and an infectious *joie de vivre*.

After introducing me to the remaining staff, Ron took me on a tour of the base. It consisted of a hangar with air-conditioned crew quarters, a library, the dispatch office, and ample cooking and sleeping facilities. Two powder-blue storage tanks stood next to the mixing pumps, which through underground piping delivered a brand of long-term retardant known as "Phoscheck" to the aircraft in their parking stalls.

When Ron revealed the secret of how to access beer hidden in the Coke machine, I knew that the two of us were destined to become the greatest of friends. So far, the facilities on this base favorably resembled those in BC, with the exception that in Canada in those days, we didn't need to hide the alcohol.

Continuing the tour, Ron led me to an adjoining field where doves roosted in the oak trees, and the blackberry bushes were full of quail.

"Are you a hunter, Ron?"

"Sure am. And you?"

"Crazy about it. But is it OK to shoot here in this field, so close to the base?"

"As long as you aim away from the buildings; shotguns only, of course."

Unbelievable! In Kamloops I had a golf course within sprinting distance of the airplane, and here I've got a stocked, private hunting reserve.

Everything was telling me that I was going to revel in this California escapade.

My first objective was to search for suitable accommodations. The process revealed that Santa Rosa, the capital of Sonoma County, was an attractive suburban community composed mostly of single-family dwellings spaced along a network of tree-lined streets, while a scattering of low-rise office buildings comprised the business center. The town lay surrounded by nut and fruit orchards, boasted several excellent public golf courses, and was the focal point of a burgeoning wine industry.

After examining several properties, I settled on a cozy, fully furnished suite in Creekside Apartments, a complex with a palm-tree shaded swimming pool and easy access to Santa Rosa Creek, which I would soon discover was teeming with crayfish. Unfortunately, there was a minor drawback: the apartment was not going to be ready until the twenty-third, so our California honeymoon would need to be consummated at the Paso Robles Motel.

I was walking on air when I reported for duty for the start of my contract on June 22.

"We'd better not get a late dispatch today; my girlfriend is arriving from Vancouver this evening," I trumpeted to anyone who would listen.

After securing my overnight suitcase in the rear compartment of my machine, I phoned Linc in Ukiah.

"Are you settled in yet?"

"Sure am," he replied in a tone that said everything.

"You won't believe it, Linc ... Rita is driving in with some chick today. How's that for a start of the season?"

"You know what that means, don't you?"

"Perish the thought, you miserable cynic. I've made a reservation in the best restaurant in town ..."

The sound of the air horn cut off our conversation.

"Where's the fire?" I yelled to Orrin as he sprinted to the freezer for his water bottle.

"They'll tell us after we start up," he shouted, running to his airplane.

My California tanker, TBM Avenger No. 24.

RITA'S VISIT AND MY CALIFORNIA BAPTISM OF FIRE

With the engine running, I turned on the radios. We were to assist a group working a turkey-shoot out of some place called Columbia, which plotted out about a 150 miles to the east. Chillingly, this had all the earmarks of an overnighter. Just in case, I asked Ron to tell Rita when she called that I had a room at the Paso Robles Motel.

As we got closer, we learned that we were joining an array of tanker types, which included a B17, several F7Fs, TBMs, and a Northrop P61 Black Widow in an area where a recent dry-lightning storm started a series of spot fires.

These were still small, which lent themselves to direct attack. The tankers were making salvo drops on individual targets, and the actions I saw immediately impressed me with the professionalism and accuracy displayed by these pilots. After each drop, we were sent to Columbia for reloads.

Sometime during the action, the Airco (contraction of air coordinator, the California equivalent of our air attack officer) pointed out two small fires about a hundred yards apart and directed me to drop half a load on each target. Although the terrain required a sharp turn after the first drop, I calculated that I might be able to hit them both on the same pass. I knew some old pros were watching, so I'd better get it right.

The first one was easy, but as I heaved the airplane into a turn, the second one came up so quickly that I had no time to level the wings and pushed the button with about 30 degrees of bank.

"Not bad, Sis-Q," a deep voice chimed in before Airco had a chance to give his assessment. I wouldn't want to bet on being able to pull it off twice in a row. It was nearly dark when I made the last of my eight drops, and as I feared, all aircraft were ordered to remain overnight in Columbia.

After we serviced and secured our machines, a bus delivered us to a motel where, before checking in, I grabbed a handful of change from the desk, beat the crowd to the pay phone, and called the Paso Robles in Santa Rosa.

"I'm so glad you called, Mr Plawski, there's a very distraught young lady here who finally convinced me to let her into your room. I hope I did the right thing."

"You did," I assured her, and presently the very distraught young lady was on the line.

"That woman wouldn't let me into your room because we aren't married. I nearly had a fit! Why didn't you tell them I was coming?"

"Everything happened so fast, I had no chance to make any calls ... no, I don't know when we'll be back, but the room at Creekside should be ready tomorrow, so if you don't mind, pack my gear, pay the motel, grab a cab, and make yourself at home ... and by the way, the phone won't be connected for a day or two, so if I get a chance, I'll call the office in the morning ... I know it's damn frustrating, but I gotta hang up now, cause there's a bunch of guys behind me biting their fingernails off ... until tomorrow, I hope ... love you, bye."

Hardly the kind of welcome I'd envisaged for our California rendezvous, but for the time being, I was starving, parched, and everyone was gathering at the watering hole across the street. I soon discovered that I had stumbled into a reunion of the most venerable tanker pilot aristocracy in the State.

Orrin knew everyone and introduced me in turn. The two who made the most lasting impression were the P61 driver, Ralph Ponte, and the B17 pilot, Don Ornbaum. Ralph was pure-bred Indian who never said a word, while Don was the natural centerpiece of the gathering and never stopped talking.

I remember him spinning hairy yarns of flying in Indochina for Air America, and hilarious anecdotes from years of firebombing with which, in his baritone drawl, he regaled his audience until closing time.

It was a raucous reunion of old buddies, and though I was the new kid on the block, they made me feel welcome, and I felt highly privileged to be accepted as a part of such a distinguished team. (Don became a legend in his time, and some of his most famous exploits are immortalized on the website firepirates.com.)

Early the following morning I called the office at Creekside to apprise them of Rita's arrival. We worked some more fires, after which Orrin and I were released to home base.

I called Creekside again; Rita had already moved in. My promise to her that I would see her that night didn't sound remotely convincing, but the gods relented and allowed me to keep my pledge.

Two days later, Rita's transport to Vancouver showed up and wrested her out of my grip, but not before we were able to do some reconnoitering of these beautiful surroundings and discovered the Mark West Restaurant, a charming, vine-draped country retreat that became our favorite eatery.

MY BEAUTIFUL AMERICANS ...

Meantime, I was becoming acquainted with my flying partner, Orrin Carr. This soft-spoken dropout from a Benedictine seminary had been a cop, a deep sea diver, and a farmer. He was also a gifted writer, erudite conversationalist, and above all, a most candidly refreshing nonconformist. Orrin was a father of four sons and lived happily with his wife and family in Santa Cruz.

My other developing friendship was with the base foreman, Ron Thomas. "Ronnie Babe" lived with his second wife, Shirley, and their four-year-old son, Jack, in Santa Rosa; he had a stunning, raven-haired daughter, Shelli, from a previous marriage, who had just graduated from high school.

This friendly and hard-working extrovert with the impish sense of humor may not have known the definition of the word *altruism* but was its living exponent. Moreover, his natural warmth, which beamed from his darkly liquid eyes, acted as a magnet for the ladies. Though he was more than willing to embrace their overtures, he returned them not only with affection but with respect. Ron was one of those rare people who had no enemies, and even with his two ex-wives, he remained on amicable terms.

Orrin and Ron soon became my lifelong friends and confidants, whose memories I will continue to cherish until the mists of my days.

My great American friends: Orrin Carr and Ron Thomas. Photo: Rita Plawski

... AND THEN THERE WAS HARRY

Harry Chafee, Sis-Q's chief of maintenance and pilot of an F7F, was a man whose reputation preceded him like a warning flag. He was a genuine enigma in the firebombing community. It was commonly known that in the early days he always carried a flask in his flight boot, and when sufficiently emboldened, enjoyed beating up Montague with suicidal recklessness for which he never suffered the consequences, possibly because he was also the town's sheriff.

He liked to be thought of as a kind of Mafia don, made no bones about carrying a pistol, and boasted to me on more than one occasion that for ten grand he could arrange a snuff job. Harry's constant companion was an unapproachable German shepherd, which observed everyone with distrust and was trained to attack on command.

My first confrontation with Harry concerned my habit of wearing stylishly chic, skin tight, kid-leather gloves. The wearing of flight gloves was sensibly inculcated in us in the training command for reasons of safety. I chose to elaborate somewhat ostentatiously on this practice by visiting the most fashionable women's glove shops in Paris, where before each season, I purchased, at great expense I might add, several pairs of conspicuously showy, multicolored examples (size eight fit me perfectly), embellished with the logos of the most famous couturiers of France. I paraded this signature conceit not only to show off but for practical reasons as well, because controls of an aircraft broiled by the sun are impossible to touch barehanded.

To Harry, this epicene sight became a personal affront, acceptable in Height Ashbury but not in the macho brotherhood of tanker aviation. Accordingly, he strode manfully to my airplane, and in no uncertain terms ordered me to desist forthwith.

Pre-warned by Orrin that, in addition to the litany of his other unseemly traits of character, Harry was a bully, I stood my ground and tactfully explained why I intended to continue the practice. This took him somewhat aback but effectively shelved the problem forever.

Harry was based in Ukiah, and it was Linc's misfortune to be assigned as his flying partner. In contradiction of the universally accepted rule of "first in, first out," Harry laid down the law that he, Harry, was always first in the loading pits.

Though Harry continued to be a dangerous and unpredictable son of a bitch, he was a competent mechanic, an excellent pilot, and by the time we met him, he had largely conquered his alcoholic demons, yet he remains the most complicated and unfathomable character I had ever known.

DIFFERENT STROKES FOR DIFFERENT AGENCIES

It was fascinating for Linc and me to observe how the tactics to achieve the common objective of delivering retardant to a fire as quickly as possible could develop so many variants. That they differed between countries might be expected, but between jurisdictions? It was a topic Linc and I discussed endlessly on the phone, as it was soon to become an important addition to his book.

California excelled in the speed of dispatch. Unlike in BC, where tankers sat empty until dispatched, California tankers were filled with retardant immediately after returning from an action and sat loaded in the pits. It was a practice that stemmed from the directive that all fire reports must be actioned immediately with all available resources. The moment such a report arrived at headquarters, the duty officer's first action was to alert the nearest tanker base. As pilots raced for their planes, the DO busily mined his resources to ascertain the nature of the target, and to determine whether it merited an aerial attack.

The DO had to work fast, because pilots were highly motivated to move at top speed since they would only be paid if the wheels left the ground. This led to more loads being jettisoned to reduce to landing weight than in BC, but paradoxically, a well saturated jettison area testified to high level of efficiency.

A further difference pertained to reloads. In California, tankers were obliged to shut down while being loaded, whereas in BC, we kept the engines running.

As we pondered these comparisons, Linc and I were amused to discover that the elementary traits of human nature in the form of jurisdictional jealousies that occasionally blossomed back home, transplanted effortlessly across the border with an intriguing twist.

The root of the problem in BC derived from the layout of regional boundaries, which, determined by topography, resulted in conspicuously irregular geographic shapes. This arrangement, worked out long before the start of aerial firefighting, may have suited the purposes of forestry management, but spawned unexpected problems for the operation of air tankers.

Although common sense dictated that the group closest to the fire should initiate the attack, the location of the target within a region often led to bizarre examples of aircraft flying great distances to fires that were within spitting range of a tanker base of an adjoining jurisdiction.

I remember the giggles we shared as we flew 120 miles from Smithers to a fire 50 miles from Prince George, but I haven't forgotten how we bristled with indignation anytime we became victims of such an incursion. Forestry personnel were intimately aware of this fatuous convention, yet in BC, the problem wasn't completely solved until the introduction of central dispatch in Kamloops in the early nineties.

California developed its own version of this inanity, which was caused by the division of the State into two competing and intertwining jurisdictions.

Areas controlled by the California Division of Forestry (CDF), now renamed Calfire, lay side by side with those where the federal government's United States Forest Service held sway. Each operated its tankers within its area of responsibility and guarded them with proprietary jealousy, which produce the same inefficiencies as in BC, but our American friends added a sinister spin: the two agencies despised one another with a vengeance.

Not only did they employ different tactics, but they used different radio bands. To contact a federal Airco, you couldn't just change frequencies—you needed to carry a separate radio!

The most significant difference between the two agencies, however, lay in the techniques employed by their respective birddogs. The CDF birddog pilot flew a right-hand orbit one thousand feet above the fire from where the air coordinator directed the action. The Airco identified the target, chose the type of drop, and determined its accuracy, but his aircraft never left its orbit to demonstrate or to ascertain the safety of a run, which was left entirely to the pilots' discretion.

On the other hand, the air attack officer of the federal lead plane flew the airplane himself and did nothing but lead-ins. Both methods used in California lacked the flexibility we had built into the system in BC.

A further difference between BC and California lay in base attire. Whereas in Canada, appearing shirtless and sunbathing on base was entirely acceptable, in California it was strictly forbidden: political correctness compelled Forestry personnel to be in uniform at all times, while the pilots' only concession was the wearing of shorts.

FISHING FOR CRAWDADS, AND LINC'S EMERGING OPUS

Life in Santa Rosa soon assumed an agreeable routine. One of my most enjoyable off-duty pastimes was fishing for crayfish in Santa Rosa Creek, immediately below my motel. Nature equipped crawdads, as they were called, with a unique habit of escaping danger by flipping their tail and streaking away backward at blinding velocity. Challenged to take advantage of this proclivity, I constructed a wire-mesh counterpart of a butterfly net and armed myself with a long stick. The trick was to wade carefully upstream, and upon spotting a crawdad, to gently position the mouth of the net a couple of feet behind the Crustacean. Tickling its whiskers with the stick resulted in an explosion of mud, instantly followed by violent thrashing in the back of the net. A deft flip of the wrist deposited the animal in a bucket permanently attached by a string to the waist.

I also learned that crayfish liked to forage at night and were attracted to light. To profit from this habit, whenever Linc visited me from Ukiah, which was an hour's jaunt on the freeway, we worked as a team. I did the gladiatorial work while Linc operated the flashlight, carried the bucket, and dispensed whatever beverage we chose as the drink *du soir*.

Thirty specimens were the minimum requirement for a meal, which I learned to prepare in the form of pasta marinara and served with fresh asparagus and a sufficiency of Riesling. The remainder of the evening was invariably devoted to the examination of ideas for Linc's book.

There wasn't a pilot, AAO, forestry employee, dispatcher, mud mixer, firefighter, or arsonist who wasn't fair game for his obsessively inquisitive mind. His focus on the subject was unquenchable; it was common to see him climb out of his cockpit with the knees of his flight suit and the back of his left hand a tapestry of notes, jotted hurriedly between drops and ready to be copied as the content of the next chapter.

Rita has never forgiven me for accepting to proofread his galleys, which I carried on our worldwide peregrinations. She was particularly annoyed when, while ignoring her as she lay expectantly on the pristine sand in the shade of a palm tree in a sequestered area of a Cape Town beach, I spread out his notes and began to wrestle out loud with the forest of solecisms, repetitions, and non-sequiturs that characterized his grammar and syntax. In retrospect, it was all worth it, but I can't help wondering how Linc could have unwittingly become such an accomplished student of the style of Gertrude Stein.

Early in July, after a successful action on a fire at the Korbel Winery, the owner, Adolph Heck, as a token of gratitude, issued a standing offer to Orrin and me to order a case of each of the winery's products at cost once per season. I immediately put in a request for their unique Sparkling Burgundy, California Champagne, a Riesling, and a Cabernet Sauvignon, which the winery religiously filled every year.

A review of my life in these new surroundings revealed that I had every reason to be delighted with my new lot. I liked the crisp military efficiency in the fire environment; the flying was steady, my machine worked well, I was genuinely attracted to my new friends, and on a daily basis I relished the sheer thrill of being in California. Besides, whenever she had a few days off, Rita flew to San Francisco and connected with a commuter airline that deposited her in Coddingtown, a strip practically downtown in Santa Rosa. How could life get better than that?

Crawdadding in Santa Rosa Creek.

LAST CRASHES OF THE YEAR

Early in September, the taciturn Ralph Ponte was involved in a spectacular crash while attempting a takeoff from Hollister on an unusually hot day. The length of the runway, given the conditions of high temperature and humidity and the lack of wind, proved insufficient for his P61Northrop Black Widow, a twin-engine WWII night-fighter that was the last operational example of the breed.

Ralph was late to abort his takeoff and ran through a vegetable field until he hit an embankment, which tore off his landing gear. Continuing sideways, the airplane caught fire, and as Ralph scrambled out of the cockpit, an alert TBM pilot who had just taken off returned to the scene and dropped a load of retardant on the burning machine, possibly saving Ralph's life.

The story gets picked up by Al McDonell, who was the base engineer.

Al saw the crash, jumped into a truck, and arrived at the scene within minutes. He spotted Ralph sitting under a tree in his pink, retardant-soaked flying suit a hundred meters from the smoking wreck, coolly considering the recent events.

"Are you OK?" Al asked as he ran up to the dripping survivor.

Ralph took his time answering the question; finally, after a couple of ponderous shakes of his head, punctuated by meaningful clicks of his tongue, he offered this terse evaluation: "… click … click … dangerous son of a bitch."

Al was able to fill in the details sometime later.

When he recognized that he was running out of runway, Ralph sensibly tried to punch out the load, which would have neatly solved his problem. That's when he realized he hadn't armed his switches. To arm them he needed to take his hand off the throttles, which he couldn't let go of because he had failed to tighten his throttle tension lock. By the time he cut power, he was committed to trundle off the runway.

Sloppiness in following checklists can sure lead to an embarrassing situation in a hell of a hurry. However, Ralph wasted no time in retraining in the F7F, which he flew to the end of his career.

I followed Ralph's mishap with one of my own. Just before the season came to an end, my TR6 suffered an unfortunate confrontation with the highway divider while I was returning to Santa Rosa from the Playboy Club in San

Francisco. As this occurred vis-a-vis a conveniently located Shell station, I was readily able to arrange a tow home and organize the required repairs, which only delayed my return to Vancouver by a few days. Rita was not amused.

1968–1969, M.A. THESIS PRODUCTION,

ENTERTAINING MR. SLOANE

Immediately upon my return to Vancouver, I located Nigel, who was eagerly anticipating his bi-annual assignment, and with his faithful assistance, I was soon installed in an apartment on Comox St.

This address was a gigantic anti-climax after Laurier House. It faced north onto the alley, had no balcony, and deservedly met with Rita's disapproval, but it was immediately available and I needed to apply myself right from the start, because this would be the semester during which I was required to direct my MA thesis production.

The play I had chosen was Joe Orton's *Entertaining Mr. Sloane.*

Though the prurient and bawdy nature of the piece did not meet with BJ's approval, he found himself in a quandary, since Professor Klaus Strassman had chosen to direct *Loot*, an equally lascivious work by the same author, which was to run concurrently on the main stage. Setting aside his misgivings, BJ obtained the performing rights, and my production in the Dorothy Somerset Studio would be the North American premiere of this play.

To earn a Master's degree in directing, in addition to passing written and oral exams, a candidate needed to meet critical standards in the staging of a play, which then became the subject of a thesis. This required the director's in-depth interpretation of the author's intent, examination of the play's mood, theme and tone, along with a forensic analysis of each character's role and motivation.

I needed to provide floor plans, sound and lighting plots, and detailed descriptions of costumes and props, along with a diary of each rehearsal.

However, the worst horror of all was the need for a minutely itemized list of expenses. Without access to a team of secretaries, my dossier bloated to alarming proportions, but I remained pacified by the knowledge that, in their wisdom, my superiors had allotted a generous term of three years for its completion.

On the positive side, I was fortunate to be able to cast strikingly close to type with matronly Kathy Webb, punkish Nick Kendall, curmudgeonly Wes Taylor, and threatening Peter Burgis in the principal roles. We commenced rehearsals early in December.

The set design was the MA project of the flamboyantly precocious Ellis Pryce-Jones. His most extravagant contribution was an art nouveau, William Morris-like wallpaper, whose patterned floral motif he assiduously painted by hand.

The play opened on January 11, 1969, for a four-night run. The carefree excitement, glitz, and glamour of opening night were feelings reserved for the audience. For the creators, it was a time of nail-biting apprehension, while Rita's Germanic soul, after having been subjected to a succession of crises and hair-tearing frustrations, had become a scarred amalgam of *angst* and *Weltschmertz*.

All these frustrations vanished when we discovered that our production was accepted, which for Ellis and me constituted the first stage leading up to the investiture of a Master's degree.

1969, FIRST PROFESSIONAL PRODUCTION, ARTS CLUB

It was while I was still rehearsing *Sloane* that Rod Langley informed me that he had just finished writing his first full-length play, which he named *The Veterans*, and was eager to put it on the boards.

Following the well-trodden path familiar to anyone who remembers the impetuosity of youth, Rod rushed off to the Arts Club and rented it for a week-long engagement, opening on February 10. (The Arts Club was still located on Seymour Street at that time and was in the process of becoming the venue Bill Millerd took over on the way to his remarkable career.)

Rod proposed to cast the leads with Equity actors and managed to persuade the theatre to accept a promissory note, which he planned to cover with proceeds from the box office. This cockeyed optimism was considerably bolstered by the substantial warranty represented by his wife, Coleen, who was gainfully employed as a nurse.

With this shaky proposal strung together, Rod asked me to direct. How flattering. How complimentary. And how bloody inconvenient! After the torturous exertion of directing *Sloane*, I needed to refocus on my coursework and begin preparing for final exams, not to mention the start of my thesis. To top it all, there was that beautiful girl I was living with who expected at least a ration of my life.

It's for times like these that we come equipped with innate powers of rationalization. The thesis can wait, and exams are still months away, so how could I forgive myself for turning down this God-sent chance to work, for the first time, with professional actors? Someday my biographers may recognize this decision as the inseminating moment of my epic theatrical career. It was *nolo contendre* from the start.

"I'll do it, Rod. Give me the script."

Rita processed the events through a different prism; she foresaw a month-long whirlwind of chaos, which she had no appetite to live through. A week in Antigua with her ex room-mate, Anna, would take a bite out of the time span, but to fill the remainder, how about a solo sojourn in a jungle retreat in Kenya? That should do the trick.

Rita, in fact, was doing us both a favor. I was free to hold open readings in our apartment and was lucky to cast two seasoned veterans of the Vancouver theatre scene, Ted Stidder and Derek Ralston.

We started rehearsals in a vacant classroom at UBC.

Veterans was set in a hospital ward; to furnish it with authentic detail, Coleen scrounged a hospital bed and filled the stage with all the life support paraphernalia required by the script. During the run of the play, Vancouver audiences witnessed a courageous theatrical first with an unimpeded glimpse of a well-filled colostomy bag, which prompted one critic to invent a new category: "The Theatre of Nausea."

However, Rod became recognized as a "playwright of promise," and though the influence of Orton and Pinter was tediously bantered about in the radio and press, the reviews were encouraging, and I might be forgiven for privately indulging in favorable comparisons to Orson Wells.

Sometime in February, I read an announcement that a one-act play festival was to be held in Kamloops in June. What caught my attention were the generous cash prizes offered to the winners. Accordingly, I proposed to the original cast of *Strip Tease* to revive the play, to which all enthusiastically agreed.

With this prospect on the shelf, I focused my attention on the upcoming exams. I scarcely remember that tangle of sleepless nights and exhausting days that marked the climax of this grand finale. What I *do* recall clearly is the delirious sense of relief and jubilation following the morning-long oral exam with Dr. Soule. It was a feeling that, on a euphoric scale, must have rivalled a reprieve from a firing squad.

Of course, the Master's degree was hardly a *fait accompli*, as there was still that little detail of the thesis. Apart from that, I couldn't help reflecting on how much had happened from the time of nervous insecurity when I left the Navy with no prospect in mind except to finish my BA. It all seemed an eternity away as I now stood perched on the threshold of a vastly different future.

To be involved in a uniquely stimulating profession, to be free to indulge my theatrical passions, and to live with a radiant creature with whom I dared to imagine companionship for a lifetime was a bouquet of gifts impossible to imagine a scant five years ago. If, out of sheer amazement, this frenetic *modus vivendi* should someday motivate me to record its discordant progression, *Never a Dull Moment* might serve as an appropriate title.

STRIP TEASE IN KAMLOOPS

A palpable feeling of excitement rippled through the room when the team of Jace van der Veen, Dermot Hennelly, Nigel Turner, and I convened to prepare for our provincial theatre debut. We learned that a contest to determine the two groups that were to represent the lower mainland was to be held at the Metro Theatre.

Our first job was to construct those pesky hands. With Nigel providing a workshop at the Emily Carr School of Art, and Rita's sewing expertise, we repeated the original design and obtained Jack Darcus's permission to start rehearsals in his studio under the Granville Street Bridge.

With a well-prepared script, but unwilling to undergo the expense of constructing a set that would have to be transported to Kamloops, we presented the play on a bare stage. The adjudicator, Paddy Malcolm, was sufficiently impressed with the actors' work to award us second place. First place went to a superbly polished offering by the Chilliwack Players Guild of Jean-Claude Van Itallie's intriguing *America Hurrah*, directed by Derek McCooey.

For the finals, however, Paddy strongly suggested that we should build a set. Accordingly, on a Sunday early in June, an advance guard composed of Nigel and me drove to Kamloops and set to the task. After obtaining permission to construct our set in the Kamloops Secondary School auditorium, which was where the festival was to take place, I bought the lumber and accessories. Two days later, not only the set but two dollies on which to mount the hands were complete.

The festival was a four-day event during which the nine survivors of province-wide eliminations were to present three plays per night starting on Wednesday, while on Saturday evening the three finalists were to compete in a playoff. *Strip Tease* was to be presented on Thursday.

On Tuesday evening, a stack of suitcases with two huge hands waving out of the rear windows rolled into the motel parking lot. Three paralytics tumbled out of the front seat, one of whom was Rita.

On Wednesday morning, we were allotted two hours for our tech and dress. We erected the set, which had to be struck immediately afterwards to make way for other groups. This gave us a chance to paint it.

Our presentation on Thursday was flawless, but we would have to wait until Friday before we knew if we'd made the finals. When the finalists were announced, we were pleased to discover that ours was to be the closing show.

Our competition was the dangerously well-prepared company from Chilliwack, and a home-grown group under the direction of Tom Kerr, the adjudicator of this festival. The actors spent Saturday morning toying with the nuances of the script, occasionally amusing themselves by reversing roles. Thinking back on it today, I don't believe I've ever had a play as meticulously prepared as this presentation of *Strip Tease*.

As the evening approached, though we were all eminently aware that this was small-time in the cultural backwaters of BC, nobody could have convinced us that we weren't about to open at the Winter Garden. We experienced the same anticipation, stage fright, goose-bumps, and insecurity— all those familiar little torments so accurately lyricized by Berlin in *Annie Get Your Gun*: "… the headaches, the heartaches, the backaches, the flops … the openings when your heart beats like a drum …"

We had all invested tons of time and energy in this enterprise, and for me there was a tad more at stake, because as the only gainfully employed member of our company, I was paying the bills.

I remember nothing of the two competing shows on the final night; my mind was otherwise engaged helping Nigel to oversee the local stage crew as they erected our set, after which I took up my post as stage manager, leaving Rita to judge the show from the auditorium. I knew the actors were spot-on, and the audience was lapping it up. The prolonged standing ovation was appropriate and flattering, but everything depended on the adjudicator.

It was only when Tom Kerr began to analyze each category that we began to understand the scope of our achievement. One-by-one he pronounced his verdict: best production, best visual presentation, best director, best play, and best backstage work. The titles multiplied until he came to best actor. The roles were so evenly intertwined that Tom had no choice. Jace and Dermot split the award.

Later in private Tom told us that he'd never seen a script so minutely explored and competently delivered, and he asked me for my translation. I was pleased to comply and gladly threw in the two hands for his future use.

It was a worthy achievement, and turning over some $700 in prize money to Nigel and the actors, a considerable sum in 1969, gave me enormous satisfaction.

On return to Vancouver, Nigel's fortune was further enhanced with the customary transfer of my furniture, which to our mutual regret closed the cycle of musical apartments.

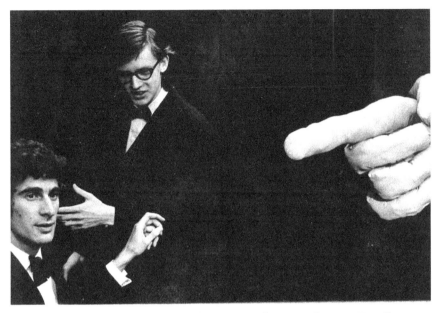

1967, Directing Strip Tease in Kamloops. Jace van der Veen and Dermot Hennelly; Nigel Turner operates the hand.

1969, CALIFORNIA FIRE BOMBING

The feeling of liberation after the five-year grind made my spirit sing all the way to Santa Rosa, where I arrived in an ebullient mood to start my second season with Sis-Q.

I was delighted to discover that Orrin was my flying partner again and that Ron was in fine fettle. After moving into Creekside, I felt right at home.

Following nearly eight months without touching an airplane, it felt terrific to slide into the cockpit, wipe off the dust, and inhale the familiar smells. I took the time to re-establish a comfort zone in the crowded space by arranging the seat, pedals, and straps precisely to my liking, and relaxed for a while fondling the controls.

"OK, old buddy, I'll treat you with tender loving care if you behave," I proclaimed out loud, heedless of anyone listening. You'd be surprised how many pilots talk to their machines; I certainly did, because physically and mentally it was an extension of my being. Like any thoroughbred, it required guidance, encouragement, cajoling, and occasional praise, as well as the odd rebuke over some foolhardy maneuver that the reckless brute needed to be warned never to attempt again.

A thirty-minute test flight and one practice drop, and I was ready for action. Firebombing contracts in those years commenced in July, when the fire hazard triggered by the yellowing grasslands rose to incendiary levels, and usually ended in mid-October. Global warming deniers might note that presently the season extends by several months in both directions.

The 1969 fire season started off at a gallop, highlighted by a lightning bust on July 23. Lightning strikes, which started fires all over Humboldt and Mendocino counties north-west of Ukiah, quickly swamped the resources.

Situations like this called for a particular procedure used only in the States. Called "lone wolfing," this technique came into play when there were too many targets for the Airco to handle. It applied to tanker pilots with a minimum of one year of experience who were permitted to attack fires independently. Launched into the area, we were free to choose a target, carry out an attack, and report the fire's position along with an assessment of the drop. The remarkably high levels of accuracy amply testified to the success of this procedure.

Late in the afternoon, to relieve the congestion in Ukiah, Orrin and I were sent for reloads to the Rohnerville tanker base, which abutted the ocean near the town of Eureka. As we got close, we saw that a blanket of sea-fog that stretched inland from the shore thoroughly obscured the coastline.

The visibility at Rohnerville was below VFR minimums, but since the airport was equipped with a radio beacon, this allowed us the use of an unorthodox procedure. With Orrin leading, we departed the beacon westward over the ocean and descended on instruments until the water was visible at about three hundred feet. After turning around, we flew back until we could see the airport and joined downwind left. I saw Orrin turn base and heard him call: "Tanker two-five gear down on final," but a glance at his airplane showed no wheels in sight.

"Tanker two five your gear is up!" I hollered into the mike. A split second later, wheels sprouted from his machine a moment before touchdown.

When we landed in Santa Rosa that evening, Orrin sheepishly thanked me for saving him a lifetime of embarrassment.

Early in August, my father took his holidays and drove with my mother to Santa Rosa. I introduced them to the staff, showed them proudly around the base, sent them for day trips to San Francisco, and happily spent a week in their company. When they returned to Canada to use up the rest of my father's leave, they headed for their favorite summer watering hole of Osoyoos, where my father suffered a urinary blockage. Diagnosed as an overgrown prostate, he was admitted to the Penticton Hospital, where he underwent an immediate operation. It proved to be the start of the decline of his health.

ORRIN'S TRAGIC DAY

The tragedy that destroyed Orrin's life forever occurred at the end of the Labor Day weekend. Orrin's wife and four sons were leaving Santa Rosa after a visit when some stoned hippies on the wrong side of the road smashed into their car. His wife died instantly while four graves were dug for the sons.

Although all boys eventually recovered, the consequences were dire. The oldest son suffered brain damage, and while he was in a drug-induced psychotic spell, he brutally murdered a woman in her home. He became a double murderer after a similar offence against a man he'd met in a bar. Convicted of these crimes, he barely avoided execution when California rescinded the death penalty for capital offences committed before 1972.

Orrin's agony increased each time he visited his son in San Quentin, where he was incarcerated in a cell next to Charles Manson. Orrin took the rest of the season off, but we all wondered if he would ever fly again.

My new flying partner, whom Bud Davis transferred from Hollister, was a highly atypical product of the United States Navy: a taciturn, born-again abstainer. Though our relationship remained distant, it was nevertheless cordial, and his flying skills could not be faulted.

September marked the beginning of the hunting season, and since Ron knew nearly all the farmers who owned orchards and fields, we had permission to hunt the entire county. Though pheasants were becoming rare, for the second year in a row we each shot a brace, which I offered to Ron's parents.

The most challenging targets, however, were doves, which migrated through the area in enormous flocks. Doves emit a characteristic whistling sound in flight that betrays their location, but they fly swiftly and erratically and are wary of hunters. Our most unforgettable shoot occurred one morning in dense fog. This created ideal conditions. Though we could hear the birds coming, they couldn't see us until they emerged from the mist, perfectly within gunrange. Our bag that day equaled the season's limit. Cooked in white wine with olives and veggies until the meat fell off the bones, and served over wild rice accompanied by Korbel Champagne became one of Rita's favorite meals.

THE EARTHQUAKE IN SANTA ROSA

It was October 2 when I went to the local cinema to see the rage of the season, *Butch Cassidy and the Sundance Kid*. Partway through the film, the theatre went dark and a pronounced shaking brought me to my feet.

When eventually the emergency lights came on, I discovered to my amazement that I was the only person in the house! I was stunned. How could this place have emptied like that in about ten seconds? The mystery unraveled when, like prairie dogs after the hawk had passed, bodies began to pop up in the aisles.

Of course! Everybody in California is genetically predisposed to hit the deck during an earthquake. I drove through darkened streets to my apartment, and in the light of my car's headlights, opened the door. Chunks of the ceiling littered the bed, bathtub, and floors, but the cruelest blow of all was the loss of my entire liquor supply, which lay smashed in a sticky mess on the kitchen floor. A second look exposed a startling revelation: the impact of the bottles on the floor was laterally displaced two paces to the left of where they were stored in a cupboard above the refrigerator.

After sweeping the debris, I decided to inspect downtown Santa Rosa. What struck me immediately was the remarkable level of readiness displayed by the inhabitants and local authorities. Flares marked cracks in the road, and shopkeepers whose windows were smashed were already in the final stages of installing plywood inserts clearly pre-constructed for such an eventuality.

The quake measured 5.7 on the Richter scale and had taken one life.

This experience instantly entered my subconscious, and from then on, its impressions joined the tapestry of horrors that the spiteful part of my brain occasionally enjoys inserting into my otherwise fascinating and generally untroubled dreams.

Two days before the season's end, following a convivial evening at the Jack London pub in Napa County, my car chose to repeat the previous season's reckless behavior. This time, after speeding through a perfectly marked T-junction and flattening a blackberry thicket which caused an explosion of panicking quail, it came to rest ignominiously in a farmer's field.

Although the required repairs only took a few days, this delay was particularly inconvenient for Rita, who had just rented a thirtieth-floor apartment on Bidwell Street and would have appreciated some help with the move.

The new address was a fortuitous choice. Compared to the dark and claustrophobic first-floor suite she'd been renting on Cardero Street, this lofty aerie was bright, boasted a balcony, and afforded 270 degrees of unobstructed view over the West End and Kitsilano. Until we splurged on a wall unit, bricks and boards served as shelving, Rita's paintings adorned the walls, and the sparseness of furniture lent an agreeable air of open livability. We saved the hippy look for the bedroom. The mattress rested on the floor, books, clothes and shoes lay handily disposed within easy reach, while theatre posters and Rita's collages stood disposed around the perimeters.

Our decision to live together not only disappointed Nigel's expectations of a bi-annual boost to his coffers; it also risked Rita's dismissal by Air Canada, which in those days held a proprietary interest in the morality of its employees. To disguise this transgression, we installed a second phone with an unlisted number that we disseminated to our friends, while the listed one remained in Rita's name and was reserved strictly for crew scheduling.

We would occupy this address for nine years, and both of us agree that this was the happiest time of our lives.

Our happiest hippie days on Bidwell St.

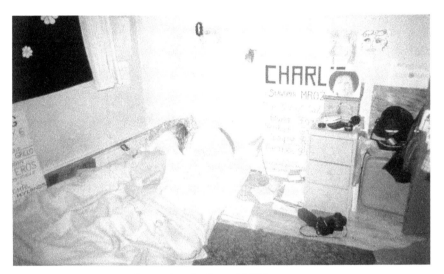

Our version of a Greenwich Village garret.

WITH THANKS TO THE CANADA COUNCIL

'69

Sometime in November I received news that my application for a Canada Council grant to study Polish theatre had been approved. It amounted to some $1,660, and when I communicated this to my parents, my father inquired if this was to involve a trip to Poland.

Yes, I enthused, that's what it's all about.

This was when my father felt compelled to sit me down for a drop of detail.

Though he never spoke of the specifics of his job as a translator with the RCMP, we had always known that his duties in the special branch involved dealing with classified material. He was now forced to reveal that if I chose to go to Poland, he would be compelled to terminate his employment.

With Poland in the grip of the Communist occupation, my visit risked being exploited by the authorities to put pressure on my father, which rendered the trip unthinkable. On the other hand, returning the money seemed somewhat premature, so I decided to profit from this windfall in some other way.

I knew that a professional Polish theatre group was thriving in London.

This seemed like a sensible place to start, which was a particularly attractive idea, since Rita happened to be working the London flights.

On hearing of my plan, Rod Langley, whose familiarity with cheap accommodations worldwide was legendary, informed me that it was possible to obtain lodging at London House, a graduate student center near Russell Square, for ten bob a night.

I flew to London in December and, following Rod's advice, moved into a private room in the dormitory, from where I commenced to live up to the purpose of the grant by meeting with the director of the Polish Professional Actor's Association (ZASP).

He treated me with great cordiality, allowed me the use of the library, and invited me to several engaging symposia, which included the well-known Polish writer and critic, Adam Tarn. This was a most fortuitous encounter, because Mr. Tarn was the creator, editor, and publisher of *Dialog*, the Polish monthly literary magazine dedicated primarily to the theatre, in the pages of which I had discovered *Strip Tease*. Moreover, Mr. Tarn was a personal friend and mentor to his fellow émigré, Mrożek, with whom he was engaged in continuous correspondence.

I profited greatly from my time in the company of this venerable gentleman, much of which was devoted to listening to his particular understanding of Mrożek's style and his place within the context of Polish drama.

Though my student lodging was more than satisfactory, it was no place to host Rita when she flew into town on her weekly layovers. Air Canada crews were staying at the posh Britannia Hotel in Grosvenor Square, which was recognized as a venerable bastion of Victorian respectability. To defend this reputation and to guard the morals of its guests, an impenetrable *cordon sanitaire* surrounded its premises. Though the layers of security were tricky to breach, determination fueled by a permanent state of hormonal candescence breeds ingenuity capable of outfoxing the most dedicated teams of house-detectives. Evading them added a satisfying level of accomplishment to the enjoyment of the classy comfort of this stylish abode.

When Rita left, I resumed my favorite routine of traipsing the streets of this beloved town and occasionally revisiting once familiar pubs. During one such stroll, as I passed the British Leyland showroom on Piccadilly, my attention was captured by a rakish yellow TR6 sporting the intriguing conceit of wire wheels. As I stood staring at this beauty, I became spectrally aware of an ethereal tap on my shoulder.

Haven't we all imagined being able, once in a lifetime, to act on the spur of the moment and do something wildly rash? Since a sufficient number of my friends who tend to classify some of my decisions as impulsive had not had their opinions recently refreshed, I chose not to strain their patience any longer.

Sauntering inside, I beckoned to a salesman, pointed to the car and said:

"Wrap it up!"

After a period of recovery, he informed me that this was a special order that would be ready for pickup at the end of January, and the cost, including shipping to Montreal, was in the vicinity of $3,000.

Assuming a sports car to be an awkward fit on a Canada Council audit, I paid with my summer earnings. The January date dovetailed conveniently with Rita's leave, during which we decided to take our new car on its maiden voyage to Morocco.

START OF MY LOVE AFFAIR WITH PARIS

Rita's next flight included a three-day layover in London, during which she decided to visit her family in Paris. It was a perfect opportunity for me to meet her mother, Maria, and stepfather, Leon, who had recently moved into an apartment in the suburb of Villejuif, a community approximately mid-way between Orly Airport and the city center.

Rita and I flew to Orly, from where I expected we would grab a taxi, but Rita's local knowledge dictated otherwise. Taxi drivers who may have been waiting at the airport for hours were unwilling to take fares halfway, so to avoid the inevitable squabbles, she decided to take public transport.

The number 285 bus passed through a tunnel beneath the airport along the *Nationale Sept*, the main artery leading south from Paris. To reach the bus stop, passengers needed to haul their luggage down fire-escape-like iron stairs to a narrow, improvised sidewalk where the din of the speeding traffic became magnified to eardrum-splitting magnitudes. It was worth the discomfort, since this bus conveniently passed through Villejuif, where we registered in its only hotel. We did this not out of propriety, since Leon and Maria weren't harnessed in marriage either, but because their apartment was too small.

Villejuif in those years still resembled a typical French working-class suburb. The streets were lined with specialty shops that offered a staggering variety of merchandise, most of it focused on the national fixation on food and drink, and nothing about the busy streets suggested that this municipality was one of the last strongholds of communism in the République.

After circling a thirteenth-century church next to the *Mairie*, we traversed a small park, soon to be named after the Chilean communist writer Pablo Neruda. We walked, mindful of Rita's warning to tread carefully through the fallen leaves because they treacherously concealed canine *billet doux's*.

The apartment nestled on the top floor of a new fifteen story high-rise on a well-kept property named *Les Jardins de Villejuif*, which offered an unparalleled vista of Paris. Meeting us at the door was a furry, black object that bounced off the walls, yelping paroxysms of joy, and it was only after Rita's dog, Wotan's (pronounced *Vo-tan*), energy subsided that humans were able to exchange greetings.

Maria, who spoke French with a German accent, was fifty-one. She was taller than her daughter and exuded an impression of quiet but friendly dignity.

Maria's partner and Rita's step father, Leon Znaty, came from a Sephardic Jewish family from Morocco. He was somewhat shorter than Maria, nine years her junior, and his handsomely swarthy North African face radiated an amicable charm. A refreshing lack of formality made me feel instantly welcome, and the dog's emotional excesses were agreeably offset by the languid affability of Pom-Pom the cat.

The apartment contained one bedroom, a living room, a narrow kitchen, a separate bathroom and toilet, and a full-length, north-facing balcony from which to admire the Parisian panorama. The 180-degree view encompassed a sweep from the hills of Versailles in the west to the Bois de Vincennes in the east, and included all of the most famous landmarks of the city. Dominating the horizon from left to right were the new sky-scrapers of La Défense, the Eiffel Tower, Arc de Triomphe, Tour Montparnasse, Opera Garnier, St. Sulpice, Pantheon, and Notre Dame, while the Byzantine shape of the Basilique du Sacré-Coeur topped the Butte de Montmartre in the distance. Continuing further right stood the twin towers of Les Mércures, beyond which one could see the control tower of Charles de Gaulle airport.

One of the traditional activities after Rita's arrival in Paris was her ritual fitting session. Leon was the manager of a garment factory near Meaux and prepared for Rita's visits with an accumulation of apparel to be pinned, tucked, measured, and draped on her highly compliant physique. It wasn't long before I joined Rita as a willing mannequin, which elevated me from steerage to peerage in a single session.

An essential part of this visit was my initiation to authentic French cuisine. It was thanks to Maria, who à la Julia Child embraced the art as well as the spirit of French cooking, which elevates a meal to the status of a sacrament. In working-class households, this practice was necessarily limited to weekends, but its celebration received the same devotion lavished in palaces of kings or at the tables of the Tour d'Argent, which amply reflects the willingness of the French to consecrate 60 percent of their salaries to gastronomy.

Our visit was short, because I was slated to start rehearsals in Vancouver and Rita needed to rejoin her flight in London, but it was a joyous beginning of a family relationship and the dawn of my fascination with Rita's home-town.

Rita with Wotan.

Rita and her mother, Maria.

Rita's stepfather, Leon Znaty, sewing her trousseau.

1970, VISITS TO MOROCCO AND ZERMATT

We opened *Lovers* on January 15 at the York Theatre on Vancouver's Commercial Drive, on completion of which, for the first time in six years, I found myself with nothing to do.

Conscience: "Hold on there! What about the thesis?"

Me: *Get off my back, C! There'll be time for that later. Rita and I have more important plans; we're going to tour Morocco in our new convertible.*

Accordingly, Rita flew to Paris while I bought a ticket to London and contacted the dealership.

"Oh yes ... Mister Plawski. We're awfully sorry, but there's been a bit of bother about that; you see, your car was ready to be delivered from Coventry yesterday, but a strike by the beastly delivery people has stranded it in the Leyland factory parking lot ... No, we have no idea when this might end ... I'm afraid you'll simply have to stay in touch. Ta Ta ... and do cheer up, old chap, it's bound to finish sooner or later."

I flew to Paris, where Rita and I checked into a tiny hotel in the busy little Rue des Canettes, just around the corner from the Église St. Sulpice. On learning of our predicament, Leon immediately offered us the use of his Volkswagen Beetle. This generous gesture not only saved our holiday, but the car's sloping shape would prove a godsend in shedding the urchins of Morocco who piled onto any passing vehicle *en masse*. Also, not having wire wheels would take the worry off negotiating the crumbling trails along which we chose to cross the Atlas Mountains.

Our trip did not start well. We spent the first night in Tours where we staged a giant row, continued it through a stopover in Biarritz where we vowed never to travel together again, and made up in Madrid wondering what the hell *that* was all about.

After a night in Seville in a hotel perfumed by a surrounding orange grove, we crossed the Straits of Gibraltar and headed for Rabat, Casablanca, and Mazagan, which is now known as El Jadida. Mazagan was the Znaty family's hometown, which Rita remembered from a previous visit.

The only hotel was closed for the winter, but luckily Rita located the last remaining family member, who convinced the owner to open his establishment where we spent the night.

The following day we drove all the way to Agadir and then reversed course for Marrakesh. After two days in this vibrant city, famous for the crowded souk and the red brick forts, we took what appeared on the map to be the most direct road to Fes. It turned out to be a single-lane goat trail carved into the mountainsides on which it was impossible to turn around, and which in keeping with the law of shortcuts, extended our journey by a day. The royal city of Fes charmed us with its mixture of medieval tanneries and magnificently tiled shrines interspersed with modern French architecture. As we quickly discovered, the town was also famous for the refinement of its Moroccan cuisine.

After crossing the Straights of Gibraltar, we stopped in Torremolinos, where I looked up a friend of my father's from the St. Petersburg Naval Academy. Mr. Fedorovsky and his wife invited us to their home, where we spent an evening admiring his watercolor impressions of Spain and listening to their recollections of the agonies of the post-revolutionary Russian debacle.

Our next stop was Barcelona, where we swiftly established a reputation in a neighboring restaurant, Los Caracoles, where our evidently romanti deportment caused the staff to greet our arrivals with calls of: "Bienvenido Romeo y Julietta!"

Floods inundated the south of France that winter, and it saddened our hearts to see such damage wreaked on this rich and fertile land.

I contacted Leyland immediately on arrival in Paris and learned that the car was still strike-bound. Since Rita had to return to work, I needed to find somewhere to wait on this side of the pond until its release. With uncanny timing, a confluence of circumstances lined up that determined my agenda.

To begin with, two of my Navy friends, Hal Hallaran and Malcolm McCulloch, happened to be starting a skiing holiday in Zermatt. I decided to join them for a week and then continue to London, where Rod and Coleen Langley, on their way back from Australia, had rented a house.

I spent my time in Zermatt watching my expert friends glide effortlessly down the mountains while I thrashed clumsily in their wake on my recently acquired, two-meter Fischer skis, which some spiteful SOB talked me into buying as the most appropriate equipment for a beginner. Surviving this ordeal, I bid adieu to my friends, packed my skis, and made my way to Geneva for the flight to London.

Rita and me after the tiff in Biarritz

LUNCH-HOUR THEATRE; A SEED IS SOWN

After boarding the flight, I relaxed in my seat as I perused the theatre section of the *London Times*. Among the reviews was a write-up of a Tom Stoppard play, *The Real Inspector Hound*, which was being staged in Soho in what was described as a "crowded sub-terrenial warren" located under a restaurant called The Green Banana, at lunch-time. Instantly intrigued by the unconventionality of the arrangement, I resolved to explore it on arrival.

With my new skis and boots in tow, I made my way to South Kensington, where the Langley's had settled in a condemned Victorian mansion while Rod attempted to raise interest in his new play. I was welcomed to sleep on a rolla-way cot in the absurdly spacious, high-ceilinged, and brutally frigid front room, which I discovered was also occupied by a lady they had befriended on the sea journey who had already taken possession of the couch.

Rod hadn't seen the Stoppard play, so the following day we made our way to the Green Banana. The "theatre" was a cavernous cellar furnished with a motley collection of sofas and chairs that encircled an acting area. In these cozy quarters, with some of the audience standing, crouching, or sitting on the floor, nine actors and one cadaver brought the play to life.

There was something immutably unifying in this experience, which made everyone feel drawn together, as if partaking in a conspiracy. Silently, a seed was sown, and I resolved to investigate this lunch-hour theatre scene more thoroughly.

Impulse purchase, Triumph TR6, London, 1970.

ROD AND I VISIT A CERTIFIED BRITISH ECCENTRIC

Another call to Leyland: "Hello, this is George Pla ..."

"Ah, Mr Plawski! We finally have good news; your lovely car will be ready for you in the morning."

Coincidentally, Rod, who'd been taping interviews for the CBC radio program *Matinée*, received an arresting assignment. An inventor in Devon had adapted the engine of his car to run on methane gas. Nothing original, of course, but the intriguing aspect of this undertaking was that he obtained the gas from chicken manure. This sounded potentially amusing, and since the shipping date for my car was a few weeks away, it presented an opportunity for a few laughs and a chance to break in the new engine—not over fifty mph for five hundred miles, admonished the manual.

We loaded up Rod's recording equipment and started out for the West Country, stopping en route at Stonehenge. Today, practically all of Salisbury Plain is out of bounds, and the actual site is guarded by a fence, but at that time we just drove up to the menhirs and, recklessly dismissing the Druids' avowed curse, clambered all over them with great abandon.

Another photo-op presented itself in a rural Norman church where Rod, who had been a Divinity student, delivered an inspiring sermon, the subject of which sadly escapes me, but judging by the ardent look on his face captured in my photo, it delved deeply into themes cautionary and Hadean.

We arrived in Torquay in the evening, where our day ended with unprecedented heroics when, armed with a set of deplumed rag-tag house-darts, we demolished the local champs.

The following morning, we arrived at a farm somewhere near Totnes, where the inventor, Mr. Bates, lived with his wife and daughter. A collection of friendly mutts spilled out of the thatch-roofed house, followed by a chap in muddy gumboots whose tweed jacket barely covered the remnants of a blue sweater that bore signs suggestive of an encounter with something dangerous.

Dignified in speech and manner typical of a British gentleman farmer, he invited us to follow him to the fermentation tanks where his neighbors deposited the chicken excrement. On route, Mr. Bates informed us that he was the holder of numerous patents that found application in physics and submarine technology, and from the incongruous combination of dress and style we quickly recognized a quintessential example of a certified English eccentric.

I have always venerated this exotic species for its beguiling unconventionality, and though this phenomenon materializes in every culture, I am convinced that it reaches its apogee in its English expression.

Mr. Bates explained how, after a suitable period of maceration, chicken manure exuded the gas, which he then collected into oversized bags mounted on the roof of his ageing Hillman. Although he willingly conceded that this was a throwback to WWII technology, the crucial difference, which he embroidered with graceful understatement, lay in the fuel's source, which offered the dual benefit of ameliorating the global energy shortage while presenting a profitable side-line for struggling chicken-farmers.

Our demonstration ride revealed that one of the drawbacks of this installation was a persistently offensive odor, which the vehicle had insufficient chicken-power to outrun. The inventor dismissed this as a trivial inconvenience easily overcome with a supply of nose-clips, and attributed the absence of pep directly to his neighbors' miserly habits of providing their broods with sub-standard nutrition, which contributed to the inferior octane of their poultry's egesta. We returned to London with the double success of Rod being in possession of a saleable interview, and me with a properly broken-in engine.

Conquering Stonehenge.

Rod Langley interviews a certified British eccentric.

EXPLORING LONDON'S LUNCH-HOUR THEATRE

Continuing to profit from Rod and Coleen's hospitality allowed me to con-centrate on exploring the unfamiliar territory of lunch-hour theatre, where I discovered an unexpectedly vibrant and prolific arena. My exploration revealed that there were several established lunch-hour venues in London pubs, such as The Orange Tree in Richmond, The Lamb and Flag just off the Covent Garden, and the recently opened King's Head in Islington. The majority of lunch-hour plays, however, were being staged by small companies, groups, or individuals at whatever locations could be rented, borrowed, or occupied, which opened a venue to a lucky few of the enormous supply of untapped talent thirsting for exposure.

Some of the material was improvised and some blossomed as happenings, but the vehicle ideally suited to this enterprise was the one-act play.

It suffices to look at the early works of Chekhov, Beckett, Pinter, Albee, Miller, Williams, Stoppard, Ionesco, and Mrożek, among others, who cut their teeth on this format. They employed it because it optimized the opportunity to experiment with structure, subject matter, and style, and could be fitted into a short time-frame. Furthermore, a frequent turnover of plays provided a vital training ground for all the other disciplines involved in the making of a theatri-cal production.

One of the thriving lunch-hour groups was The Soho Theatre; it was directed by Frederick Proud, whom I buttonholed after a performance. How, I wanted to know, does one go about getting to do a play in this town?

"Are you a playwright or performer?"

"Director," I replied.

"Hmmm … pop over to my place tomorrow and we can discuss it."

Fred met me on Archer Street in Soho and led me up an implausibly claustrophobic staircase to a space furnished floor-to-ceiling with nothing but pillars of books. Taking care not to touch anything that might result in a catastrophic domino-effect, we arrived at a small clearing that a single burner and sink identified as the kitchen. It was occupied by Fred's beautiful partner and co-director, the novelist Verity Bargate, who unconcernedly continued to breastfeed their infant.

Fred inquired about my experience and asked what I had in mind. I told him about Mrożek, with whom he was unfamiliar but expressed an interest in reading his work. I promised to forward it to him on my return to Vancouver.

"In case you were wondering," he added, "there's not much money in lunch-hour; it's pretty well done pro bono."

"No problem," I assured him. "I'll be in touch."

Judging by my ebullient mood, Rita was convinced that I had landed a life-long contract with the Royal Shakespeare Company.

"All this excitement … isn't it a touch premature? What agreement? As you like to say, it's all written with a stick on water."

I could not be calmed down.

"One small step for Plawski, one giant stride for Theatreland, yes … no?"

After delivering the car to Leyland for shipment to Montreal, Rita and I decided to spend a few days in Paris with a stop-over in Amsterdam. Naturally Rembrandt and Van Gogh occupied much of our time, but we also enjoyed a memorable adventure at a well-known restaurant, d'Vijff Vliegen (The Five Flies). Evidently smitten by my blonde, the urbane and charming owner, Mr. Nicolas Kroese, joined us at our table, and after closing his establishment at midnight insisted on hosting us, lavishly and hilariously, until three o'clock. I always loved sensing men lust for my little treasure; it made me puff up with pride and did wonders for my vanity.

From Paris, we flew to Montreal to wait for the delivery of my car; we moved in with one of my closest friends, Gaston Beauchesne, after which Rita had to return to work.

With a Little Nudge from Gaston and His Friend

Gaston was a practicing chemist; we befriended as cadets in 1953 when we were embarked in the Frigate HMCS *Swansea* on the way to the Queen's coronation. Following this cruise, Gaston and I were sent to Royal Roads near Victoria to continue summer training. He became a frequent visitor to our house, where he spoke French with my parents, and by the end of the summer we became each other's best friend.

Gas was two years older but a lifetime more experienced than me. He took full advantage of his good looks and the fatal attraction of his operatic baritone voice. It was a gift he could easily have exploited professionally, but apart from a guest appearance on the *Ed Sullivan Show*, he chose to reserve it as a showstopper at sing-alongs in bars and in lounges where opera singers came to show off their talents.

In the fall of 1955, we spent some time together in Montreal, where it amused him to observe my spirited but futile attempts to shed the inhibiting stranglehold of my virginity. Apart from a few furtive dips in some dark and sweaty tropical haciendas that could never count as *The Real Thing*, it clung to me like an unconfessed sin.

He'd finally had enough, and realizing that my ineffectual efforts might trail me until doomsday, decided to formally assist in the uncoupling of this embarrassingly unnatural condition. Accordingly, he arranged for one of his lady friends to recruit a compliant accomplice to take me to bed.

It amuses me to recall how smoothly she lied to Gaston the next morning when she pronounced my performance as very good.

I was twenty-one years old!

But then, it *was* the fifties.

Tragically, Gaston's exquisite voice, though not his memory, was forever extinguished in 1985 in the senseless sabotage of Air India flight 182, in which he and his lady friend were passengers.

My irrepressible friend, Gaston Beauchesne.

Gaston visits my parents, Victoria, 1954

A TOUCH OF CHUTZPAH

Meanwhile, as I awaited the arrival of my car in Montreal, I was told that the ship was three days late, having been damaged by a grand-daddy of an Atlantic storm. Anxious to start on my way, I was there to watch it dock when it eventually arrived.

"How soon can I expect my car?" I inquired of a foreman who appeared to be in charge. His answer was not encouraging; the storm apparently caused damage in the hold, and since there was no way of knowing where my car was stowed, it could be several days.

What happened next could not even remotely be imagined in our tight-assed, security hidebound world.

"I served in the Navy, and I'm familiar with ships," I offered. "Would it be OK for me to go on board to see if I can find it?"

He looked me over. "There's over six hundred cars there on four decks, but if you want, go ahead."

Stifling disbelief, I mounted the ramp, and dodging the first vehicles that were being offloaded, entered the hold. Endless rows of cars stood chained to the deck, but it wasn't long before I encountered the first significant debris field.

A car had come loose in the storm, and like a deranged bull charging in all directions, progressively enlarged its enclosure by reducing everything around it to scrap. In the process, it became compressed it into an unrecognizable clump of metal now resting amidst a clutter of smashed bumpers, flattened hubcaps, and broken glass. There were several such scenes on each deck, but these were other people's problems. A half-hour later, I came across my yellow beauty, covered in dust but otherwise unscathed, keys in the ignition. I reported its position to the foreman, who called one of the drivers.

It wasn't long before I drove my prize to a liquor store and rewarded my savior with two bottles of single malt.

En route to Vancouver, I stopped in Kingston where my Navy friends, Charlie Poirier and Jake Freill, were stationed with their families while attending Staff College. We were joined by Larry Washbrook, who with his wife, Eli, drove in from Ottawa. Larry was still a lieutenant and was studying computers, which eventually formed the backbone of his civilian career, but Charlie and Jake were now lieutenant commanders.

With the notorious Washbrook-Poirier-Plawski triad reunited again, we briefly considered pulling off some prank for which we'd become famous, and the flag on top of the administration building presented a tempting target, but sadly our appetite for such shenanigans had suffered an irreversible detumescence. Nevertheless, it was a joy to get together again and wipe some mildew off the memories of our brazen early years, but the meeting reinforced my conviction that leaving the service was the absolutely right thing to have done, and I wouldn't swap places with my friends for all the gold braid on the planet.

When I last drove across the country in 1964, I was a sorry amalgam of uncertainties and doubt. It was a different person at the wheel of an eye-catching yellow convertible who was crossing the Port Mann Bridge into what had all the earmarks of a bright new future.

Immediately on arrival I sent four of my translations to Fred and Verity, secretly hoping that *Strip Tease* would be their choice.

My parents were dutifully impressed with my new status symbol, and my prospect of directing a Polish play on a London stage gave them great satisfaction.

1970, HEROICS IN CALIFORNIA

I spent a languid month with Rita and my parents until the day Linc arrived from Red Deer, where he was the manager of a ski school in the winter.

The hibernation was over; I bid goodbye to my loved ones, and we drove in tandem to Santa Rosa.

It was good to greet my American friends again and to get back to the job I loved. Bud Davis welcomed us with his usual grace and immediately got to the point. An F7F seat had become available at Willows. Were any of us interested?

To fly that incomparable twin-engine beauty was every pilot's wet dream. Just the look of this lissome vixen, the glamour-queen of any assembly of flying machines, was enough to make any red-blooded pilot ready to burn his vows and slip the surly bonds of earth in her throbbing embrace forever.

There was just a single, solitary drawback that stood between me and the consummation of this lust: Willows. Not even an offer of Marilyn Monroe as the season's bed-mate could make me consider a summer of counting jackrabbits from a trailer isolated in the searing armpit of the Sacramento Valley.

Linc didn't need MM as bait. He was ready to pledge celibacy, if that's what it took, to get his hands on that silky siren. For the next two weeks in Santa Rosa where Linc did his checkout, I burned with envy listening to those powerlants making the air vibrate with all that unleashed power. For the remainder of the season we only met in the air, but Linc was in seventh heaven, and it was easy to share in his euphoria.

The fire season started briskly that year with daily dispatches to targets in the counties of Napa and Sonoma. One of the fires was started by a Navy A7 that crashed after the pilot bailed out, and the other was a most unwelcome callout one morning at dawn. This flight required an IFR climb out through a blanket of fog, which with malice of forethought used to roll in from the ocean exclusively on mornings after a tanker base party.

Sometime in August, the California Division of Forestry approved my friend Ron Thomas' request to be trained as an air attack officer, and he started to accompany our dispatches. He became certified on September 21, and it was good to welcome a personal friend to the executive team.

His baptism of fire came early in the afternoon on the following day.

Taking advantage of an easterly wind, an arsonist set a fire on Grizzly Peak Boulevard, a road that follows the top of a ridge above the city of Berkeley from where several well-defined valleys open westward toward the Bay. The wind quickly spread the flames downhill through the tranquil community, where hundreds of residences nestled on the forested slopes.

By the time Ron arrived, the smoke had blanketed the area, making it impossible to pick out a target. As tankers converged from all over northern California, each received a number and joined the expanding orbit, where I counted four TBMs, one B17, and two Tigercats, one of which was piloted by Linc.

It was easy to imagine the frustration of the people below as they listened to this armada circling impotently over their heads. Occasionally, a space cleared enough for Ron to send a tanker down for a drop, but sniping was all we could do, as there was no way to lay a retardant line. During one of my passes, I recall seeing people with garden hoses watering their roofs and waving feebly as they watched me fly by.

Each time we returned with a load we reported: "Three minutes out" to Ron and took our place in the stack. As we waited our turn, an occasional black plume penetrated upwards through the lighter wood smoke, signifying that someone just lost their home.

I was number three in line when from my wide orbit I caught a glimpse of a situation developing beneath the smoke. A brisk fire was climbing up a steep slope toward some houses. This required immediate action, but I knew that Ron couldn't see it from his position.

"Airco Eight, Tanker Two Four, I have a priority target: clear me for a lone-wolf attack, Ron … now!"

Ron cleared me without hesitation.

I peeled off to a position on the opposite side of the valley level with the houses; there was still about a hundred feet of clear air between the roofs and the base of the smoke, but it was impossible to gauge how long this condition could last. I had only one option: hug the left slope and fly as far as possible up-canyon into the smoke, then make a 180 degree turn to the right and hope to find my target on the other side. To deliberately enter smoke under these conditions was sheer insanity, but an instant calculation that a 30 degree level turn a hundred yards into the smoke should fit into the contours of the valley determined my course of action.

With my target at my altitude on my right, I tucked my left wing into the hillside, memorized the heading, finished my bombing check, armed for a salvo, and with my thumb on the drop button took a deep breath as my world narrowed to attitude gyro, needle, ball, and airspeed.

The further I could force myself to fly on this heading, the more distance I would gain for any corrections on final, but my nerve vaporized almost immediately and I rolled into the turn.

"Nail that VSI!" (vertical speed indicator) I yelled to myself out loud, my eyes straining to pierce the murk as they flicked back and forth from gauges to windscreen.

Through the 90 degree position I started to breathe again, but I was still in smoke. As I rolled out on the reciprocal heading, everything happened at once: I broke clear, saw my target level a short distance ahead, knew I was too low but couldn't pull up yet or I'd be in the smoke, then adding full power and lifting my left wing to miss the roofs, I triggered the load in a steep climbing turn, hoping to place it below the houses.

No one observed my drop, and there was no way to check its accuracy.

When I broke out, I reported to Ron that I was clear of the target.

"OK, Two Four, reload and return."

On the way back to base I had time for a quiet debriefing. It wasn't hard to conclude that these kinds of heroics are the ones that make people reading accident reports shake their heads with disbelief. For the first time in my bombing career, I broke the most basic rules of safety and got away with it— but no fire is worth a life, particularly if it's mine.

Forty-five minutes later I made the customary "Two Four, three minutes" report and fitted into the stack. The smoke was now clearing, which afforded a view of the devastation below. Standing out prominently within the burned out area were the charred remains of what recently had been people's homes.

One-by-one, I started to pick out the landmarks, searching for where I dumped the last load. After identifying the canyon and scanning its south slope, I saw it—two adjoining houses stood intact above a vast puddle of retardant, which separated them from the burnt out hillside below. A short distance beyond my drop, the fire climbed the hill unimpeded and consumed someone's house.

Suddenly it all appeared worth it, though it wouldn't have been if not for an extravagant dose of luck, which is a useful but unreliable commodity to tap into when judgment should have been the wiser choice.

It was getting dark, and I was the last tanker to drop. I don't recall where Ron had me place the load, but as soon as I was empty, I asked him to clear me for one low pass. Camera in hand, I flew by the two houses, clicking away, then after a show-off departure over the Claremont Hotel, made my way home.

After the debriefing, I leapt into my TR and headed for San Francisco. This was one action I needed to see on the ground. I took the San Marin-Richmond Bridge to Berkeley, then proceeding by instinct, climbed in the direction of the fire until I was stopped by a police roadblock.

"Only residents are permitted beyond this crossing. What is your business here?"

"I'm one of the tanker pilots who worked this fire, and I've been appointed to ascertain the effectiveness of our drops," I brazened importantly, flashing my California Air Tanker certificate. He bought the line without question and waved me through.

A constant lament of sirens tormented the calm night air, which hung saturated with the sweet medicinal smell of burnt eucalyptus. Fire trucks dousing smoking remains that smoldered eerily in the night seemed to be everywhere. I bumped over their fire hoses and passed a group of people with flashlights grubbing through some rubble. The scene briefly reignited the memory of my mother, brother, and me sifting through the charred remains of our home in Warsaw in 1939.

Eventually I reached a road that snaked along the north slope of a canyon. There were several such valleys, but at night from the ground nothing looked familiar. When I passed two houses perched on a steep hillside, and a short distance later saw two fire trucks hosing a wrecked property, I decided this had to be the place.

After turning around, I pointed the car at the house and knocked on the front door in the light of the headlights. It was opened by a lady of Japanese descent, flashlight in hand.

"Good evening," I said, "I was the pilot who dropped the load below your house. I just wanted to know how it turned out."

She looked at me for a long moment in silence and then uttered the words that still reverberate in my memory: "God bless you; you saved my home."

We hugged, and both of us cried.

She led me to her balcony, which was splattered with pink overspray, and shined the flashlight down the slope. The retardant was now almost dry, but the vegetation still flattened by the low drop showed evidence of massive pooling. It's likely that a release from a more reasonable altitude may have dispersed the drop too much to stop the grass-and-Manzanita fueled fire.

A group of people stood gathered on the balcony of the house next door. Their Japanese neighbor told them who I was. Come on over, they waved. Again, tears mixed with hugs. Once more we inspected the retardant. The load had stretched sufficiently to provide a guard for their home as well. A B17 drop could easily have reached their westerly neighbors, but a TBM only carried six hundred US gallons: unguarded, that home went up in flames.

Would I care for a drink? It was then that I became aware of the bottles on a table in the corner of the balcony. As bizarre as it seemed, a celebration under the circumstances was not only appropriate: it seemed mandatory. With a glass in hand, I listened to their story.

The fire started up-canyon to the east, and smoke quickly filled the valley.

Tell me about it, I thought.

City fire trucks, reinforced by California Division of Forestry, showed up quickly, but sparks driven by the wind jumped hundreds of yards, starting new conflagrations that entirely overwhelmed the resources. They could hear the planes overhead but never saw any drops, and when they spotted the fire climbing up the slope, they knew there was no choice but to evacuate.

Then they heard the roar that changed everything.

They only saw the airplane for a few seconds as it emerged out of the smoke, but all at once, they realized that the most pressing danger threatening their lives was not the fire but that berserk madman about to smash into their homes. Ducking, they covered their heads from the rush of wind and the shower of pink goop that splattered the area, but by the time they looked up, the apparition was gone.

Slimy overspray covered the decks and rolled down the windows and walls, but when they peered down the slope, they could see that, incredibly, the fire front was stopped.

It was true that these peoples' descriptions and gratitude made me feel giddy inside, but privately I swore never, *ever*, to contemplate anything like this again. The arrival of a *Deus-ex-Machina* just in time to forestall catastrophe was a convention of Greek Tragedy that I would be well advised to leave to the dramatists.

A few days later, Bud called me into his office. If he'd heard about my antics in Berkeley, I could anticipate a well-deserved rocket.

"Sit down," he said. "How would you like to check out in the F7F?"

Something resembling a drum roll rumbled in my chest.

"There may not be a seat available next season," he added," but I'd like you to be ready if one comes along."

Though I had no intention of accepting a seat out in the boonies, this was hardly the time to equivocate.

"When do I start, Bud?"

He'd make a plane available when the season was over, but first I'd need to get an FAA multi-engine rating, which meant extending my stay in Santa Rosa by about a month. I knew that Rita would understand; it was an opportunity I just could not pass up.

When I phoned Linc to tell him the news, he, in turn, informed me of the continuing developments of the appealing offer he'd received from a Toronto based company, Kenting Aviation. It stemmed from the decision by the Ontario Department of Lands and Forests to enhance its water-bombing operation with a group of multi-engine tankers using long-term retardant.

Since Kenting had considerable experience in aerial survey but none in firebombing, it was natural that they should approach Linc to oversee the program, since his recently published *Pilots' Notes For Firebombing* had already established him as an authority on the subject. Seeing this as a career opportunity, Linc obtained Bud's blessing to cut his ties with Sis Q, checked out in the twin-engine A26 Invader at Rosenbalm Aviation in Oregon, and was en route to Toronto to report to his new employer. I had no way of knowing how significant Linc's decision would be for my own career.

Meantime, having to stay beyond the end of the fire season in California could not be classed as an arduous fate. Though much of my time needed to be spent preparing for my checkout, there was plenty left over for hunting with Ron. We could now add turkeys to our usual quarry of dove, quail, and waterfowl. Hunting turkeys was a particular thrill, because sneaking up on these wary birds tests the hunter's skills to the limit. It also gave me a chance to play golf with Bill Park, even though his visits tended to devastate the mornings after.

Linc in cockpit of a guided missile.

Linc's F7F Tigercat outclassing my TBM.

MY FIRST SOLO IN THE F7F TIGERCAT

After four dual flights in a twin-engine Apache, I passed the multi-engine ride and began preparing for my checkout. The first glance into the impossibly narrow F7F cockpit wedged into the pencil-thin fuselage announced unequivocally that this baby was built for speed, not for comfort.

The Tigercat, designed by Grumman, was the first twin-engine fighter built for the USN, and its two 2100 HP engines propelled it at over 400 kts, or 740 mph, making it one of the fastest piston engine airplanes on the planet. Once snug in the seat, with those monstrous power-plants thrusting defiantly on either side of the canopy, I might have been in the nose-cone of a spaceship.

To become familiar with this new office, I spent long hours in the cockpit with the manual in my lap making rippling noises with my lips. Bud and Harry Chaffee generously shared their considerable expertise in this machine, and as soon as I learned how to start those Pratt-and-Whitneys without backfiring, I ventured that I was ready to solo.

November 12 was to be the memorable day. My checkout in the patrician silver beauty with the number "23" on her tail was scheduled for after lunch. However, my first duty that day was to jettison the retardant with which my Avenger was still loaded to prepare it for its winter hibernation.

As I prepared for this flight, Ron stuck to me like a shadow. I knew he had always wanted to go up in a Turkey, but we weren't authorized to take passengers, and we'd be in deep kaka if we got caught. Of course, if I didn't know that I had a stowaway …

"Are you there, Ron?" I whispered before starting the engine.

A knock on the fuselage confirmed his presence.

After jettisoning the load, I headed for the coastline to do some flat-hatting near Stinson Beach for the benefit of one of Ron's lady friends before returning to the field.

On landing, we discovered that a coterie of kibitzers had already gathered at the base, which unfortunately included some SIS-Q management and Forestry brass, effectively trapping Ron in his hiding place.

It must have seemed like an eternity for him as he crouched in the back while I went about last minute preparations for the flight, which included an extended briefing from Bud, the most carefully monitored pre-flight inspection of my career, and the longest run up ever recorded while I built up courage for takeoff.

After triple checking the checklist, I was cleared to go, and now there was no turning back. I advanced the throttles at my usual measured pace on the way to full power of fifty-two inches of manifold pressure, when at barely forty inches this demon was already flying. Though I was well aware of the enormous power of these engines, it still caught me off guard. It does the same for everyone on their first takeoff. I caught up to the airplane somewhere around five thousand feet.

"Wow!" I kept repeating out loud. The responsiveness of the controls, unlimited visibility, and prodigious performance was a revelation to someone accustomed to the more temperately attuned examples of the *genre*. It was the most exciting experience of my aviation career.

Ron was in the group of people who welcomed me back into the pits. There were lots of handshakes and backslapping, which made me feel like Chuck Yeager after breaking the sound barrier.

"Did anyone see you get out of the airplane?" I asked Ron when I got a chance.

"No way! When you were on takeoff roll, the Dallas Cowboys cheerleaders could have done a number stark-naked on the tarmac and not a fucking soul would have noticed."

Appreciatively, I savored the image so typical of my great friend, but my day was not over yet as Bud called me aside.

"Harry is going to take you to Hollister in the [Cessna] 310; I'd like you to pick up Orrin's machine and drop the load on the way home."

"Jesus Christ, Bud, it's already getting late. Can't I do it tomorrow?"

"They want to shut down the base, and you're the only TBM pilot I got."

The Tigercat I "tamed" in 1969

SCARY NIGHT WITH GEAR PROBLEM

It was dark when we landed in Hollister, but Harry helped to get Tanker 25 ready and waited until I took off. I jettisoned the load at a safe altitude, and with San Francisco Center guiding me through their control area, I relished an unforgettable flight over that magnificent city at night.

The fun was not over yet, because when I entered the pattern to the Sonoma County Airport, one gear wouldn't lock down. I told the tower of my predicament and climbed out to the west where there were no mountains while they called out the fire brigade. Night gear-up landings were not on the syllabus in the training command, so it would be more prudent, I reckoned, to get that effing thing down.

After a nervous and untidy struggle doing whatever those emergency procedures called for while trying to keep the airplane right side up, the moment of deliverance arrived with a clunk accompanied by the precious glow of that Elysian green light. With a voice in a register that could be the envy of *La Divina* Callas in her prime, I reported my success to the tower controller, whose relief almost matched mine as he gave me a course to steer back to the field from somewhere over the uncharted blackness of the Russian River.

"We've got the fire trucks on standby just in case," he added reassuringly, while what I really wanted was a bucket of beer and a fresh box of pampers.

"TAMING" A TIGRESS

The following day my checkout continued. The next four flights were devoted to practicing stalls, slow flight, single-engine work at altitude, and all the emergency procedures, as well as rejected takeoffs, single engine approaches, and lots of touch-and-goes.

It wasn't all work, however, because though aerobatics were technically forbidden, this slinky hussy begs to be treated according to her purpose. Luckily, the nearby ocean offered an ideal arena where this foreplay could be consummated well out of sight of disapproving eyes.

On the last day, Bud approved a couple of water drops, which this airplane performed smoothly with just a slight pitch up, and I joined Linc in believing that this had to be the world's most successful air tanker conversion.

The type-rating flight was scheduled for November 18, and I hoped that I would be luckier than Linc, who after the obligatory feathered-engine flyover performed for the benefit of the FAA examiner watching from the ground, could not unfeather the prop. As a result, Linc was called upon to demonstrate more skills than are typically required by having to land with a frozen left engine.

Things went quite smoothly for me, and since I happened to remember to extend the gear for the landing, this was judged by my examiner to exemplify sufficient mastery of the machine to issue me with my type-rating, which possibly made Linc and I the only Canadians who could proudly boast this honor.

If, on the drive home, I had taken the time to compose a *flimsy* of my life so far, I would have been able, without hesitation, to record, "… to my entire satisfaction." A *flimsy* is the name of a naval document that registers the commanding officer's opinion of the character and progress of a subordinate officer on the occasion of his promotion, or of leaving for another appointment.

For reasons known only to their Lordships, it is written on an eponymously flimsy piece of paper, which encourages succinct and pithy commentary.

"To my *entire* satisfaction" is the highest possible accolade, while "to my satisfaction" is its less complimentary counterpart.

This form also lends itself to highly original assessments at the other end of the spectrum, as exemplified by: "While serving in my ship, this officer has conducted himself to *his* entire satisfaction," culminating in the cruelly waspish:

"This officer has used my ship as a convenient form of transportation from one brothel to another."

My personal contentment rested on a constellation of factors. I was privileged to have been a part of the august brotherhood of Canadian Naval Aviators; I had survived five years of academe; I held an enviably exciting job; I radiated health and vigor; and I could boast loving parents and devoted friends.

Most of all, I was returning to a beautiful, cultured, talented, headstrong, self-confident, and passionately loving girl, with whom I was ecstatically, flat-out in love, and who, if she agreed, I could contemplate living with for the rest of my life.

There was much to catch up on with my little blonde in her thirtieth floor eyrie where she had been busy creating collages and painting more of he naïf motifs, which adorned the walls. Rita paints with her heart and her instinct. She is a gifted colorist, and her work reflects not what she sees, but what she feels, which is the basis of a genuine artistic temperament.

I was also relieved to discover that my father had recovered from his medical travails and was back at work.

To add to my joy, a letter from Fred Proud arrived from London. Fred invited me to direct *Enchanted Night* for a two-week run at the King's Head pub in Islington, opening on May 3. It was a venue in the process of gaining a foothold as London's new experimental theatre under its visionary American founder, Dan Crawford. The timing suited me perfectly, and the chance of being a part of something new and avant-garde in the theatrical capital of the Anglo-Saxon world created a mind-warp of excitement.

Rita's *Smoking Fish*, [oil.]

Rita's *Esprit de Famille*, [gouache.]

A FATEFUL LAST-MINUTE DECISION

Just before Christmas, our Air Canada friends, Carl and Trudy, invited us to dinner, which unexpectedly became an event with life-transforming consequences. It began with their announcement that they planned to spend a week in Grenada in January and wondered if we'd like to join them. Tempting indeed, we agreed, though I baulked at the cost of my ticket.

"Mere bagatelle," offered Carl. "Why not stage a quick wedding and travel free as the husband of an employee?"

Seeing that I was taking a long count recovering from the jolt of this idea, he clinched his point by suggesting that, to restore the relationship to its liberal respectability, it would only cost fifty bucks for a divorce.

Rita and I exchanged a meaningful look; this was something we would need to discuss in private. After all, we had defied convention by living together for four years and solemnly proclaimed that our commitment rested on a foundation fundamentally more durable than any mere marriage certificate could offer. On the other hand, we were forced to admit that our friends had a point. The question was: How to commit wedlock without shattering a closely guarded self- image?

When principles need to be compromised, history reveals that the reason behind the apostasy is often a question of money. After sorting out the ethics involved, we agreed that a traditional wedding was out of the question; however, a snap ceremony without any trappings retained enough of the cachet of defiance to render the artifice feasible. There would be no wedding rings, of course, and except for informing our parents and Air Canada, this stratagem would remain a secret. Accordingly, we made arrangements to tie the knot privately on December 30.

Although our families were aware of our living arrangement, their attitudes were poles apart. Maria and Leon, who were also cohabiting unharnessed by marriage, unquestioningly accepted Rita's choices as long as she was happy. My father, who came to love Rita, adjusted to the situation with worldly grace, but my conservative mother remained in a state of embarrassed denial.

Since Rita had a three-day layover in London starting on December 26, this would allow her to hop over to Paris to make the grand announcement. I made mine offhandedly at my parents' house after supper in a tone of studied informality between the second and third periods of a Canadiens and Maple Leafs hockey game. The horrified silence that met this disclosure made me aware of the abject insensitivity of this approach. My parents felt rightly appalled by the tactlessness of my announcement, and I'm deeply ashamed of it to this day.

Meanwhile, on the other side of the Atlantic, Rita engendered a somewhat different reaction.

"I'm getting married!" she cheerfully announced to her mother upon arrival.

Maria paused, visibly intrigued; "Oh? To whom?" she inquired.

Rita was scheduled to work the flight from London to Winnipeg on December 29, and then to fly as a passenger through Edmonton to Vancouver. On arrival in Winnipeg, she found a land paralyzed by a mature manifestation of a classic Canadian winter. Though she made it to Edmonton, on entering the terminal she encountered the very thing she feared the most: an impenetrable backlog from previous flight cancellations, which made further progress impossible. The crews would have to lay over in Edmonton until further notice.

The chances of making it to the wedding the next morning vanished in the white-out. Was this Providence throwing her a life-line? A meaningful tap on the shoulder advising a pause for a sober second opinion?

To try to inform me, she joined a queue of equally desperate travelers lined up for the phone booths, but when her turn came, she failed to get through.

Meanwhile, I was bouncing off walls wondering if I should cancel the ceremony. Though heaven might sanction a wedding with an absentee bride, I was not confident of its acceptance by civil authority.

Unknown to me, miracles were happening in Edmonton; through some inexplicable sorcery, Air Canada conjured an aircraft and crew and scheduled an extra section. The urgency of the situation required an instant decision. Standby was out of the question, so Rita rushed to the ticket counter and bought the last remaining seat in first class. With no time to phone, she asked the agent to contact crew scheduling to give me the news and ran to the airplane. The word got through, and sometime near midnight, I drove to the airport to collect my exhausted future bride.

The wedding took place on schedule the following morning at ten, in the private home of the justice of the peace, forebodingly named: Dangerfield. Attending were our witnesses, Richard and Heather Mossakowski, along with my parents, whose demeanor suggested that they were about to witness a beheading.

Mr. Dangerfield conducted the ceremony with an *hauteur* befitting his six and a half foot frame; with grave authority, he enumerated the list of obligations to which we supplied a litany of "I do's" until he reached the phrase requiring Rita to *obey*.

Presuming the prolonged pause was caused by a lack of understanding, he repeated the phrase with increased emphasis and lingered meaningfully awaiting her response. A split second before I could nudge my betrothed to accede to this directive, the silence was ruptured by a plosive discharge of captive air.

When I looked at Rita, her shoulders were shaking and her hand shielded a face contracted into a spasm of ineffectively stifled laughter. To his credit, Mr. Dangerfield navigated safely away from this perilous moment by bringing the ceremony to a close, and this commitment remains unexpressed, and I might add, unpracticed, to this day.

1971 JANUARY HONEYMOON IN GRENADA

With our cohabitation now sanctioned by the state as well as by Air Canada, we prepared for our honeymoon in the tropics. However, before being able to make use of travel privileges as a husband of an employee, I needed appropriate documentation, which using normal channels would take too long to acquire. The only way to accelerate the process was to show up in person at Air Canada headquarters in Montreal.

Accordingly, I flew to Montreal one day ahead of our group, obtained the required blessings, and the following day we all landed in St. George's, where I was pleased to discover that my newly acquired status entitled me to the delivery of my luggage.

Unfortunately, this was not the case for the remainder of our party. With assurances from the airline that the bags would be delivered to our address immediately on their discovery, we rented a *Mini-Moke* (a stripped down version of a jeep), and proceeded to our accommodations.

Arriving encumbered by layers of Arctic overwear caused considerable surprise to our housekeeper, who interpreted it as apparent ignorance of the local climate. Rita's tropical trousseau, after we shared the contents of my suitcase, turned out to be my Skyway T-shirt, which portrayed a tanker dropping a load, underscored by the politically questionable caption: YOU LITE 'EM, WE FIGHT 'EM. By the time the clothes arrived five days later, we had become cheerfully accustomed to their absence.

Tourists had not yet overrun Grenada. With our housekeeper's hand-drawn map to Morne Rouge Beach, after driving through a vast colony of instantly vanishing land-crabs, we discovered that we had this pristine stretch to ourselves in which to skinny dip to our hearts' content.

One afternoon, as we relaxed in the shade of the conveniently located palm trees, we observed a rowboat crewed by three young locals who, as they slowly cruised by, displayed an inordinate interest in our group. After rowing about a hundred meters, they reversed course and passed by again: we were obviously being cased. Turning once more, they came abeam and stopped.

Suspecting something more sinister than mere voyeurism, we were contemplating a prudent retreat when one of the occupants stood up in the boat and casually disrobed. Naked, he jumped into the water, and after collecting something from his companions, struck out toward us. On reaching the beach, he rose from the sea like a Pelagic Poseidon, and with our sartorial kinship unequivocally established, unraveled the contents of the bag.

"Would you like to buy a lobster, man?" he inquired, proffering an impressive specimen while sporting an enormous grin.

Indeed we would; after shaking hands all around, he placed the money in his mouth and swam back to his companions, who helped him climb into the boat. He then re-donned his attire, and with a friendly wave, the group rowed contentedly away.

Not all of our encounters had a similarly happy ending. One of these occurred when a local gent, on passing our foursome, waspishly commented that frolicking naked on beaches was not done in Grenada. On returning to our *Moke*, we discovered four flat tires.

We knew there were some houses hidden in the jungle high above the beach to which we made our way, hoping to find a phone. Following the unmistakable smell of smoking weed, we approached a house, where a cheerful group of young American hippies waved us fondly inside. From there we called the renter. It turned out to be a party-house where we would enjoy several mellow and laughter filled evenings.

We relished walking under the lush canopy of the unspoiled tropical vegetation that covered the expanse of this western peninsula, the south side of which opened on a black, volcanic-sand covered beach, home to colonies of lizards and diving birds. (When we revisited the island twenty years later as guests aboard my Navy-friend Brian Moorhouse's yacht, to our immense disappointment we found that the Maurice Bishop International Airport had swallowed up the majority of this pristine land.)

On return to Vancouver, I was quick to visit my parents with my new bride to try to make amends for my unforgivable *faux pas*.

The dreary January rains that followed our sun-drenched Grenada honeymoon afforded a chance to ruminate on the events of the past two weeks. It was sobering to consider that an unpremeditated impulse motivated by monetary considerations precipitated such a life-altering decision. Rita would have to get used to being Mrs. Plawski, and I would have to think of her as *the wife*. It was all embarrassingly conventional and smacked of betrayal of the teachings of our guru, Bertrand Russell, and our self-evaluation as free thinkers.

On the other hand, the benefit conferred by our new alliance became instantly reflected in my cost of travel. As Rita's husband, I inherited her seniority and the right to fly on standby, which in those days was a fraction of the regular price. I resolved to roll-over quietly and live with this arrangement, while Rita's paintings would defiantly remain in her maiden name as the work of R. Schumacher.

So long as there are eyes to see us thus, so long lives this, and this gives life to us
(with apologies to the bard).

RITA'S NEW FAMILY AND THE START OF A BOARD GAME

My first duty before directing *Enchanted Night* was to obtain the rights to Mrożek's play from his London agency, which arrived promptly in the mail and thoughtfully included the authorized version of the script translated by Nicolas Bethell. I kept my mouth shut about having no intention of using this version and got on with preparing to direct the play from my translation.

Though this is a highly time consuming stage for a director, apparently this overload failed to plenish a restless brain, whose underused lobes demanded further stimulation. The result began to materialize in the form of a board game based on football. I knew little about the sport, since I had never played it, but the concept intrigued me enough to begin constructing a prototype. It would be a cards-and-dice game, but to create it I needed statistics. Accordingly, I approached the management of the BC Lions, who were most generous with reams of information, to distribute which on the cards required at least a rudimentary knowledge of mathematics.

In spite of my previous problems with this subject, necessity awakened an unexpected connectivity within the synaptic structure of the brain, which with the assistance of a prototype calculator costing $140, allowed me to master it sufficiently to create the bell curves I needed to produce realistic results for each given play.

Prototype of Quarterback.

Rita feeds Scrapper, or vice-versa.

LONDON: LAUNCH OF A VAUNTED DIRECTING CAREER

The prospect of directing a play in London kept me in a state of perpetual agitation. I was itching to start, so five weeks before the opening, I flew to London and rented a spacious, high-ceilinged flat in Sloane Square.

Fred agreed to show me the theatre the following day; we took the tube to Islington, got off at a station named Angel, and after a short walk reached the Victorian building that housed the King's Head pub, a distinctly un-glamorous and somewhat grubby example of the species solidly reflecting its blue-collar surroundings.

Inside, Fred introduced me to the artistic director, Dan Crawford, one of a group of Americans who helped to launch fringe theatre in London. Dan's ambition was to have his own theatre, and after convincing the Arts Council to furnish him with a grant, he set out with his wife, Joan, to find a suitable location. He settled on the King's Head principally because he judged that a space at the back of the house that had previously served as a boxing ring could be adapted to create a stage.

Though he'd only been staging plays since December, his reputation, choice of material, quality of work and sheer chutzpah had already stamped the venue as a committed presenter of original work. The auditorium consisted of a collection of tables set with checkered plastic tablecloths and surrounded by a motley conglomerate of chairs that faced a raised platform cluttered with the props of the presently running show.

Backstage, a manual light-box, which controlled the handful of lights mounted on a grid above the audience, rested next to a tape recorder used for sound effects. Tucked in behind a curtain were a sofa, a sink, and a mirror, which identified it as the green room—an area that would later be unkindly described by actor Sheridan Morley as "a space which made the hole of Calcutta look like a five-star hotel."

Dan assured me that a qualified stage manager and staff would look after the construction of sets, the handling of props, and all technical requirements, and he finished the tour with an expansive, "There you have it; all the accoutrements required to transplant *Aida* from the Royal Opera House, camels and all." I silently agreed that this would be an apt venue for this opera, since in this space no one would notice whether the animals were house-broken.

Working here would be challenging, but at the same time there was something immutably exciting about the prospect of creating theatre in these conditions, and I couldn't wait to begin.

During a production meeting convened for the following day, I met the backstage personnel, to whom I presented the floor plan along with the sound and lighting plots. I explained that the play required a realistic rendition of a cheap hotel room with a functional door and a window, two single beds, a desk and a chair, all of which were judged to be well within the theatre's capability.

On the way home, Fred briefed me on the casting process, which he assured me was facilitated by the enormous pool of talent eager for work. He supplied me with some prospects from his personal lists and gave me the addresses of talent agencies, where for a fee I could peruse albums containing *curriculum-vitae* of every performer in the British Isles, along with their agents.

It was an enormously ego-inflating feeling to enter the offices of *Spotlight*, where on announcing that I was casting a play, I might as well have been Darryl Zanuck. Informing the staff that I required two middle-aged men and one attractive young female, they served me with several albums from which it wasn't long before I completed my cast: it would star John Gielgud, Laurence Olivier, and Diana Rigg. Just in case these actors were otherwise engaged, I stuffed my notebook with a selection of alternates, whose agencies I planned to call in the morning.

The half-price ticket venue on Leicester Square was just around the corner; on the way by, I bought a seat to that evening's performance of Christopher Hampton's *The Philanthropist*, which had won the Best New Play award and was playing at the May Fair Theatre. I enjoyed the piece thoroughly, but what especially caught my attention was the work of one of the actors, Edward de Souza, who seemed to me ideal for the leading role in my play.

When I called Fred the next morning, he described De Souza as an actor with a strong reputation in the West End who was very much in demand, and Fred doubted that he'd be interested, but I decided to contact his agent anyway. On hearing that this was to be a lunch-hour production that wouldn't interfere with his client's present engagement, the agent agreed to deliver the script.

I received a call from Ted the next day; he loved the play, and we agreed to meet in my flat to discuss it. Ted, as I would soon discover, was a deeply cultured man, brimming with humor and energy, and his black, wavy hair and swarthy complexion handsomely reflected his Portuguese ancestry. A convivial interview confirmed that Ted was perfect for the part, and I was elated to become the subject of a subtle role-reversal when he agreed to cast me as his director. Fred was astonished that I had made such a prestigious catch.

After organizing my *Spotlight* selections and amassing a sizeable collection of twopenny bits, I established an office in the cramped confines of a nearby telephone booth, which made the task far cheaper than having to pay the usurious prices charged to the phone in my flat, and began to make appointments for the following week.

It was genuinely humbling to discover that well-known actors were eager to read for a complete unknown. My list includes contemporary luminaries such as Frank Middlemass, Michael Logan, Judi Matheson, as well as Leslie Anne Downe, whose career remained undamaged as she went on to star with Sean Connery in *The Great Train Robbery*, among others, in spite of my dismissal of her as "very beautiful, but not much personality, really."

I completed the cast with the highly experienced Gordon Sterne and a most attractive film actress and dancer, Irene Gorst.

Our first rehearsals took place in my apartment. I was immediately impressed with Ted's professionalism, whose preparation included the habit of recording the dialogue of the other characters to tape, leaving appropriate gaps that he filled with his lines on long walks through Richmond Park.

We moved to the King's Head as soon as we were able, and I was proud of my cast for choosing to disregard the conditions in favor of concentrating on the show. Working with dedicated professionals drove me hard to refine each moment of the script, and soon the rhythm, flow, and well defined characterizations convinced me that we had prepared a polished offering.

I particularly enjoyed how the tight-lipped petulance between the two incompatible strangers who are compelled to share a hotel room achieved such perfect pitch when delivered with a crisp British accent.

On opening day, the usual mixture of thrill and terror filled my being as I watched the theatre fill. As Dan, Fred, and Verity introduced me to some of the guests, I realized that this would be a sophisticated and discerning audience.

The stature of this remote little theatre became evident by the arrival of London's most prestigious reviewers, which included Michael Billington and the venerable Harold Hobson.

How I wished that Rita could have shared this moment with me, but her schedule didn't allow it. The other person who was sorely disappointed with

Rita's absence was Ted, whose frank infatuation with her led him to make a delicious fuss over her every time they met.

The English reviewers favorably noted Mrożek as a uniquely talented writer, and tickled my vanity with a complimentary mention of the fluid translation, while Michał Chmielowiec, the head of the Polish Professional Actors Guild, wrote a flattering article that was published, along with my picture, in the Polish weekly *Wiadomości*.

Mrożek's English agents, who did not fail to notice the difference between the dialogue on stage and its authorized version, chose not to interfere because of the positive way the production served their client.

I was especially pleased that the actors were well rewarded in print for their work, since the pittance Fred was able to pay them scarcely covered their tube fare.

I left London with a standing offer to direct with the resident professional Polish theatre group, ZASP, and though this never materialized, it still made me feel that, even if indirectly, I fulfilled at least the spirit of my Canada Council Grant.

1971, ONCE MORE TO BATTLE THE BUDWORM

On return to Vancouver, my father showed me the lump of his recently installed pacemaker that had allowed him to return to work. My stay at home was necessarily short, because Sis-Q had obtained a contract to supply three TBMs to Forest Protection Limited (FPL) in New Brunswick for the budworm spray program, which owing to my previous experience, Bud appointed me to lead. He allotted me a dream-team composed of Jerry Sward, an easy-going, ex-US Navy pilot; my friend Orrin Carr; and the best imaginable mechanic, veteran of many a budworm campaign and my avuncular confederate, Al McDonell.

I arrived in Santa Rosa early in May, fondly greeted Ronnie Babe and the rest of my firebombing family, and our first task was to calibrate the newly installed spray system.

We departed on May 17, and though I had a highly experienced team who were not, like Kenny Owen, likely to lose sight of the leader, I chose to keep a paternal eye on my charges from behind. Visibility was unlimited that day, and as we overflew the Tahoe National Forest, we were enchanted with wonder at the beauty of this land and with our luck of being paid to admire it.

About twenty miles past Reno, I observed what appeared to be a faint wisp of smoke trailing Orrin's machine.

"Slow down, Orrin, I need to look at you," I radioed as I added power. As soon as I got close, I could see that his problem was an oil leak. The underside of his plane was black with it.

"We're going back to Reno," I told my team and declared an emergency.

Even at low power settings in descent, Orrin began to notice that unsavory combination of decreasing oil pressure and rising cylinder head temperature. While Jerry and I remained in orbit, Orrin glided to a safe landing and stopped in front of the terminal.

As soon as we joined him, Mac leapt out of my airplane and ascertained that Orrin's engine had blown an oil line. The dipstick showed a bare gallon in the tank, while the remaining thirty-one marked his flight path and blackened the belly of his machine. Engines overheat and seize without oil. We caught the problem just in time, because the rocky mountain valleys east of Reno are known to be highly unreceptive to wheels-up visitations.

While Mac was fixing the problem, we received the good news that there was plenty of the right kind of oil to be had at the airport. The bad news was that there was no bowser. It meant that we'd have to replenish the tank by opening 138-quart cans and pour the oil in by hand, a task annoyingly complicated by a steady thirty-knot wind. In fact, it required 160 of them, the remaining oil leaving a wind-driven swath across the tarmac and into the grassy field beyond.

We could only make it to Elko, Nevada, that evening. This suited Mac well, because the small but flourishing red-light district kept him usefully engaged until morning.

I kept in touch regularly with Rita and my parents while we were en route, and somewhere along the way discovered that on May 19, my father was diagnosed with cancer of the stomach. To use this as an excuse to stop work was for him unthinkable, and he was soon back at his desk at Brock House in Kitsilano.

We continued hopping across the country through towns with Wild West sounding names like Rock Springs, North Platte, Des Moines, and Fort Wayne. After a stop in Buffalo, we made it to Burlington, Vermont, from where, after three days grounded by weather, we flew to Blissville, which would be our base of operations.

This romantically named facility lay in the center of the vast and unpopulated expanse of the Camp Gagetown Army Training Area. It consisted of two small buildings next to a runway; one was the home of an army helicopter detachment that boasted a solitary Bell 47, while the other was leased to FPL and contained a radio room and sleeping quarters for the spray crew and the loading team.

Our group would commute to the airport from our accommodations in the village of Oromocto, which was located next to the army barracks, where Mac instantly befriended his counterparts at the sergeants' mess.

A few days later we were joined by a group of tankers belonging to Conair Aviation. This was a new company that had evolved from Skyway in 1969 and employed most of its original tanker pilot contingent. The team included John Truran, who was flying my reliable old Tanker 12, along with the ubiquitous Kenny Owen. Kenny could still fly in Canada after having his bombing card pulled in California, but he remained restricted to the spray program.

By coincidence, I happened to have witnessed the incident that led to this event in 1968 when I found myself working a fire with a group of TBMs from

Oregon, among which Kenny was instantly recognizable by his high pitched drawl. Being the next tanker behind him gave me a good view of his action.

The fire was below the crest of a hill. We all watched dumbfounded as Kenny flew perpendicularly at the peaks, then pulling up as he dropped his load, made a snazzy wingover turn, contouring the slope back out into the valley. An impressive maneuver to watch, but everyone knew that bombing uphill was the most basic taboo in this business.

"That was a bullseye, Kenny, but you made an uphill run!" transmitted the Airco.

"Ah could see the target real good from there," Kenny squeaked back. "What do you want me to do now?"

"Santa Rosa and reload."

After my drop, I was also sent for a reload in Santa Rosa, but there was no sign of Kenny ahead of me. It wasn't until after I was airborne again that I heard Kenny call for landing clearance. *Typical of him to get lost*, I thought.

Some days later we learned that, after another uphill drop, CDF pulled his tanker card, and Kenny's career in firebombing came officially to an end.

Mac was authorized by Sis-Q to rent a truck, but because engineers operate in a different time zone from pilots, I decided to free myself from this inconvenience by following a scheme that had worked well during the 1967 spray season. That's when Linc and I had bought a car from a dealer in Newcastle with his agreement to take it back from us at an agreed-upon price at the end of the season. I was pleased to find an equally compliant car dealer in Oromocto, from whom I "leased" an aging clunker for $350 with the explicit understanding that he would take it back for $250, which brought us some welcome independence.

Before the budworm larvae were ripe for our ministrations, we received an agreeable assignment to spray the mosquito-infested Mactaquac golf course, west of Fredericton. The following day I drove to the course and innocently inquired if the spray application had been effective. On hearing of the miraculous results, I owned up to being one of those responsible, which resulted in a hearty celebration and free golf for the day. (I still have the scorecard; it was a par 72 layout with a course rating of 73, where I manufactured a 77, acceptable for a tight and unfamiliar track.)

The oil-slicked belly of Orrin's Avenger. Reno, Nevada, 1971. Jerry Sward and Orrin Carr.

JERRY CRASHES IN A SWAMP

When the spraying started, we settled into an enjoyable routine. We loved the flying and the local pub scene; my team was quick to master the tricky turn-around at the end of each swath, while Mac basked in the *bonhomie* of the sergeants' mess, where he held court every night.

On chilly mornings, it was common to find our airplanes covered in hoar frost. We had no choice but to start up, taxi to the pits, pick up a load, perform our run-ups, and then shut down and wait for the frost to melt in the sun.

A curious event occurred one morning when, after the rest of us shut down, Kenny taxied his machine onto the button of the runway. What is this fellow up to? We wondered. But not for long, because Kenny lowered his flaps for takeoff, added full power, and began to roll.

We all watched mystified as Kenny's machine trundled down the runway until well past the place where he should have been airborne. A couple of backfires announced that Kenny had abruptly cut his engine, after which he continued to the end of the runway, turned around, and with the brakes still smoking, taxied back to his parking spot and shut down.

"What were you doing, Kenny?" we inquired as he calmly descended to the tarmac.

"Ah jist wanned to see if it would flaahy," he answered with a sheepish grin. Then after a pause, somewhat unnecessarily added, "It wouldn't."

I rest my case.

On June 18, we were assigned to spray a considerable stretch of woods terminating at the edge of the army property, which promised at least five hours of work. We flew to the starting point, where I took up my station under the lead planes, with Orrin in echelon starboard as number two and Jerry outside of him as number three.

The end of our swath was clearly defined by a swamp. Upon reaching it, I would turn off the booms and start a level, 45 degree turn to the right, followed by a hard left turn to the reciprocal of the previous heading to line up on the lead planes that had previously made the turn above us. Each of my wingmen then climbed sufficiently to stay out of the slipstream of the plane ahead. After completing their 180 degree left turns, they descended elegantly back into formation on my right. At the other end of the swath, we swapped ends again and once more headed for the swamp.

Just after completing my jog to the right, as I started the turn to the reciprocal, our earphones registered a cryptic call: "Lost my engine; going in!"

I looked over my left shoulder and saw Jerry's airplane, its cowling spewing smoke, making a bee-line for the swamp. Pulling up in a hard left turn, all I could see of Jerry's machine were the wingtips protruding from a rooster tail of flying mud and grass.

As the machine slowed and the spume behind it collapsed, the pilot could be seen exiting the cockpit, timing his egress onto the wing to coincide perfectly with the stoppage of forward motion. All that was needed to cap this performance was for Jerry, after a dramatic pause, to take a deliberately slow and exaggerated bow.

After broadcasting "Mayday" on the guard channel and requesting a helicopter, the pointer planes remained in orbit over the crash site while Orrin and I returned to Blissville, picked up Mac, and drove to the base hospital, where we knew Jerry would be taken by the chopper.

It wasn't long before he was released. He was unscathed, and my picture of him in the parking lot shows his clothes bespattered with drying mud from head to foot while his eyes lift to the sky in grateful acknowledgment of providence's benign participation.

Seconds earlier he would have crashed into the trees, and an instant later would have led to the same result, as he wouldn't have been able to turn back to the swamp. Though some credit for the masterful handling of the emergency must appertain to the excellence of Jerry's US Navy training, the occurrence of the incident at the dead-center of the envelope that permitted his flawless heroics leaves ample room for divine intervention.

A muddy post-crash cockpit.

Jerry's devout vote of thanks.

SALVAGING A TBM; MAC'S FINEST HOUR

Because the site of the crash was a hundred yards outside of the perimeter of Camp Gagetown, this effectively put it beyond the army's jurisdiction; it meant that Sis-Q would need to engage a private contractor at enormous cost to remove the machine from the swamp. Enter Al McDonell, whose subsequent actions spawned what I've always considered to be his finest hour.

Taking advantage of his new friendships in the sergeants' mess, he began a spirited campaign to convince them that salvaging the airplane presented the army with a unique opportunity as a training exercise. Should such an incident occur on army property, he argued, having men with previous experience would be of invaluable help. Straining his powers of persuasion to the limit, Mac finally gained their assent when he clinched his argument with a promise of unlimited beer for the duration of the job. That did it.

Beer, as previously noted, possesses the power to move armies irrespective of national origin, and ours proved equal to its allure. Presently, a trailer with an industrial-size fridge and portable generator stood parked near the site to act as the control and command center. Trucks loaded with chainsaws and tons of excavating equipment soon followed, along with two flatbed trucks. One of these carried a crane, while the other piggy-backed an impressively muscular vehicle on tank-tracks.

Mac took charge of the entire project, the first step of which was to stock the fridge with beer.

The crew's first job was to cut a clearing from the road to the swamp through two hundred yards of woods, which necessitated the felling of numerous trees. Once this was done, the tracked vehicle hauled the airplane out of the swamp to firm ground with wire ropes attached to the propeller. This allowed the crane to lift the machine onto the flatbed truck, which enabled Mac to fold the wings.

To transport the airplane to Fredericton Airport was a tedious task, because the height of the tail required the lifting of 147 electrical wires. The entire evolution took four days, during which time Mac covered the cost of the beer out of his own pocket, which saved the company a fortune.

Al McDonell in his finest hour.

Al gets the army to haul Jerry's machine out of the swamp.

A TASTE OF PETTY REVENGE

Jerry flew home with commercial airlines, which left Orrin and me to finish our assigned blocks. Once we were done, I drove the car back to the garage to collect the agreed-on portion of my down payment. Unexpectedly, the dealer flatly refused to live up to the deal.

I don't want the car back; it's all yours, buddy, was the gist of his argument.

Such mendacity was not to Mac's liking. Girding his considerable loins and puffing his chest out to a measure that fairly challenged his Falstaffian gut, Mac strode ahead of me to the garage. The stratagem worked sufficiently to convince the fellow to agree to a refund of a hundred bucks, take it or leave it. We were due to depart the following morning, so I had no choice.

Still seething from this injustice, I recounted the story loudly at the bar that night to anyone who would listen and discovered that I had a local ally.

"That cheating son of a bitch … he's a well-known swindler hereabouts," said my new friend. He also knew that the fellow lived in Fredericton, and we soon had his phone number.

When the bar closed, with his indignation sufficiently primed, my accomplice walked to the pay phone. It was after one in the morning, so there was a good chance our victim would be deep in la-la land. It took a few rings before a sleepy voice said hello.

"Is that Mr. … ?" asked my buddy, his baritone trembling with authority. "This is the RCMP detachment in Oromocto," he continued. "I'm afraid, Sir, that your garage is on fire. The local boys should be on it soon, and we're waiting for backup from the army. I suggest you come right away."

Replete with vindictive glee, we giggled at the thought of the panic-stricken owner speeding twenty miles to witness what he imagined to be the demise of his business.

"Serves him right," said Orrin as we prepared to depart in the morning.

We left Mac with the stricken machine and flew back to Santa Rosa, where we arrived three days later. Apart from qualifying as a grand adventure and logging nearly a hundred revenue hours, the trip proved to be especially therapeutic for Orrin. It served to distance my cultured, erudite, and lovable friend from the scene of his tragedy, which also gave me a welcome chance to contribute to his healing process.

Bud was not happy with me when I returned. After checking me out in the F7F, he expected me to bid a Firecat seat this season. However, lifestyle for me always trumped money, so not even the opportunity to fly this exquisite bird could tempt me away from Santa Rosa, where the TBM was my only choice.

Luckily, the same apartment at Creekside into which Rita moved me three years earlier became available again that summer, and I wasted no time in getting her to join me. By a fortunate coincidence, she arrived on the same day that an electrical fire shortly after takeoff forced me to jettison the load and return to base. Because this caused the grounding of my airplane for repairs, we profited from an unexpected holiday by spending a second honeymoon exploring the scenic settlements along the Russian River Valley and the seaside beaches. My photos of Rita are crowned by a contest-winner of a shot that catches her standing on a rock just as a breaker explodes against it, almost sweeping her off into the sea.

Although being deliberately cruel is normally alien to my character, a flash-back to that SOB in New Brunswick prompted the resident Buddhist in my soul to nod understandingly before withdrawing to a sound-proof corner of my conscience to allow me to make a satisfying exception.

Throughout the summer, whenever I felt so inclined—which often coincided with the closing of some bar—I would saunter over to a pay phone and dial the garage owner's number. Given the time change, his phone would ring some-where between three and four in the morning. Not wishing to provoke him unduly, I made a point of hanging up after two or three rings, quite content that the act had its desired effect. I charitably discontinued the practice when I felt that I'd had my $150 worth of petty revenge.

When Jerry brought Mac home in his repaired machine from New Brunswick, Mac discovered that Chaffee would not authorize a refund of the $600 he claimed as expenses for the beer he supplied to the army. Eventually, Orrin, Jerry, and I convinced Bud to resolve the problem, but Harry's intran-sigence served to deepen the growing rift between the two men, which would result in Mac leaving SIS-Q the following year.

At about this time I made contact with Linc, who revealed some arresting developments. In keeping with its intent to introduce long-term retardant to the province, the Ontario Government had acquired a surplus Navy Tracker (CS2F-2), which it planned to turn over to Kenting to test as an air tanker. The conversion was taking place in Sault Ste. Marie, where my good friend and ex-squadron-mate, Bill Nash, was now flying choppers for Dominion Helicopters.

On discovering the Tracker's projected new role, he applied to Kenting for a job. His timing was perfect: Kenting hired Bill to check Linc out in the Tracker, who in turn would instruct Bill about firebombing.

The two of them flew to Kamloops, demonstrating the airplane's capabilities to Provincial Forestries along the way, which upon its certification became the first of an avalanche of Trackers that would form the backbone of air tanker fleets worldwide.

"In the fall I'm collecting a couple of A26s in Arizona," Linc continued. "A seat could be available—I'll stay in touch."

I thanked him profusely, but leaving California was the furthest thing from my mind.

Rita on the rocks.

SINISTER STUFF AT SIS-Q

July and August were relatively quiet months that year, and just as things started to pick up, Dick Rank, a recent friend flying for Hemet Valley, became a fatality when he crashed his TBM on takeoff out of Placerville. Dick was young and enthusiastic and had an insatiable desire to see Paris, which I promised to show him at the end of the season.

Meanwhile, an ominous undertow of events began to rise to the surface on tanker bases in California caused by Teamster Union reps who were putting pressure on pilots to join their union. Two of these gents had approached Linc the previous summer, and without equivocation threatened him with the loss of his green card if, when the time came, he didn't agree to sign up. One of these was now reportedly looking for me.

Recognizing this as a danger, some of the senior pilots started a whispering campaign to discuss the possibility of forestalling this threat by mobilizing into a bargaining unit on our own, but this plan remained strictly confidential.

SOUTH AFRICA: INTRODUCTION TO APARTHEID

We returned to Vancouver in mid-October. Rita had a month-long leave, which we hoped to spend in the Seychelles, provided we could find seats on the freshly created route from Nairobi. Following a stopover in London, we arrived in Paris, where the dog was so happy to see Rita he waltzed with the cat, and Leon presented her with a new trousseau. Maria went out of her way to eclipse the famous chef, Bocuse, with something delicious.

Getting to Nairobi wasn't a problem, but the jaded jet-set in search of new titillations had already sniffed out this route and instantly filled all the seats. After examining numerous options, and in spite of severe misgivings on Rita's part concerning Apartheid, we settled on South Africa.

Rita's instinct was a formidably honed apparatus whose frighteningly perceptive powers I was just beginning to discover. Her apprehensions began to materialize in the South African Consulate on the Champs Élysées, where we were processing our visas. As we waited for the completion of our paperwork in the handsomely appointed consular office, we gained the impression that a similarly engaged couple was taking more than a cursory interest in our conversation. Our suspicions were confirmed when they followed us into the street.

"Are you going to South Africa?" they wanted to know. When we affirmed it, they insisted we join them in a café. Young, educated, and highly personable, they told us that they were on their honeymoon; both were recent graduates from university, he with a medical doctor's degree, and they wanted to know if we would agree to hand-deliver a letter to the bride's parents in Johannesburg.

Why couldn't they just put the letter in the post?

Here the paths of Rita's and my memories diverge. Mine tells me that the contents of the letter contained information this couple wished to conceal from possible censors. Though Rita's imputes a less sinister purpose, the result was the same—we took down the address and agreed to deliver the envelope on arrival.

Following a three-day stay in Nairobi, we continued on British Airways to Johannesburg. Immediately after arriving in a foreign land, Rita's routine was to buy postcards to send to her mother. Accordingly, we found a drug store next to our hotel, where, upon hearing our accent, the clerk inquired into its origin.

"From Canada," we answered brightly. "We just arrived an hour ago."

She paused momentarily before uttering this chilling remark: "You won't like it!" she said with a shake of the head—a sobering sentiment to hear from the first person you speak with on arrival in a new country.

Though somewhat discomfited, we followed her directions to the post office, an imposing stone structure with a vaulted, cathedral-like ceiling, where I joined one of the queues to buy stamps. As we looked around, we began to sense that we had become an object of interest to the other customers, but an attempt to nod and smile was met with tight lips and piercing eyes.

What the hell? we wondered, starting to examine our appearance when the penny dropped. Without realizing it, we had positioned ourselves in a "colored" lineup. Rita and I exchanged knowing glances, but we both knew we'd be damned if we now changed queues. As we weathered the withering looks, we became aware that the blacks were showing just as much discomfort.

Presently, an officious looking individual in a gray hat and trench coat arrived and began pacing at a distance in an apparent attempt to gauge if we were troublemakers trying to make a point. We held our ground until I found myself facing the white teller.

"You are in a colored only lineup," she hissed through clenched teeth.

"I don't give a shit!" I blew up. "Are you going to sell me some fucking stamps or not?"

As if slapped in the face, she pushed the stamps forward, taking the money.

We strode out of the building to the sound Rita's footfalls which echoed like gun-shots off the stone walls and created a sound I can still hear to this day.

The drug store lady's prophecy was shaping up as predicted.

When we returned to the hotel, we phoned the parents of our Parisian acquaintances, who on hearing that we carried a letter from their daughter, immediately insisted that we come to dinner. We were unprepared to be met on arrival by members of both families, who had eagerly congregated to hear news of their progeny.

As the recipients of a most gracious welcome, we soon relaxed in the company of urbane and educated people in the home of Mr. Mickey Janks and his wife, accompanied by Mr. and Mrs. Woolf, parents of the groom. Dinner was served by a black woman who was treated with the utmost civility, and who we later learned had been the governess of the daughter. She lived with the Janks family during the week, spending weekends in her home in Soweto.

On hearing that I played golf, Mr. Janks avowed that he had been the South African Open golf champion in 1948 and amateur champion in 1952 and 1953. He wondered if I might be interested in meeting his friend, Gary Player, who was in town to take part in the Professional Golf Association Tournament, the South African PGA.

Would I?

Gary was one of my stable of idols; I watched him for the last two days of the Master's I attended while in flight training in Pensacola in 1959.

The Joburg press was bursting with the controversy surrounding the historical significance of the upcoming tournament in which, owing to Gary Player's insistence, a black golfer was to be permitted to break the color barrier for the first time in a national event.

Pictures of Player and his wife meeting Lee Elder and his wife at the Smuts airport became the front-page scream of the week. The Elders stayed at the Players' home, and Gary made sure that Lee would play with him for the first two rounds.

It was acts like this, along with his sponsorship of the black tennis player, Arthur Ashe, that caused the South African government and the press to label Gary as a traitor. Gary Player's uncompromising ethics undoubtedly influenced the eventual reversal of the Apartheid policies, which during our visit had already begun to show significant cracks.

On the eve of the tournament, we drove to the site of the event. After exchanging warm greetings with Gary in the practice area, Mickey introduced Rita and me to the moral ambassador of his tortured land. Washing my right hand was out of the question for the remainder of our stay.

Before bidding goodbye to our congenial hosts, we added to our pyramid of adventures by attending a Formula One race. Our dominant impression of this event is the deafening howl of those engines, and the reckless way the spectators leaned over each other to get a better view of the racers who sped inches away along unprotected roads.

It was now time to start the next leg of our journey in an Avis rental, destination: Cape Town. We planned to drive to the city of Durban and then to continue along the coastal highway known as the Garden Route.

Starting early in the morning, we decided to stop for lunch in Ladysmith, which was about two-thirds of the way. We were parched to the core when we rolled into this somewhat non-descript town, but we soon found a pub attached to an attractive country hotel into which, like desert survivors, we staggered through the door.

It was a busy place, not unlike a noisy western saloon, but like John Wayne's entrance in a John Ford film, our arrival caused an immediate and dangerously uncomfortable silence. *What the hell?* I wondered, checking to see if we had again blundered into some segregated zone, but the clientele here was exclusively white, and each stared at us with undisguised animosity.

It can't be our attire, I thought, glancing at Rita, who looked like a million bucks in her jeans and checkered halter. I walked uneasily over to the barman, who was staring daggers.

"Can we get a couple of beers?"

"We don't serve women in bars; it's a male-only establishment," he explained in painfully cryptic tones.

Hello! A new surprise around every corner.

"Where can we get a drink?" I asked.

"Go around to the hotel; I'll send some over."

So where did the eponymous Lady Smith go to drink? we mused as we waited in the empty lobby. Tippling alone in her smithy, we concluded, and after finishing the beer, proceeded to Durban.

From here, the mostly uninhabited coastal road introduced us to scenes of Africa we had previously only imagined. Fabulously rich vegetation draped lushly over the road, concealing troupes of baboons that leapt out at the approach of a car, looking for handouts. I slowed down sufficiently to let them jump out of the way, but this allowed several adventurers to hitch a ride on the hood and the roof.

We chose to overnight in the idyllic village of Port St. Johns, where except for the company of a stray dog that sprinted like it was possessed up and down the length of the superb beach, we had the vastness of the sandy estuary of the Mzimvubu River to ourselves. We spent the night in an elegant resort, where amiably stoned and casually dressed, we dined in a classy restaurant where the elderly and formally attired clientele amused us with their ill-disguised disapproval.

From Port St. Johns the road led inland to Port Elizabeth. Except for occasional settlements composed of a scattering of round clay dwellings with thatched roofs, this stretch was equally empty of habitation. Since considerable distances separated these villages, when we passed an elder trudging barefoot along the road, we stopped to offer him a lift.

He looked at us round-eyed when we opened the door but eventually responded to our beckoning and scrambled uneasily into the back seat, where he sat visibly trembling with fear. Conversation was impossible, and our friendly demeanor not only failed to melt his misgivings, but made us suspect that he must have interpreted our invitation as a command, and that the entire episode likely smacked to him of abduction. When we stopped at the next village, he opened the door and bolted out of the car like a hare from a cage, leaving us with an unambiguous understanding of the depth of the racial divide.

The drive to Cape Town led through rolling savannahs punctuated by magnificent baobab trees, many of them with cave-like crevices in their trunks, which were teeming with birds. The city lived up to its reputation of beauty; playing the role of tourists, we enjoyed the views from Table Mountain, adopted a charming waterfront restaurant as our watering hole, and became *habitués* of the local beaches.

As expected, we also found the city marred by institutionalized segregation; in accordance with Newton's third law of motion, oppression, wherever it occurs, always produces an opposing reaction, which lends itself to outpourings of creativity specifically appropriate for satire. We observed an exemplary expression of this trend in a revue that lampooned government policies in a manner so outrageously derisive, we feared a raid by the police.

I particularly recall a skit based on the dilemma faced by the government caused by a law that prohibits blacks from attending movies. Since the job of usher is too demeaning for whites, the authorities stumbled on an ingenious solution by passing an amendment, presumably with a straight face, which permitted blacks to act as ushers, provided that while leading patrons to their seats, they remained with their backs to the screen.

The murmurings that would eventually lead to the dissolution of official Apartheid were being emphatically voiced in 1971, and it was impossible not to become passionately involved in this process. We remember cheering for a columnist and Member of Parliament, Helen Suzman, who courageously vilified the system in the press. In a governing body composed mostly of calcified Calvinist Afrikaner men, she was a remarkably brave beacon of hope illuminating her cause.

When the time came to leave this beautiful but broken land, we were faced with a mini-dilemma. British Airways, which flew us to Johannesburg, did not operate out of Cape Town. Trains were expensive, so Rita decided to see if we could get a reduced rate ticket from Cape Town to Joburg with South African Airlines (SA).

Upon checking her airline ID, the gentleman in the SA office graciously accommodated her request by issuing a pair of tickets.

"How much do we owe you?" we inquired.

"Nothing at all," he replied. "Compliments of South African Airlines."

Overwhelmed by this unexpected generosity, we exited into the street, where I was struck with an idea: "Rita! South African flies to London. Do you suppose we could …"

"I can't just go in and ask," Rita baulked.

"Well, I can," said I, while running back up the stairs to the agent who served us.

"Excuse me, but I believe you operate to Heathrow …"

"No problem," he interrupted, breaking into a grin as he reached for the tickets.

A few minutes later, I descended the staircase, and bowing gracefully to my bride, presented the tickets like a bouquet.

The following day we boarded a new SAA 747. Next to me sat a young Catholic priest. In the course of the flight, he got totally ripped, which Rita remembers as a poor example, because we attempted to follow him drink for drink. But it wasn't until we were a long way north of the South African border that he dared to open up about the conditions he'd experienced in that conflicted country. Change the accent and alter some of the specifics and he could easily be talking about Poland under the communists.

When we arrived in London, we called Mickey's daughter and her husband. After we thanked them for the invitation to meet their families, they surprised us with the news that they were in the process of obtaining employment in London and would not be returning home. I wondered if that was the information we took to their parents in Johannesburg?

AU REVOIR SIS-Q, HELLO KENTING AVIATION

Rod Langley: portrait of a playwright.

Rita's leave was over, so we parted company in London, from where she flew home while I proceeded to Halifax to visit the Poiriers. I then stopped off in Ottawa to see the third member of the triad, Larry Washbrook, and his wife, Eli.

My next stop was Montreal, where Rod Langley was working on his MA at McGill. He and Coleen had rented an apartment on Grosvenor Street, where I snapped an iconic image of a burgeoning playwright in his surroundings.

"What's on your agenda these days?" I wanted to know.

He told me he was thinking of writing a play about Dr Norman Bethune.

When Rod told me about him, I wondered why I'd never heard of this remarkable Canadian.

"And what about your theatrical career?" he asked in turn.

I eagerly updated him about the critical triumphs of my recent London debut, but ducked his queries about my thesis, the very thought of which made me break out in uncontrollable sweats. I also mentioned that I was spending my spare time creating a knockout board-game based on football, which was going to make me rich.

Continuing to hopscotch across Canada, I stopped off to see Linc in Red Deer to deliver my notes on his book, for which he now had a title: *Air Attack on Forest Fires*. The handsome cover, with an obvious nod to the American market, included a B17 flying over smoke. Everything about the proofs had impressed me, and the years of meticulous preparation and a deep understanding of his subject showed on every page.

"How is the job with Kenting?" I wanted to know.

He described his harrowing experience while delivering the A26s from Arizona. The airplanes he was to collect had been parked in the desert for years.

After some rudimentary fixes, Linc flew the first machine without incident, but the second had a surprise in store when the port engine erupted in flames somewhere over Illinois.

Only the absence of a baptismal font stood in the way of an instant cockpit conversion, but shutting off the fuel, which extinguished the flames, followed by a successful single-engine emergency landing in Peoria served to neutralize the impulse.

He then brought me up to date on the situation in Toronto. Linc was proposing that Kenting's two Invaders should form a team with the provincial Tracker to introduce the use of long-term retardant to Ontario. He would run the program and fly one of the Invaders, and Bill would fly the Tracker. Would I like to fill the other seat?

It wasn't the first time we'd spoken about this possibility, but now that the offer was official, I faced a Solomonic dilemma. Here was an opportunity that positively reeked of fresh adventure. New surroundings, a type-rating on an exciting brute of a machine, and the company of personal friends was a formula tailor-made for my acceptance. But how could I even think of giving up California? That's when Linc brought me up to date on the latest news. Bad things were happening at Sis-Q. Apparently the Teamsters Union had been stirring the pot, threatening everyone's jobs, and Linc suggested I should make some inquiries. I immediately put a call through to Ron.

"Bum news, Palawski," he announced in his familiar fashion. He then told me that the pilots' secretly formed association to defend against the meddling of the Teamsters was being misinterpreted by the company. He advised that I should call Orrin, who knew more about it.

Orrin described the unexpected developments. When Bud got wind of the association, he became convinced the pilots were starting a union. Kennedy and Alford, our most senior pilots, had been fired for trumped-up reasons because somebody reported them as the ringleaders, and nobody's job is safe. Even Orrin himself, along with Ed Real, were contemplating a move.

The hissing sound was the oxygen getting sucked out of the room. I told Orrin about Linc's job offer. Given the circumstances, Orrin unequivocally suggested I should leap on it.

My next call was to Rita: her feelings matched mine. We were both deflated by the prospect of leaving our beloved California, but we were enormously relieved that I had an alternative.

"Welcome to the team," said Linc as we embraced.

Before I left for Vancouver, Linc decided to teach me how to hang glide on skis. He had already become proficient in this new sport and would in the future reach a high level of expertise, but at that time he was flying on proto-type wings with a dismal glide ratio of 1:4.

Since I was a lousy skier, my main problem was reaching rotation speed in the upright position. On the few occasions when I managed to get airborne, I sailed like an albatross, but my landings inevitably resulted in spectacularly graceless pileups.

Back in Vancouver, we settled into a happy routine. Rita was painting some of her most inventive naïf creations between flights, and we often visited my parents, but most of my time was spent developing Quarterback.

I designed it to be packaged in a nifty, compact box, which unfolded to become the field. Ideally, it was to be played by teams of two or four, but it could also be played solitaire.

Buoyed by the promising nature of this endeavor, I also designed a baseball game, and since I was at it, in partnership with Rita, we had enormous fun in creating a game we named Jailbreak. The participants in Jailbreak were prisoners whose objective, via cunningly provided stratagems of bribes, betrayals, and deceptions, was to pull off an escape. (Based on identical principles, I considered a game to be called Wedlock, but somehow it never came to fruition.)

The ongoing newsworthy item of the year was the increasing unpopularity of the Vietnam War precipitated by the leaking of the Pentagon Papers, while the radio was alive with Janis Joplin knocking it out of the park with "Bobby McGee."

On the home front, the *scandale-du-jour* trumpeted by the Progressive Conservatives (PC) and their proxies focused on the profligate waste of tax-payer dollars being squandered by the governing Liberals on something called The Local Initiatives Program, or LIP. This vote-grabbing racket, the PCs proclaimed with self-serving outrage, doled out funds to support proposals like fielding teams of indigents to count squirrels in Stanley Park, or producing T-shirts adorned with the Canadian flag. Instantly intrigued by the prospect of easy money, I decided to make inquiries at Canada Manpower, the administrative agency for this program whose office was on Howe Street.

The LIP, a Manpower staff member explained, was a Canada-wide federal initiative designed to absorb the growing ranks of the unemployed. The program would consider funding any proposal by individuals or groups that guaranteed employment for one or more people in any endeavor judged by Manpower to qualify under its specifications.

"How about a theatre group?" I inquired.

"Ideal," was the reply.

HOW ABOUT LUNCH HOUR THEATRE?

I left the Manpower office with my brain on fire. Since my most recent theatre experience was in its lunch-hour iteration, my mind naturally gravitated to such a venture. Given that nobody will walk more than three blocks during the lunch break, the most daunting requirement of such an objective was a central location.

It would also mean assembling a production team: stagehands, set designers, stage managers, house managers, technicians, costume and props people, a publicity section, and a co-director to take over during the summer, since I wasn't prepared to quit my flying job.

All of these thoughts tumbled inside my head as I walked up Howe toward Dunsmuir Street when, before I even reached the end of the block, a sign in a storefront arrested my attention: FOR RENT, it proclaimed, a phone number conveniently supplied.

When I peeked in through the window, I could make out a high-ceilinged space with a skylight and a door at the back. I called the number and arranged for an inspection on the following day.

"You won't do anything rash, will you?" Rita's raised eyebrows admonished as I left the apartment.

A well-dressed real estate agent opened the door to the long and narrow room, which was two stories high and bore unmistakable aromas of recent occupation.

"This was a doughnut shop until a month ago," my guide informed me, "but most of the appliances except the sinks have been removed."

These had been housed in a box-like construction at the back, the roof of which formed a first-floor deck accessible by a set of stairs. A corridor leading to the back alley separated this area from a full-service toilet on the left. Climbing the stairs revealed a large space with a window facing the alley and a railing across the front.

Like a balcony! I thought, and almost instantly Juliet's voice awakened in my subconscious; "By whose direction found'st thou out this place?"

"By Love*," replies Romeo, which was a fair metaphor for my mission. "Let's talk about this," I proposed as we descended the stairs, Rita's caution vanishing into the ether.

"What do you plan to sell here?" the agent wanted to know.

"Tickets," I answered.

"Tickets? To what?"

"To a new theatre."

He looked at me quizzically. "Where is the theatre going to be?"

"You're standing on the stage," I said with a broad grin.

The price was $700 per month. I managed to talk him down to $625 and wrote out a cheque.

"I've just found a theatre!" I announced, startling the Manpower officials and their clients as I rushed in through the door.

Clutching an envelope containing the application forms, I hurried home to Rita.

"We've got a theatre!" I hollered, flaunting the keys and spinning her off her feet. "You won't believe it. It's right in the bullseye, Goldilocks, dead-center, cross-hair middle of downtown!"

I imagined it as a renaissance of the vastly successful Federal Theatre Project launched by Roosevelt in the thirties as part of his New Deal which revitalized American theatre.

Though Rita shared my excitement and would soon throw her support wholeheartedly behind the venture, at the time it seemed to her that I had just signed adoption papers for a baby elephant.

The first and most pressing assignment was to find a partner. Some obvious candidates, like classmates Judi Freeman and Judy Penner, had vanished. Fellow MA student Ken Livingstone had moved to Ontario; John Gray was busy with the Gallimaufry theatre; John Juliani had his Savage God; Bill Millerd was on the cusp of becoming the nation's most notable theatre success at the Arts Club; and the last time I'd seen Ray Michal, he was running Playhouse Holiday, the touring company started by Joy Coghill.

I was becoming increasingly desperate, when out of the blue, I ran into Wes Taylor who had acted for me in *The Station* at UBC, and in *Lovers* at the York. Not only was he available, but he was living with Jane Mushet, a lady who

---

* William Shakespeare, *Romeo and Juliet*, Act 2, Scene 2, l. 78.

professed to have some experience in directing, and importantly, they were willing to share expenses until we got the grant.

Teaming up with a competent actor and a director was a fabulous start.

With the core of the organization firmly on board, we filled out our application and delivered it to Manpower.

"How long will it take to get the confirmation?" we wanted to know.

"We fully approve of your project," they replied, "so we'll do our best to speed it up, but the final decision has to come from Ottawa."

Though we knew this program had many detractors, and some of us may likewise have privately harbored philosophical objections to such a transparent, vote-grabbing scheme, it wasn't too strenuous to prorogue such reservations as long as we stood to gain from this initiative—at least until it became clear that we would not become its beneficiaries.

While we waited, we laid down some basic plans for the *modus operandi*. We agreed to alternate directing duties, with each play running two weeks. The awkward need to find my summer replacement was something we would have to tackle when the time arrived; in the meantime, we sat back and read reams of one-act plays, and I must have sorely tried the patience of our supporters at Manpower, where I practically camped on their doorstep.

Why, we wondered, are those blockheads in Ottawa dragging their butts? Can't they recognize the immense value of a project that's destined to enhance Vancouver's cultural image forever while concurrently bestowing a stamp of legitimacy on a deeply maligned program? Moreover, think of all those unemployed actors fleeing to Hollywood to work as parking lot valets, never to be seen on native shores again, while those gubernatorial dimwits disseminate grants to flower arrangers and basket hangers on the Burrard Street Bridge. Patience, counseled our Manpower allies. Unfortunately, this was the very commodity that was long past its "use before" date.

Not all was lost, however. I spent my time usefully engaged in amassing a stack of exciting material I was dying to work on, among which were my Mrozek translations, some short works by Pinter and Orton, and a script by John Grillo entitled *Blubber*, which utterly charmed me when I saw it performed by the Soho group in London.

My partners were likewise compiling lists, and it was time for an exchange of ideas to settle on some choices. On perusing the plays submitted by my associates, I became intensely disappointed with the uniform blandness and banality of their proposals. Since an engaging curriculum was the backbone of such a venture, I approached our next meeting with much trepidation. The thorny topic of the timidity of their choices never came up, however, because my partners were not only shocked by my selections, but they found my favorite, *Blubber*, patently offensive.

The script contains a scene in which a distraught Wilfred Blubber is contemplating suicide by drowning in a river. Unexpectedly, he finds himself in the company of a similarly dissatisfied vagrant, who turns out to be none other than God.

Wilfred stops knee deep.

"If you are God, why commit suicide?"

"How would you like it if nobody believed in you?" God replies.

However, it wasn't this perceived sacrilege which exceeded my partners' tolerance: it was because the script called for Wilfred, before entering the water, to remove his clothes.

We all realized that this impasse was a classic case of artistic incompatibility, which made it impossible to continue as a team. When I agreed to refund their portion of the rent, we dissolved our partnership with as much civility as could be mustered, but I had to admit to Rita that our project was in peril.

Fearful that it could jeopardize the entire enterprise, I was a nervous wreck when I felt compelled to tell Manpower about this managerial shuffle. Fortunately, my proposal had become something of a pet project for our neighboring bureaucrats, so they agreed not to report this schism to Ottawa until I found a replacement, or until I was forced to abandon the venture entirely.

The real bummer was that I would have to shoulder the cost alone, and the February rent was now due. In spite of Rita working as an Air Canada goddess, our funds were severely depleted by our recent extravagances, and I wouldn't be getting a paycheck for another five months. I coughed up the money to keep the ball in the air, but unless something changed, the prospects were most discouraging.

Erecting City Stage. Ray Michal, center, Henry Yeager on his right.

THE BIRTH OF CITY STAGE

We were into the first week of February when, as Rita and I passed Freybe's Deli while shopping on Robson *Strasse*, a tall, dark, and angular figure materialized from the crowd. It was Ray Michal, and that place of hould be commemorated by a brass plaque in the pavement.

"How's Playhouse Holiday?" I asked.

"I'm finished with that until next summer."

A quick exchange of glances with Rita.

"So you're between engagements?"

"For the time being."

After stifling a mini cardiac arrest, I reached for my gravest conspiratorial tone.

"I may have a proposal for you, Ray. How soon can you come over to discuss it?"

We arranged to meet the following morning.

Ray and I had been classmates in the directing program at UBC. We attended the same seminars, and I had visited him in his home in Kerrisdale on several occasions, where I met his wife, Betty, and two young sons, Carl and Paul. I was keenly aware of his work ethic and creativity and respected his qualities of perseverance and dependability. Most importantly, Ray had hands-on experience in running a theatre troupe and knew everybody in the business.

Daylight found me glued to the balcony railing, scanning the streets below. Finally, Ray's ancient black Morris sedan turned into Bidwell Street and parked in front of the building. With a coffee in hand, Ray listened to my feverish presentation. Though I cautioned that this was still a plan written with the proverbial stick on water and depended on the kindness of bureaucratic strangers, I outlined my mission and sat back for his reaction.

I didn't have to wait long. Ray eagerly committed to my vision and agreed to join as a partner. I recall how Rita and I jockeyed for position taking turns to hug Ray's craggy frame, both of us knowing that his participation was the essential cornerstone of the project. I then drove Ray to inspect the premises.

Like me, he immediately recognized the potential. The anatomy of the room dictated the location of the stage as well as the seating arrangement. It would take the shape of an L, split at the corner to accommodate the entrance.

A partition dividing the kitchen would serve as the green room and scene shop, while the upstairs would be curtained off to house an office and the light and sound controls.

Ray's considerable qualifications made a favorable impression on the folks at Manpower, and the addition of his name as co-director considerably enhanced our proposal. The next step was to start assembling a team, wherein Ray's contacts proved invaluable.

The first to come on board was Henry Yeager, whose skills ranged from carpentry to lighting design. We were then joined by Paul Robillard, who initially signed on as a stagehand but later proved to be a gifted and inventive designer. Somewhere along the way, we collected Martin Keeley, a writer, photographer, and editor of the BC Lumberman magazine. Inseparable from his Hasselblads and endowed with limitless energy and enthusiasm, which he expressed with a pommey accent, Martin took over the PR portfolio and became an indispensable member of the company. When Wendy Abbott and Mary Lou White agreed to add their expertise as secretary and house manager, the basic building blocks were in place.

Early production meetings to discuss details of programming, staging, house management, casting, advertising, the procurement of performance rights, and all the minutiae associated with a theatre were held in an adopted watering hole in Gastown. These meetings were enriched by the presence of a libidinous waitress, whose impressive carriage inspired Martin to insist that we name the theatre after her, but more sober minds had already settled on the name City Stage, which thankfully rescued it from becoming known as Stephanie's.

We had the space, the personnel, and a starting curriculum; all we lacked was the funding, but our almost daily pilgrimages to Manpower yielded nothing but sympathy and renewed appeals for patience.

All this spirited activity aroused the apprehension the Greek owner of the coffee shop next door, but appeals to his thespian heritage fell on deaf ears. He remained firmly convinced that the existence of a theatre adjoining his premises was guaranteed to attract a flotsam of indigent lowlife with a catastrophic effect on his business and neighborhood property values.

As the weeks dragged by, I was compelled to level with our Howe Street sponsors that our coalition, held together by gossamers of hope and imagination, was, after two months, soon bound to dissolve, and I was beginning to attract unfavorable attention from my live-in banker.

Presumably their intervention paid off, because approximately mid-February I received a phone call: "Congratulations, City Stage. Please come to the office, your application has been granted."

Everyone at Manpower was in a festive mood. This bureaucracy came equipped with a face. We were presented with Project 511696, whose aim, copied precisely from my application, was "to commence permanent popular theatrical entertainment at lunchtime, in an accessible location, for employees and shoppers in the downtown area of Vancouver." Progress reports, along with precise accounting, were to be submitted according to a given schedule, etc.

The amount granted was $27,846; it expired on May 31, at which time it could be considered for renewal. Not only was this enough to transform the store into a theatre, but now I could refund our rent, and we were able to pay ourselves a salary. I recall that we agreed on a wage of $100 per week, the same as the actors' Equity minimum for the size of our house, while Ray, who had a family to feed, would take $140.

The job at hand, which required a considerable amount of carpentry, was entirely beyond the capability of our team. Manpower again stepped up to the breech by providing us with four men with construction experience to whom we could guarantee several weeks of work.

Concerned that the construction noise would disturb the neighboring businesses, we decided that most of the heavy work would be performed at night. In addition, we upped our neighbors' ante with a standing offer of free admission once we opened, an act of largesse that we were saddened to note left the proprietor of the coffee shop singularly unmoved.

Finally, all those days of planning spent at Stephanie's' were about to come to fruition. We agreed on the colors and assigned everyone's duties, and soon the blueprints drafted on napkins and cigarette boxes could begin to assume physical shapes. However, nothing demonstrated our commitment more emphatically than the arrival of the industrial-size garbage container, which anchored into place in the alley posed as an implacable symbol of our intent.

Everything in our space was to be dismantled and re-framed. The upper balcony needed to be screened off, and all the windows, including the skylight, had to be light-proofed. To build a lighting grid, Henry Yeager moved into a crow's nest atop of some sixteen-foot ladders, where he had his food and mail delivered for three days. When he descended, he had not only created a grid spanning the entire ceiling, but he had also managed to light-proof a swimming-pool-sized skylight. That could not have been an easy job, someone remarked while admiring his work when he finished.

"If Michelangelo wanted to make it easy, he would have painted the fucking floor," was his unforgettable reply.

A colossal stride toward legitimacy arrived when BC Tel responded to our urgency and installed a phone line. At about that time, word reached us that Metro Theatre possessed a spare lighting board that they were willing to loan. This ancient monstrosity, impossible to fit into the trunk of my Triumph, practically deflated the tires of Ray's Morris. It was a clunker bristling with eight manually operated levers, each of which governed a single reflector, and when we muscled it into its upstairs location, it looked like a prototype of the throttle-quadrant of Howard Hughes' *Spruce Goose*. In retrospect, it proved ideal for the task, because eight lights were all we could borrow from the Playhouse. Once we cleared the rubble, we could start the construction of the seating risers.

Emboldened by the progress, I now dared to inform the street of the reason for all this secretive activity by displaying a large cardboard sign in the window which proclaimed:

CITY STAGE
LUNCH-HOUR THEATRE OPENING SOON
A LOCAL INITIATIVES PROJECT

I rejected the temptation to add: at least *some* of your taxes are going to a useful cause.

While this was going on, Ray and I settled on the agenda. To take advantage of Ray's administrative skills, he would assume the role of the managing director and take care of much of the paperwork. Though we envisaged occasional guest directors, Ray and I would alternate directing duties.

Each play would run twice a day for two weeks, Mondays through Fridays at 12:15 and 1:15, and on Saturdays at 12:30 and 1:30. We would start with lighter fare at lunchtime, eventually moving to more experimental work for evening productions.

Entry fee would be $1, while twenty seats for each of the Saturday shows would be free for old-age pensioners and to anyone with a convincing story of indigence. Rita's favorite sausage provider, Freybe's, agreed to prepare a selection of Kaiser Rolls at fifty cents each, which we would sell for sixty cents at the door.

It was now time to select a program and go into rehearsals. We agreed that I would direct the opening play, and because I would have to leave for Toronto at the end of April, the third and fourth slots would also be mine. After careful deliberation, I chose to open with Mrożek's *Enchanted Night*. This was partly because, given our frenetic preparations, directing a piece with which I was intimately familiar would be a good fit for the limited time I could spare for rehearsals, but primarily because we reasoned that presenting an almost unknown playwright would set the right tone for a new theatre.

Before we could open, we needed to pass two vital inspections. The building inspector gave his approval provided we gussied up the toilet with a new seat, while the fire inspector set the maximum seating capacity at seventy and directed that a lighted "Exit" sign be displayed to indicate the route to the alley. Thanks to diligent preparation that had gone on day and night, we passed these tests with ease.

Although much still needed to be done, confident that we could meet this deadline, we announced that we would open on March 13, which gave me two weeks to mount the production.

The casting took place in my apartment. I was thrilled to engage the highly esteemed Australian actor Graeme Campbell, along with an unknown to me prospect whom I'll call John, who was physically and vocally a perfect counterpart to the character to be played by Graeme. The nubile Brigid Johnston would portray the object of their dreams, and Michelle Bjornson, whom I knew from UBC, was engaged to design the set. To rehearse the play, I obtained permission to use a common room in my building.

After five days, Graeme and Brigid were off the script, but John's progress was distressingly slow. I repeatedly expressed my concern, but with a week to go he was still on the book. This was the stage when we needed to work up nuances of the script, but with one actor holding us back, progress was impossible. Highly alarmed, I asked Ray to attend a rehearsal.

"You have no choice but to give him an ultimatum," said Ray during a break. "If he doesn't know his lines, you'll have to let him go."

My feelings precisely, I agreed, but how do I find a replacement?

At the end of the rehearsal I took John aside and made it clear that unless he was off the book the next day, I'd have to release him. As soon as he was gone,

I called an emergency meeting with the cast and staff to examine our options. There were just two: postpone the opening or find a suitable replacement.

The humiliation of having to postpone such a well-publicized debut was equally unacceptable to opening with a piece that might not be ready for the boards. This was the kind of dilemma that makes a gripping story in retrospect but was a bitch to have to live through.

After deciding that a replacement was the lesser evil, Ray suggested an actor he knew, Owen Foran, who was ideal for the role, though at the time he was appearing in a play at the Arts Club. Since we could rehearse mornings and afternoons, that may not be a handicap.

Ray dialed his number and then passed me the phone. Trying not to sound desperate, I smoothed over the critical aspect of the timing, concentrated on the historic nature of this venture, and succeeded in getting Owens's agreement to read the play. On delivering the script, I discovered Mr. Foran to be a soft-spoken, somewhat rotund gent in his late thirties who perfectly fitted the character. He agreed to let me know his decision post-haste, and called me at supper time.

Owen loved the script and was prepared to give it a try. If he'd been in the room, I would have kissed him on the mouth.

Last minute paint job.

AN ONEROUS CHOICE

The following day, since I owed it to John to give him his last chance, we asked Owen to wait in the car while we played out the charade. It wasn't long before I called a halt to the rehearsal and gently took John aside to give him the news. To his credit, he didn't contest my decision and voluntarily dropped all claim to pay. After an embarrassment of apologies, we all shook hands, and the moment John was gone, Owen took his place.

For the next two days, with the cast's co-operation, Owen allowed me to treat him like a puppet. No director ever wants to be a mere manipulator, but we had no choice.

"Trust me," I said, mechanically maneuvering him through the action.

"On this line, you move here ... this beat belongs to Graeme ... here we need a pause ... a loud train whistle will sound here ... and when Brigid appears, in your imagination she is naked ..."

Further complicating the issue was the temporary space where tape on the floor marked the location of doors, beds, and furniture.

On the fourth day, the Saturday before our Monday opening, the scenes began to gel, but we were still ages away from performance levels. Understandably, Owen was still shaky, but with help from Graeme and Brigid, he showed encouraging progress.

While this was going on, our entire crew engaged in preparing the house. There were programs to print, advertising to be arranged, and signs to be painted, while documenting expenses for the weekly Manpower report was an ongoing chore.

I gave interviews to the press while Ray was busy auditioning for his upcoming show, but whenever possible, both of us pitched in to help with the construction. Benches and risers began to take shape, electrical cables littered the floor, and while Henry Jaeger continued his Spiderman antics aloft, Michelle did her best to navigate through this chaos, constructing the set.

Creating a sound plot was a tricky assignment in the days befor digitalization, as cues needed to be recorded to tape in sequence from a sound effects LP. During the performance, while peeking through a slot cut in the curtain, Henry used one hand to operate the lights while the other ran the tape recorder. He needed to turn it on and off for the precise duration of the effect, because running into the next cue would turn it all into a dog's breakfast. This would have to be Henry's *modus vivendi* for the first half of the year until we constructed a light-and-sound booth at the rear of the house.

On Saturday evening, Henry and I conducted a technical rehearsal without actors, which ended after midnight. After sending him home for some shuteye, I joined the staff in stacking all the furniture in the middle of the room to make the walls accessible for painting. We had chosen a dark blue, non-reflective color that four of us applied using long-handled rollers. The paint was dry when we returned in the morning. After we pushed the seating risers into place, for the first time we could stop to admire the final effect. Dressed with light, Michelle's set looked terrific; all the backstage props were in place, and we were ready for the first technical rehearsal with actors, scheduled for after lunch.

I remember it as a horror show. We walked through it endlessly before the sequences smoothed out and the actors took a breather to prepare for the full tech and dress. If the adage that a disastrous dress rehearsal foretells a dazzling opening were true, then we had a runaway hit on our hands. After the last run-through, we agreed that we could benefit from a refresher in the morning and retired for the night full of foreboding.

Should we have postponed the opening? I stayed behind to help with the final prep, and I remember the horror on Rita's face when I came home in the morning to grab a shower and a bite, then rushed back to the theatre before eight. The run-through was smoother, except for Owen, who inexplicably suffered a marked regression.

Careful not to let my repressed terror show, I concentrated my final briefing on the positive, reminded the cast that every motivational beat had been thoroughly assimilated, and bid them relax and have a good time.

MARCH 13, 1972: CITY STAGE OPENS TO THE PUBLIC

Outwardly cheered but each harboring their private misgivings, the actors withdrew to the green room, leaving the rest of the crew to finalize their duties. Michelle fussed endlessly with details of the props and set, Henry in his cockpit fine-tuned his switches and throttles, and Ray stood by the door, ready to hand out programs and welcome the arrivals. Wendy, in charge of ticketing and sandwich sales, huddled over the cash box; the ubiquitous Mary Lou whirled about stage-managing everything, while Martin pirouetted in the middle, firing his Hasselblads in all directions as if in self-defense.

As Paul and I finished a final sweep-out under the benches, word spread that there was a sizeable line up several storefronts long forming on Howe Street. We all took turns sneaking a peek. Wow! *Just like a real theatre*, we thought … until someone observed that the actual test would come when they start hanging around the stage door waiting for autographs.

After taping "Reserved" signs on four seats in the front row, two for my parents and two where Rita and I would endure the agony, I addressed the company: "We are making history today; let's all enjoy it!" I shouted as Ray opened the door.

A happy looking throng came in from the cold and took their time chattering and looking around before settling down. I escorted my parents to their seats, and though Rita put on a brave face, I could sense her inner turmoil.

Soon the familiar hum of an audience filled the house, its members thankfully unaware of the tension gripping the crew. When the door closed, I made some opening remarks welcoming the attendees to this historic premiere, introduced Ray who said a few words about our vision and our hope for continuing support, and concluded with our acknowledgment that it was the Liberal government's foresight that enabled this worthwhile project.

Rita gripped my hand as I took my place beside her, and as Henry dimmed the lights, I switched on the tape recorder under my seat and resigned myself to the fates.

The stage lights came up revealing two men unsuccessfully attempting to disguise their discomfort at being compelled to share a hotel room as they jockey for possession of the best bed while changing into their pajamas. The audience tittered and then openly guffawed at the slap-stick absurdities of Mrożek's script, acted impeccably by the actors.

Not only was Owen entirely on top of his role; technically, everything was working like clockwork. The trains rattled everyone as intended as they roared by on cue just outside the window, and when Brigid, the fulfillment of men's dreams, materialized in the room destabilizing the established realities, I found myself relaxing enough to start enjoying the play. At the end of the show, Rita and I joined the audience in an enthusiastic standing ovation. We couldn't bask too long in the warmth of embraces, which we all exchanged backstage, because the house was already filling for the 1:15 show.

The second performance was as fluid and polished as the first, and each time I play back the recordings I made that day, they fill me with wonder at the unimaginable reversal of what appeared to have been a guaranteed debacle in the making. There would be plenty of adventures during my tenure at City Stage, as well as at other theatres, but nothing would ever equal the intensity of emotions experienced in the five days leading up to our debut.

The next morning's reviews glowed with encouragement as both Chris Dafoe of *The Sun*, and James Barber of *The Province* laced their comments with praise and good wishes. Judging from the quality of the opening, they wrote, City Stage stood poised to take its place as a major downtown attraction and presented a welcome addition to the Vancouver theatre scene. They might have added that, since there were very few theatre venues that paid actors for their work, this in itself was a refreshing novelty.

The major employer of professional actors before 1972 was the Playhouse, which under David Gardner's and Paxton Whitehead's directorship alienated the local acting community by regularly importing the leads from Toronto.

A second source of income was the Arts Club, which under Bill Millerd's visionary leadership was in the process of establishing its space on Granville Island. The Frederick Wood Theatre at UBC used Equity actors in leading roles, but progressively acting students were taking over roles previously cast with professionals.

The other sources of decently paid work were the CBC and the filming of commercials, while the burgeoning film industry, though it provided plenty of opportunities in technical fields, generally only tapped into the local acting talent for minor roles.

Though the Equity minimum salary of a $100 per week hardly represented a living wage, City Stage took pride in paying above scale, and performing at lunchtime allowed us to engage actors already appearing in evening productions.

We all had reason to be pleased with our debut, but my satisfaction derived from deeper roots. For my parents, City Stage presented a concrete justification for my leaving the service, and the presentation of a play by a Polish playwright reaffirmed for them my acknowledgment of my national origins.

Their attendance was particularly timely; my father's health had been deteriorating from advancing cancer of the stomach, which had forced him to retire from his job with the RCMP in October of the previous year at the age of seventy-six.

With the major teething problems behind us, we settled into a semblance of a routine, still manic in tempo but acquiring a sense of order. On the day after we opened, Ray went into rehearsals with a quirky piece by David Cregan titled *Transcending*. His cast included Duncan Regehr, Carolyn Hunt, the comely Yvonne Adalian, as well as Owen Foran and Graeme Campbell, who were well on the way to melding into a polished comedy-duo, a combination I exploited with my next presentation.

It was easy for me to forget, having become immersed in this maelstrom of activities, that another world existed outside of the confines of this theatrical ghetto. The reminder came in the form of a call from Toronto. It was Linc. I had obliterated him from existence. The Ontario Forestry appeared to be ready to field three retardant-carrying aircraft. When, he desired to know, might I deign to show up for my checkout in the Invader?

It took me a while to make a connection to this parallel universe with which I had severed all contact. I vaguely remembered that it had something to do with earning a living.

"Sometime in May," I told him, gradually returning to my senses.

"Should I send you the manual?" he inquired.

"I won't get a chance to look at it, but when I get there, I'll have it memorized in a trice," I promised, hopeful that the application of Einstein's discovery of the elasticity of time, which seemed to work equally well at City Stage as well as in the universe, could transplant to the other arena.

When Ray opened *Transcending* on Paul Robillard's colorful set on March 27, we were pleased to notice a repeat clientele. The show also garnered excellent reviews, and I was impressed by Ray's enrichment of the play with the addition of background music of the Stones'"You Can't Always Get What You Want," which supplied an effective emotional dimension to the script—a trick I'd put to good use in future productions.

While it was running, I started rehearsals with *Madly in Love*, a hilarious piece by Paul Ableman. It would star our resident duo of Owen and Graeme, complemented by the gifted Daphne Goldrick, Bill Buck and Brigid Johnston.

In his review, Chris Dafoe wrote that "for two weeks, City Stage would become a scene of cheerful lust."

[It was a smash hit, and such a box office success that Ray reprised it two years later for a three-week stint, though with a different cast.]

While my play was running, I was already rehearsing an intriguing adaptation of a television play by Joe Orton entitled *The Good and Faithful Servant*. Typically Ortonesque, bitter-sweet, and darkly humorous, it was scheduled to start on April 24 and would be the only play for which I designed the set. My cast included a repeat appearance of Daphne Goldrick, along with Carolyn Hunt, Duncan Regehr, Joyce Sobell, and the excellent David Glynn-Jones.

In the course of one of our production meetings at Stephanie's, we came to the alarming conclusion that, following that frenetic start, we were beginning to suffer from the onset of creative doldrums. We had always envisaged that the role of City Stage would need to eclipse its mandate of producing digestible fare at lunchtime, and it was time to ramp up the pace.

To realize this plan, we conceived a more mature program for our evening debut, for which Ray chose *Sweet Eros*, by Terrence McNally, to run as a double bill with my production of a wistful one-hander, *History of a Poor Old Man*, by British playwright John Grillo. The evening program would run in tandem with my lunch-hour staging of the piece by Orton.

Ray's cast, in addition to Sharon Kirk, included the well-known film actor Scott Hylands, who deliberately delayed his scheduled return to Hollywood to appear in our theatre, while I engaged Owen Foran to play the old man, a character he interpreted with nuanced understanding. While these shows were running, Ray was rehearsing *The Lover*, one of Pinter's fine early pieces familiar to me from having directed it as a student exercise at UBC.

I regretted having to abandon City Stage for the duration of the summer, but with Ray at the helm of a smoothly running team, I was confident that we had laid the foundation of a viable and significant cultural contribution to Vancouver theatre.

1972, KENTING AVIATION, TORONTO

The time was now ripe to start refocusing on the other plane, so to speak, of my existence. I could finally revel in the prospect of joining a new company, exploring an area of Canada unknown to me, working with my friends Linc and Bill, and experiencing the thrill of learning to fly a powerful new machine.

We had no idea where we would be based, so I decided to take my car. I departed Vancouver full of trepidation over my father's deteriorating condition, but knowing that Rita would be a frequent visitor made it easier to bear.

In Toronto, Linc introduced me to General Manager Frank Smith, Chief Pilot Jim Monteith, and Head Engineer Tony Arsenault. I was impressed by the friendly informality of the office staff, but the seedy appearance of the airplane I was slated to fly was highly alarming.

The Douglas A26 Invader had entered the United States Army Air Forces in 1943 as a light bomber designed for ground attack. Mounted on the slippery, laminar flow airfoil were two Pratt and Whitney, 2,000 HP radial engines. Very impressive, but this specimen looked like it was about to fall apart. When I checked the maintenance log, I noticed that most of the unservicabilities Linc had recorded on his delivery flight remained unaddressed.

"They haven't had time to get at them just yet," Linc explained. "The engineers have only just installed the tank. It holds a thousand Imperial gallons".

A thousand imperial? Linc's only had an eight hundred imperial gallon tank. A thousand gallons amounts to a retardant load weighing nearly eleven thousand pounds. In comparison, the powerful F7F carried eight hundred US gallons, which weighed about seven thousand pounds. Presumably, the Ministry of Transport would not issue a certification if this amount exceeded the weight-and-balance parameters.

I climbed into the cockpit. Cockpits of military airplanes are not known for their refinement, but this one looked like a boar's nest. However, this was not the time to fuss over aesthetics. Before the checkout, I would need to memorize all the information in the manual. I was intensely engaged in this task when I learned that my father was in the hospital and that his condition was grave.

DEATH OF A WARRIOR

Without hesitation, I discontinued my studies and flew to Vancouver.

With Rita and my mother, we sat beside my father in St. Paul's Hospital and watched as his life ebbed slowly away. On the morning of May 23, he was lapsing from sleep into moments of lucidity. During one of these moments, he counseled me to take care of my mother. During another, he smiled and said, "I just thought of Jack Benny."

When he faded away again with the smile still on his face, we chose to take a break and made our way to City Stage, where Ray was opening a play by Keith Johnstone entitled *Moby Dick*. It starred the comedy-duo of Graeme Campbell and Owen Foran, and provided a welcome respite from our grief.

When we returned to the hospital, the door to my father's room was closed and we were asked to wait in the corridor. A pair of nurses hurried past, casting furtive glances in our direction. Shortly after this, one of them approached and brought the news. My father had just died.

The Polish community, particularly St. Casimir's Parish and the Polish Veterans Association (Stowarzyszenie Polskich Kombatantów, or SPK), prepared a fitting funeral.

My parents had been prominent members of the SPK. My father had served two terms as president, and my mother as secretary, and both contributed selflessly to the organizing of many social and cultural functions of this vibrant group. After an eloquent eulogy delivered by Mr. Fus, my father's body was interred in a vault in The Gardens of Gethsemane, next to a crypt reserved for my mother.

The emotional emptiness that invades everything is familiar to all who have lost a loved one. For me it meant the loss of a loving guide, leader, an exemplar, whereas the loss of a life's companion would introduce my mother to the loneliness of widowhood.

My love for my father was always intermingled with a feeling of enormous respect. The source of this feeling stemmed not only from his considerable achievements in the Polish Navy, but also from my recognition of his character, tested so profoundly during the first years in Canada when, to earn a living for his family, all the glories of his illustrious past he readily exchanged for workmen's coveralls and a willingness to start at the bottom.

Eventually, it was his knowledge of languages—Polish, Russian, English, French, and German, coupled with a lifetime of experience that convinced the RCMP to offer him a job, but none of this was evident during those first hope-defying years.

My father was a gifted raconteur and possessor of a photographic memory. His accounts of his naval exploits and adventures, which are both historically relevant and anecdotally hilarious, were regularly published in a post-war naval quarterly, *Nasze Sygnały* (*Our Signals*). I knew that this material was screaming to be published as a book. Accordingly, in 2001, I approached the directors of the Polish Naval Museum in Gdynia with a proposal: If I were to collect and organize my father's writing in book form, would they agree to publish it as a book? It was an easy sell. Two years later, the book appeared under the title *Fala za Falą* (*Wave after Wave*). Seeing it for the first time on bookshop shelves gave me great satisfaction.

My father is remembered for his cool thinking in combat, his lifelong respect for the men under his command, his loyalty to his country and his compatriots, his buoyant imagination, and his perpetual sense of humor. No wonder naval historians single him out as one of the most colorful personalities ever to serve in the Polish Navy.

I remained with my mother several more days, but then it was time to go. As I knew she would, Rita took care of my grieving mother, something she was to continue for the remainder of my mother's long life.

My father on the bridge of the Piorun.

Cover of my father's memoir, Fala za Falą.

CHECKING OUT IN THE A26 INVADER

Upon my return to Toronto, I resumed my checkout. Though I was particularly fortunate to be able to profit from Linc's inborn proclivity as a teacher, the bedraggled look of this intimidating machine inspired zero confidence.

"I see an important omission on the emergency checklist," I said to Linc as we sat in the cockpit preparing for my first flight. "There's no procedure to describe what to do when the wings come off."

"True," he agreed. "We're waiting for you to write it up from experience."

Touché!

"Maybe we'll be able to compare notes," I retorted as we continued the familiarization.

I soon discovered an unexpected anomaly. The Invader was built for the army. Accordingly, with regard for the pedestrian nature of the customer, the manufacturer installed an airspeed indicator calibrated in miles per hour rather than in the industry standard of knots, or nautical miles per hour.

It was something one would have to get used to.

However, a dangerously discomfiting characteristic of this design was the gap between the lift-off speed, which was 120 mph, and the minimum single-engine control speed (Vmca), which the aircraft did not reach until 140 mph, a pucker-inducing interval that, particularly when fully loaded, could drag on for a highly distasteful chunk of eternity.

On the positive side, I loved the reassuringly throaty and masculine sound of those piston powerplants I've come to relish over the years. A distinct characteristic of large reciprocating engines is their clunky unevenness at idle, which like a race horse being reined back from a craving to gallop continue to pop, snort, and cavort until they feel the throttle, when they smooth out to a thrilling roar.

"You'll smell some fumes in the cockpit, but they'll dissipate once you get some airspeed," Linc briefed before takeoff.

He was right about the exhaust fumes, and though this condition did clear with lower power settings, it was something I wanted fixed before going on base.

Except for the poor visibility past the protruding nacelles and that knee-trembling interval before reaching minimum single engine control speed, the airplane handled most satisfactorily. We logged three hours of dual, after which I was ready for solo.

An arresting moment on one of my training flights occurred when Bill Nash decided to come along for a ride. I distinctly remember his cocky, show-me attitude, when with his hands clasped behind his head and his cowboy boots brazenly planted on the dash, he settled in for takeoff. The moment we were airborne, he lowered his feet and sat bolt upright.

"What's that smell?" he asked on the intercom.

"It'll clear in a moment," I answered, reducing to climb power.

"That's unacceptable," Bill agreed after we landed.

"Maintenance is supposed to fix it before we leave," Linc assured us without conviction, the unserviceability still duly noted in the log.

Since I would need some bombing training before being endorsed on type, we loaded up with water; this action immediately revealed leaks from all four doors of the tank.

"With a full load, the C of G is fairly far aft, so you'll need to roll in a lot of nose-down trim," Linc instructed.

Since the area where we could safely test the drop characteristics was a long way from the airport, we agreed to parcel out the experience by dropping one door at a time. Given the tail-heavy condition, I chose to start with a rear door, followed by the corresponding front door. I repeated the procedure until all four tanks were empty.

I was satisfied with the acceptable post-drop control inputs after two flights, following which Linc signed off my endorsement. Immediately following my check ride, with the water leaks and fumes in the cockpit still unresolved, the company hastily decided to make our presence known by positioning the fleet in Sudbury. Led by Bill Nash in the Ontario owned Tracker, we made an impressive arrival. We were soon followed by the support and maintenance group, which included my car being delivered by one of the engineers.

It wasn't long before we realized that the presence of our group was being officially ignored. Although fires were breaking out in the region, the only aircraft dispatched to these targets were the Ontario owned fleet of water-carrying Otters, which seemed to us to be contrary to the understanding reached between Kenting Aviation and the Ontario Department of Lands and Forests.

Kenting purchased the two A26s and hired Linc to introduce the "One Strike Concept" to Ontario. This concept, already adopted by most of the fire-fighting agencies in North America, involved the use of fast aircraft loaded with long-term retardant being deployed as the first response to a fire, which differed fundamentally from the "Gallons-per-Hour Concept" employed by Ontario, which relied entirely on water. Though a fast tanker fleet using retardant is more expensive, experience has shown that it's exponentially more effective than attacking fires with water.

We never discovered what turf-wars made Ontario renege on their promise to employ the Kenting group in the One Strike role, but it soon became clear that we were superfluous.

As new plans were being hatched by the company, Rita happened to be dead-heading from London through Toronto and decided to detour into Sudbury for an overnight visit. Though for once the traditional base change that customarily accompanied her arrivals did not materialize, it was being formulated behind closed doors for the following day.

Linc checks me out in the A26, Toronto, 1972.

Gearing up for first flight.

Bill Nash, Rita, and Linc before my northern adventure.

GO NORTH, YOUNG MAN

The decision reached by Kenting would mark the start of two of the most unconventional and exotic years of my firebombing career. The company decided to split up the team. Linc was to remain in Toronto, while I was to position in Fort Smith, Northwest Territories, where management judged that an aircraft without a contract stood the best chance of being called on to fly. Since Bill Nash's Tracker was on an Ontario contract, his disposal would be at the Ministry's pleasure.

Accordingly, with Rita on her way back to Vancouver and someone volunteering to drive my car back to Toronto, we loaded my machine with a season's worth of spare parts, and with apprentice engineer John Burnham occupying the right seat, I took off for my northern adventure.

Fort Smith was a settlement on the Slave River originally inhabited by local aboriginals. It stood at the head of a *portage* erected by fur traders a century-and-a-half ago to bypass a stretch of impassable rapids. I wasted no time in acquainting myself with the town's amenities, which consisted of a bank, a hospital, a general store, the remnants of a Catholic mission, and the town's solitary hotel, whose thriving beer parlor served as the region's cultural center.

My room on the first floor above the pub happened to be directly over the jukebox, which assured a continuous supply of musical accompaniment through the floorboards until two in the morning. At bar closing time, the action shifted to the parking lot, over which I owned an unobstructed view from my window. It was the arena where intellectual differences spawned indoors became settled with satisfying finality. A welcome peace underscored by the soothing hum of the fleet of refrigeration trucks' diesel engines would descend over the parking lot from about three in the morning.

The following day we were joined by Jim Cook, the chief engineer. Jim's slight frame and quiet demeanor belied his engineering skills, which along with his unbridled determination and eagerness to work were slated to be challenged on a daily basis. We needed these skills the very next morning, when after a familiarization flight, I checked myself into the hospital with a splitting headache. This machine is grounded, I told Kenting, until the repeatedly reported condition of fumes in the cockpit was rectified.

The engineers peeled the metal back from the wing-roots and spent two days patching up the holes in the fuselage responsible for the problem. Subsequent test flights with Jim satisfied me that the smoke problem was fixed and the airplane was safe to fly.

I soon discovered that Pacific Western Airlines operated a scheduled flight from Vancouver to Whitehorse every second day. Since this flight stopped over in Fort Smith, it made visiting easy for Rita.

"You've got to see this place, Rita. This may be your only chance to experience the true Canadian north. You'll see herds of wild buffalo, pelicans nesting in the rapids, and the last whooping cranes in the world," I cajoled, omitting to mention the other flying creatures found in swarming abundance, because these were easily discouraged with layers of protective clothing and massive applications of bug spray.

Bravely, she agreed, and a few days later I met her at the airport as she arrived for a two-day visit. Unfortunately, Rita remained equally underwhelmed by the allure of the local attractions as by the absence of culinary imagination exhibited by the hotel restaurant's chefs, and although on her departure I tried to convince her to say *au revoir*, she adamantly stuck to *adieu*.

As our crew sat eating dinner in the hotel that evening, we were startled by an ungodly roar. We all ran outside and saw that the source of the racket was a B25 pulling up in a chandelle after a low pass over the town, but immediately our attention shifted to another approaching machine. We couldn't see it behind the trees at first, but when it finally appeared, this one was smoking down the main drag seemingly between the telephone poles. Everyone instinctively ducked as this crazy loon thundered by at full throttle, and you could swear that if he'd had his gear down, his wheels would be mussing the ground.

It's the Gordies, the locals told me. The first would be Gordy Peel; the signature pass was Gord Sherman's. The following day, I met the two Gordies and their co-pilots at the airport. One was energetic, with a youthful, cherubic face, whereas the demeanor of the other appeared more taciturn and composed. Assuming that the former was Sherman, I started to congratulate him on his showy pass, only to discover that it was the quiet one who was the Buzz Buerling of the pair.

The B25 Mitchells, which might easily have been survivors of the Doolittle raid on Tokyo in 1942, were on contract to the Wood Buffalo National Park, which occupies a 45,000 square kilometer area in northern Alberta.

Sometime that afternoon the horn went off, signaling a launch. Since my airplane was unserviceable, I stood back to observe the activities around the B25s and was somewhat surprised to notice that after loading the aircraft, nobody exhibited the usual purposeful bustle associated with a dispatch. It wasn't until a car screeched to a stop and disgorged three females and a boy that things began to hum.

One lady ran to Gord Peel's machine, while the boy and the other two headed toward Sherman's. The pilots gallantly helped their passengers aboard, then started the engines and took off.

The look on my face prompted one of their engineers to stroll over to explain that this was standard procedure for this group.

"Even on a dispatch to a fire?"

"Only from the smaller bases," he assured me. "In Whitehorse or Watson Lake, you have to be much more discreet."

"Where do they sit?" I inquired.

"There are jump seats for two, but with more passengers, someone has to stand."

A stewardess or two is always welcome on a flight, I agreed, but where, I wondered, do they find space for the bar? Welcome to aviation's version of the Wild West!

CLOSE CALL IN WHITEHORSE

On July 6 we received the welcome news: Pack up your gear; tomorrow you are base-changed to Whitehorse. I helped the engineers tie down as many of the spare cylinders, generators, magnetos, and tool boxes as would fit into the back of the aircraft, and with Burnham following us in the truck, Jim and I took off for Whitehorse.

When we pulled into the tanker base, we were astonished at the sizeable welcoming committee awaiting our arrival, at the head of which stood Linc, who unbeknown to us had flown in the previous day. His job was to introduce the assembled Forestry brass to this new weapon at their disposal, which he was in the process of accomplishing with his customary panache when the dispatcher ran out to announce a fire report.

What an opportunity to demonstrate the new tool freshly arrived for the job. While I fueled and the loaders pumped in the retardant, Jim feverishly unloaded some of the spares from the back.

From my position on the wing, I noticed that the entire assembly had convened under the fuselage, and like a rugby scrum surrounded something on the ground. I knew it was that bloody leak, which didn't matter as long as we used water, but retardant had a habit of peeling up the tarmac, making it highly unpopular with airport managers. Jim stopped unloading and made a brave show with his wrenches again, but when I shouted that I'd taxi really fast, they agreed to release me.

There was no wind, so I chose the closest button and began my takeoff roll. Halfway down the runway, I was still well short of the speed when the nose wheel should lift off the runway. Was it just the weight of retardant, which is 10 percent heavier than water that made such a difference? Once past the three-quarter mark, I was committed for takeoff.

With my finger on the drop button, I hoisted the beast into the air at 120 mph and sat hanging on the props, gaining neither altitude nor airspeed. *How much does all that equipment still bolted into the back of this machine weigh?* I wondered as I struggled for height.

Not daring to reduce power, I continued ahead until the airspeed inched toward 140 mph, wondering what color-commentary Linc was supplying of my progress, which was still in a direction diametrically opposite to the course for the fire.

I didn't dare begin my turn until I had 160 mph on the clock, by which time I must have been just a speck on the horizon. Though it had been a most nerve-racking experience, I remained pacified by the knowledge that I had the luxury, with a push of a button, of being able to dispose of my load, which gives air tankers their unique margin of safety. It would be another thirty minutes before I'd learn the consequences of such a decision, should I have chosen to make it.

I arrived at a long and narrow fire running up a slope to the crest of a hill, on which the birddog requested a full salvo. I was happy to get rid of this load in one pass, and we agreed that the best way to stretch it was to release it just short of the crest, letting the retardant fall down the hill along the length of the fire. Such a shot was always tricky to judge, because if triggered a hair too late, the retardant invariably missed the top of the fire and overflew the target.

Respecting my overloaded condition, I made an inelegantly wide circle carrying extra speed for the wife and any future kids, which offered me a long final and a comfortable descending escape route. Everything looked good, but when I punched out the load, this immediately unleashed a most unexpected train of events.

Unlike the single door pitch-ups to which I was accustomed, the airplane bucked violently upward, followed immediately by a vicious, uncontrolled nose-dive. Since no human strength could pull back that yoke, as the aircraft arced toward the ground, my right hand flew to the elevator trim-wheel beside my right knee, and in a blur of motions like a coyote unearthing a mouse, frantically rolled it back one agonizing increment at a time.

The airplane was descending more steeply than the slope until I relieved sufficient nose-down trim, which allowed me to regain enough elevator control to be able to barely pull out at the bottom of the valley.

When my brain caged and I was able to think again, I began to analyze this aberrant behavior. The pitch-up on load release was well understood: its cause was a momentary vacuum created under the tail, whose intensity varied with speed, flap setting, and the mass of the load. However, the most dangerous component of this event was the subsequent violent dive. The positioning of the oversize tank and the excess weight of spares in the back combined to shift the center of gravity far beyond the after limits. When the load release kicked the C of G forward, the extra nose down trim required for level flight took over and caused the resulting dive. Luckily, encountering this condition with 1,500 feet of altitude to spare allowed me just enough room to recover.

We all learn by mistakes, and in retrospect, a number of these came prominently into focus. During our first loaded test flight, since we already knew that the tank installation caused an aft condition of the C of G, Linc and I should have dropped a four door salvo at altitude. Such a test would have revealed the problem immediately and grounded the airplane. Instead, we dropped a door at a time, which never exhibited this result. In addition, in a hurry to show off the airplane to the Forestry in Whitehorse, I failed to check how many of Jim Cook's spares still remained on board. By removing the spares and resolving never to drop a full salvo, I concluded that I could continue to operate the airplane.

As to the leaking tank, Jim found a neat solution. With sufficient force used to tighten the bolts, the leak could be stopped, though this produced a somewhat undesirable effect: the door would not open at all, which also meant that I would always be flying with a quarter of the load trapped in the belly.

Fuck it, we agreed. Better than having that leak, which would otherwise ground the airplane. With luck, no one would notice the difference. It would be some time before we fixed the problem for good, but in the meantime, fires were beginning to pop-up, and the following afternoon we were dispatched north to Carmacks.

Given the sad mechanical condition of my machine, we decided that I would never venture anywhere without carrying a minimum of vital essentials, of which the most important were Jim Cook and his toolkit. Because the brave lad would be compelled to sit with me on all bombing flights, I requested that Kenting should give him "danger pay." To the company's credit, this proposal was accepted, and Jim received a raise that included back pay.

A CANTATA FOR TOOLS AND AURORAE BOREALIS

Carmacks Airport consisted of a single gravel strip tucked into a bend of the Yukon River at the western end of which two shacks and a loading pit elevated its status to a tanker base. Its two-man crew was composed of a loader and a Forestry employee.

The wisdom of bringing Jim was confirmed that very same day when, after the second drop, we were forced to withdraw from the action with a blown exhaust stack. On learning that we were unserviceable, the Forestry team gratefully split, but considerately left us a radio and keys to a vehicle.

To accomplish the repairs, we needed a ladder. Though no such article existed in the vicinity, a row of forty-five gallon oil drums at the edge of the clearing provided the solution. The good news was that they would offer the required elevation; the bad news was that they were full and rested downhill from the airplane.

With the help of a pair of oars, which by luck we found in the grass, by midnight we managed to position one drum under the engine, which gave us two hours of daylight. After removing the cowlings, an operation I could by now perform blindfolded, we set to the task at hand, unaware that we were about to experience a night whose spell we would never forget.

As darkness descended on the boreal land, the overhead kaleidoscope of magical iridescence began an enchanting light-dance in its silent homage to the multiverse. Compelled to mix the mundane with the divine, we worked in respectful silence. As I passed up the tools and held the flashlight while Jim changed the stack, we took long breaks to reflect on the extravagant opulence of the spectacle unfolding above us. The spell broke at about the time we buttoned up the engine, but its memory lingers to this day.

We slept for a few hours that morning in the last available room in the convoy of trailers that made up the local motel, and then kicked rocks all day at the airport while futilely waiting for a dispatch. It finally came the following evening.

Our new base was McQuesten, a dirt strip next to the Stewart River, from where we flew until the end of the action. My last drop was at two in the morning. Though we were the only airplane working out of this base, the cook shack was always open, and a hot meal awaited us on landing.

Accommodations at McQuesten consisted of a scattering of tents with folding camp beds. I flopped gratefully into one close to the river, but Jim, as usual, had to spend several hours bolting things on that were about to fall off.

Following more bombing actions the following day, we were released to Whitehorse, where we parked between the Gordies' B25s and two A26s from Airspray.

Pilots and crews stayed at the same hotel, and since this profession is known to harbor an affinity for its kind, it wasn't long before I found the entire congregation in the bar. Flying was always the topic of discourse, but after a few convivial pints, Gord Sherman excused himself and departed in search of more alluring company.

It was about 11:30 when a highly distraught young man, whom I recognized as Sherman's co-pilot, rushed into the pub. Spotting Gord Peel, he approached our table and began feverishly whispering something in his ear.

"You did what?" I overheard Gord say as they bolted out of the door.

Puzzled by this turn of events, we continued with our libations until Peel returned and collapsed heavily into a chair. We all stared at him quizzically.

"That stupid little cunt! I saved his ass from getting himself killed."

Slowly the story began to unfold. The co-pilot, following his captain's example, decided to impress a couple of lasses by offering them a ride in the plane. After removing the chocks, with the entranced passengers on board, he started one engine but failed to set the parking brake. The airplane swerved and ended up burying a wing tip in a hangar door.

"And the idiot was trying to find Sherman to confess what he'd done," continued Peel. "Christ! If he'd found him, Sherman would have torn his fucking head off."

"Where is he now?" we inquired.

"I told him to pack his gear and get out of town; I just dropped him off on the highway."

It turned out to be a particularly sensible move, because by the time Sherman found out and took off after him in a murderous fury, the kid was gone. There was some damage to the wing tip and the door, but nothing would keep Sherman on the ground, because the following day, a newly commandeered co-pilot was with him when his team and I once again ended up in McQuesten. (I later heard that the lad, mortified with guilt, approached the employer with an offer to fly pro bono until he worked off the $12, 000 worth of damage, but his proposal was politely declined.)

Operating several airplanes out of this airfield proved to be exasperatingly inefficient, because the cloud of dust raised by each takeoff made further flying impossible until it cleared, not to mention that the stuff penetrated teeth, eyes, and bedding.

"Hasn't anyone complained about this?" I asked at the base.

It seems that nobody had, presumably on the grounds of not wanting to be tabbed as whiners by their employer. I had no such qualms, so I contacted headquarters and raised it as a safety issue. As though a complaint was all they were waiting for, an oil truck appeared and finished the job that afternoon.

"If you guys want a cocktail lounge erected near the loading pits staffed with topless waitresses, just ask me," I kept chiding until the joke wore off.

After a logging camp dinner in the main tent, some of us, mesmerized by the Aurora, reclined on the bank of the Stewart River drinking Sherman's scotch until well into the short night.

"The earth's hymn to the firmament," I rhapsodized, staring at the sky.

"Paeans from the pee-ons," Gord corrected, putting the subject to bed.

I crawled out of my bunk in the morning with a toothbrush and towel, and when I reached the river for some rudimentary ablutions, I found Gord Sherman, fishing rod in hand, sitting against a tree.

"Any bites?" I asked.

"You're the first," he said with a grin.

Our actions took us to Mayo and Dawson City that day, but disappointingly, with touching concern for our health, our minders denied us the opportunity to sample a sour-toe cocktail at Diamond Tooth Gertie's by deciding it was safer to sequester us in McQuesten. We flew several actions as a team the following day, during which I continued to marvel at how these two Klondike Cowboys, when airborne, effortlessly substituted their untamed terrestrial ways for slick professionalism and impressive accuracy.

We returned to McQuesten just ahead of a cloudburst. The torrential rain, which lasted all night, trapped us in our tents and continued relentlessly the following day.

"Tomorrow you're all released to Whitehorse," announced the radioman before we retired for the night.

Next morning, as we mopped out our cockpits and prepared for takeoff, I cast a glance down the runway and saw that a small lake had formed about fifteen hundred feet from the button. Since I was the first in line for takeoff, Jim and I walked over to inspect this watery obstacle. I waded in until the water almost poured into my flying boots while Jim threw in some stones, but it was still impossible to gauge its depth. One option was to taxi through it to the other side, but that wouldn't leave much runway for takeoff.

"I'm not happy about trying to get through this stuff," I confessed to the Gordies.

"No problem," said Sherman, strapping into his machine.

I had no idea what to expect, so, camera-in-hand, I stood on the wing of my airplane to record the impending catastrophe. Without a moment's hesitation, Gord advanced power for takeoff and headed for the pond. The moment he reached it, the airplane vanished in a towering explosion of water, mud, and foam. Implausibly, two wingtips and a rudder still attached to the rest of the machine emerged from this aqueous burst. As the cascade shredded by the prop blast splashed to the ground behind him, Sherman powered through the maelstrom, and with his airplane shedding water in all directions, lifted cleanly into the air. Gord Sherman's departure set the example for his partner, who followed in identical fashion, leaving the stage to me.

"Hang on, Jimmy!" I yelled as we hit the water.

The world instantly disappeared, and we lost about twenty mph of ground speed, but the engines were still running, and once the deluge subsided and the windshield cleared, it was just like going through a car wash.

"Nothing to it," I said to my underwhelmed flying companion, but I had to admit that I wouldn't have wanted to be first.

Dusty takeoff out of McQuesten.

Watery takeoff from the same airport.

Gord Sherman, flying buccaneer.

THE WHITEHORSE ECOLOGICAL GOLF COURSE

Whitehorse tanker base was humming with activity. Sadly, we couldn't join the fun, because, among other things, my machine needed a cylinder change. Observing the action from sick-bay, we saw that the noisy bucket-brigade included three A26s from Conair Aviation. With this much firepower, I couldn't expect my non-contract airplane to get much work, so I settled in to help Jim as much as I could and watched the flying show.

When all the pilots convened in the hotel bar that night, I was delighted that the Conair contingent was composed of Barry Marsden, Al Mehlhaff, and Al Kydd. We embraced like long-lost brothers, after which we began catching up.

"What's wrong with your machine?" Barry inquired.

"Nearly everything," I had to admit. "I'm always flying with a stack of unserviceabilities, but this time it's a jug change. My engineer flies with me everywhere I go. I wangled for him to get danger pay."

I then deliberately steered the conversation to aircraft performance. I was dying to discover how these pilots handled this airplane's discourteous post-salvo characteristics. My question was met with quizzical looks.

"We don't experience anything like that. The C of G of your machine must be badly out of whack."

Among other things, I silently agreed: like the engineer's tools and spares in the back, not to mention my golf clubs, but mainly because my airplane carried two hundred more gallons than theirs. Moreover, my drag-inducing four-door tank protruded ungracefully from the belly, while theirs had two doors and fitted flush with the fuselage.

Eventually, with help from the Airspray mechanics, Jim changed the jug, which enabled me to report to Yukon headquarters that my airplane was ready to fly. Their tepid reaction suggested that my three-door hangar-queen's role was best suited for static display.

Regular calls to Rita kept me informed of my mother's condition, and from conversations with Ray, I knew that LIP had renewed the City Stage grant, which would allow us to operate until December.

Since I hadn't swung a club for months and there was little chance of flying, I made my way to the tourist office to inquire about golf in the area. Of course, they assured me that there was a golf course in Whitehorse; all I needed to do was contact the club secretary, who doubled as the town's locksmith, address conveniently provided.

I found the artisan bent over a buzzing instrument from which showers of sparks flew toward the back of his shop. On hearing my inquiry, the locksmith shut down his machine, meticulously wiped his hands on a towel, removed his apron, and after switching his goggles for a pair of scholarly eyeglasses, approached the counter fully in character as the secretary.

He showed great pleasure at my interest in playing the course, inquired about my handicap, proffered a bucket containing a selection of tees, balls, and gloves, and informed me that the annual membership would cost $20.

Where in the world can you play unlimited golf for twenty bucks? I thought as I handed over the money. The course, he explained, was twenty-one kilometers to the west. To find it, he gave me a hand-drawn map and a key to the gate, which I was free to keep. Before I left, he drew my attention to a mark on the map that showed a specific landmark on the edge of town. This was where I should take a careful reading of the odometer, after which he presented me with a handsomely embossed card identifying me as a member of the Wolverine Lake Golf Club,* Whitehorse, Yukon, and wished me a good game.

I set out the following day, and after religiously zeroing my odometer at the prescribed spot, struck out on the logging road and stopped when the reading matched the distance. Though there appeared to be no visible change to the look of the surrounding forest that might suggest the presence of a golf course, a chain spanning two larch trees attracted my attention. When my key fit the lock, I knew I was in the right place. Pleased by the additional benefit of reserved parking conferred by the membership, I drove in through the opening, and though passing around one of the two trees would have achieved the same result, it just didn't seem like the proper thing to do.

After unlimbering my clubs, I paused to examine the challenge at hand.

An area of flattened vegetation amid trees whose branches had been deliberately cut back to allow a full swing identified the teeing-off area, but the direction of the fairway wasn't obvious.

Choosing one of my most experienced balls, I played a deliberate fade into a widening space between the timbers and set off to find it. A motion caught my eye: an enormous owl on straightened wings glided noiselessly toward me.

---

* I don't recall the exact name.

Mesmerized by its tender grace, I froze in place, and only when it whispered past me did I notice the squirrel writhing in its talons.

I followed her silent flight until she disappeared and then continued my search for the ball. Presently, I reached a small clearing where someone had leveled a circle of undergrowth by spraying it with oil. When I saw the thin snag with a red band painted on the trunk, I knew I had found a green. Such attention to detail categorically dispelled any suspicion that this was a not a bona-fide golf course.

It wasn't long before the prospect of hacking through the tranquility of surroundings that had never known the insult of bulldozer or chainsaw began to whiff faintly of sacrilege. I decided to change my plans. After stowing my clubs, I carried my lunch bag into a shady section of a fairway and enjoyed a peaceful rest in the company of local residents, which included four rabbits, two grouse, and a prolonged air-show staged by a pair of ravens showing off their aerobatic skills with undisguised joy expressly for my admiration.

On return to the city, although I always carried a Forestry radio, no call interrupted my vigil until the end of July, when a message from Kenting instructed us to reposition back to Fort Smith. *Why would they want me in Fort Smith?* I wondered, knowing that the area had no fires.

Reluctant to question management, I helped Jim Cook with the loading and we took off as directed, but on the climb the starboard engine backfired. Not able to find any apparent reason for this hiccough, we continued *en route*.

There was a saying among air tanker pilots that you should always avoid being based in any town with *Fort* in its name; Fort Smith must have served as its eponym. We were soon back in our rooms above the beer parlor, and a week later, as I was rolling for takeoff for a periodic test flight and practice drop, the starboard engine backfired, causing me to abort. Unable to pin down the cause, Jim changed the carburetor, which we hoped put the problem to bed. After two weeks of this boredom, I'd had enough.

EDMONTON; THE MCDONALD HOTEL AIR TANKER BASE

"Good morning," I said to Jim on August 11. "Pack your gear; we're out of here."

"Where are they sending us?"

"*They* are not sending us anywhere; *we* are moving to Edmonton."

With all the spares safely tied down, we headed south and landed early in the afternoon. After informing all Forestry authorities of the availability and location of our tanker, we rented two rooms at the McDonald Hotel, and after opening an account at CIBC, I phoned Kenting to report the *fait accompli*.

I had no idea how the company would react, but "I can't blame you" was the last thing I expected Jim Monteith to say. "Unless you get work elsewhere, you can expect to be there until mid-September," he said, and then added, "so have a good time."

"You won't believe this, Rita!" I shouted into the phone. "How soon can you get here?"

Rita arrived as soon as I assured her that my room was nowhere near a jukebox. Her visit coincided with my schedule of weekly test flights.

"How would you like to be my co-pilot?" I proposed.

Gamely, she cast aside her misgivings, and after a thorough briefing and a silent prayer for my right engine to behave, we taxied out for takeoff. I noted with pleasure that Jim Cook's hard-hat had never been more alluringly displayed.

We spent an hour exploring the area, chasing ducks off lakes and peeking into people's houses, all of which Rita thoroughly enjoyed. I took her up again on a subsequent visit, after which I exultantly promoted her to captain. Rita accepted the advancement with equanimity, which when combined with her unspoken marriage vows, seamlessly solidified the pecking order of our relationship.

I spent the rest of my time in Edmonton evaluating the local golf courses, occasionally as a guest of Don Hamilton, the owner of the Alberta firebombing company, Airspray (1967) Ltd., at his exclusive Edmonton country club.

Don had been a renowned bush pilot in Northern Alberta ever since he obtained his pilot's license in 1948. He would eventually join Les Kerr and Barry Marsden as an inductee into the Canadian Aviation Hall of Fame in Ottawa.

Without prospects of further flying, Kenting recalled me to Toronto.

On climb out from Edmonton, the right engine backfired again. After refueling in Winnipeg, a repeat forced me to abort the takeoff. We pulled off to a taxiway, and after a thorough run up, tried again. Robust backfiring before committing to get airborne caused another abort.

This time we decided to shut down for Jim to perform another inspection. We remained stumped by this continuing recurrence, since there was nothing left to fix. I agreed to another try, but the result was the same. After finding a place to park, I called Kenting and reported that Jim planned to take the cowlings off overnight and that I was willing to give it one more try in the morning, but if the problem recurred, I would have to leave the machine in Winnipeg, since I needed to be in Vancouver to start rehearsing a play. I helped Jim with his task until well into the night, and after several flawless full-power runups, we retired to a hotel.

All seemed normal again in the morning until partway down the runway when the recalcitrant pig of an engine let out a barbarous belch.

"It's all yours," I reported to Kenting.

My car was still in Toronto, but Jim Monteith was planning to visit his wife in Vancouver and offered to drive it across, to which I eagerly agreed. After bidding goodbye to my devoted but thoroughly perplexed engineer, I boarded the next Air Canada flight for home.

"CITY STAGE IN A CLASS BY ITSELF"

Making an overnight switch from the world of firebombing in northern Canada to total immersion in theatre was like a change of religion. I was now able to gauge the enormous progress the crew had made after a summer's effort and dedication.

From the time I left, Ray had directed four plays in a row, then engaged Richard Ouzunian to direct the next two. Peter Shaffer's *Black Comedy* was currently on the boards, while Ray was in rehearsals with Terrence McNally' *Noon*.

We agreed that I would direct the next two plays while Ray took some time off, after which Rita and I planned to take advantage of a special TWA interline offer of a trip around the world.

The plays I chose to direct would be my translation of Mrożek's *Charlie*, followed by the piece that had so shocked my original co-directors. This was John Grillo's *Blubber*, the title of which, with the author's permission, I changed to a more palatable *Wilfred Blubber's Last Fling*.

I was particularly pleased to be able to convince the highly talented Wayne Robson to make a return to the boards by offering him a juicy role in each show. Wayne had become disenchanted with theatre and was working in construction. To entice this gifted actor back to where he belonged turned out to be highly rewarding, because later in the year, as a result of his two appearances in my plays, *The Vancouver Sun* awarded him the title of Actor of the Year.

Charlie is a play that takes place in an ophthalmologist's office. I cast Owen Foran to play the character of a doctor who's harassed by two sinister characters: a near-sighted, gun-toting grandfather played by Wayne, and his menacing nephew portrayed by Robert Graham. Their objective is to force the doctor to restore the old man's eyesight so he can identify and hunt down someone named Charlie. (When this play was to be staged in France during the reign of Charles De Gaulle, because the enigmatic Charlie is the object of a manhunt, the authorities insisted on changing the title to a more innominate, *Bertrand*.)

One morning as I was handing out flyers on Howe Street during one of my routine patrols, a young man strode up and asked to speak to me. Impressively attired in a three-piece, pale gray suit, and positively reeking of Aramis, in a cultured British accent he asked what this City Stage was all about.

After listening intently to my description, he went directly to the point.

"I'm Drew Borland," he announced, proffering his hand. "I am going to work for your theatre."

"In what capacity?" I inquired, trying to regain my composure.

"I am an actor, director, designer, and playwright. I can do lighting, sound, costumes, and props. I can stage manage, house manage, or sweep the floors, and I'm willing to do all this pro bono until I prove myself indispensable," he listed off smoothly, augmenting his perfumed personality with a breathtaking dose of chutzpah.

This was hardly an opportunity to pass up. I introduced him to Ray and the staff, and before we knew it, Drew simply annexed himself to our team. It proved to be a propitious arrangement, because for many years to come, Drew ably filled most of these functions and became a highly valued member of the troupe.

At about this time, we were saddened to bid *au revoir* to one of our founding brothers, Henry Jaeger, who relinquished his position to John Woods, a most capable replacement who would remain with City Stage from then on.

Charlie received glowing reviews for the actors and high praise for the author, and I was particularly pleased with the Polish community's commendation for staging this piece.

We immediately started rehearsing *Wilfred Blubber* for which, in addition to stage managing both productions, Mary Lou White provided the choreography. The actors were Yvonne Adalian, who played multiple roles, and Robert Graham, whose portrayal of God considerably expanded His presence beyond its orthodox representation, while Wayne Robson created a memorable title role.

The set, designed by Glenn McDonald, featured a stylized setting sun, which perfectly accompanied the lyrical fantasy of the script. Although I had never used mood music in a straight play before now, the flow and rhythm of this piece seemed to reach out for such treatment. In my mind, I could hear something whimsical, bittersweet, with possible overtones suggestive of a circus. When I described my idea to Wayne, he unhesitatingly showed up with a record of Nino Rota's "Juliet of the Spirits." This hauntingly poignant music proved to be a perfect accompaniment to enhance Mary Lou's choreography, which along with my idea of using a quirky, half-faced, Kabuki-style makeup, produced an intriguing effect.

On the heel of rave reviews—one of which (James Barber's) ran under the heading: "City Stage in a Class by Itself"—I bid *au revoir* to the team.

City Stage green room. L to R: Wayne Robson, Robert Graham, and Yvonne Adalian making up for Wilfred Blubber's Last Fling.

GOLF AROUND THE GLOBE: ROYAL SYDNEY, AUSTRALIA

Ever since we met, Rita and I agreed to spend as much time as possible exploring the world, and to do it while we were still young, so this early opportunity to circumnavigate the world seemed like a reasonable iteration of this ambition. Our itinerary included Australia, followed by Hong Kong, Bangkok, New Delhi, Tehran, and Paris. Why not make this a golf tour as well? In answer to my own question, I purchased a heavy-duty, red carry bag, into which I was zipping my golf bag when Rita stopped me with a quizzical gaze.

"Of course I'm taking my golf clubs. Haven't you heard? They don't let you into Australia unless you bring your own sticks."

Rolling her eyes in disbelief, Rita knew she'd have to resign herself to this maniacal obsession.

On arrival in Sydney, we rented a car and drove to the reputedly hot and lively district of King's Cross, where we moved into a spacious room in a hotel named The Texas Tavern, which we soon discovered could be rented by the hour. Though we swung into the spirit of the place with considerable commitment, we didn't neglect to explore the city. We loved its excitement and its bustle, but how to explain the lingering Puritanism, which in those days still mandated the closure of pubs at six, was beyond us.

It was while meandering through the Circular Quay that we came across a sister lunch-hour theatre called The Q. After seeing a show and introducing ourselves as fellow practitioners, we were instantly invited to join the cast and crew for a ripping party in somebody's home. The Q, we discovered, had been operating in this capacity since 1965, and was enjoying great success.

The following day, while driving through Rose Bay in our rented Beetle, we passed a posh looking golf course. "Looks interesting," I said swinging into the parking lot.

"It's The Royal Sydney," Rita said evenly, pointing out the sign. "Anyone can tell it's a private club."

I chose to ignore her upturned eyes and headed for the pro shop.

"Good morning, gentlemen," I greeted the suddenly silent staff. *They must think I'm American*, I concluded, but choosing not to disabuse them of this impression, I got to the point. "I wonder if it might be possible to play your course?"

After a cursory appraisal of my attire, one of them offered dryly that this would be up to the club secretary and beckoned me to follow him up the stairs.

Everything about the place oozed of tradition and propriety. After leading me through an airless passage lined with glass niches displaying collections of wooden-shafted clubs, ornate silver trophies, and rows of pictures of past champions, he presented me to a gentleman occupying an impressive office. If my careless appearance offended him, he had the breeding not to notice.

"From Canada, you say? One of your chaps saved my butt during the war, but that's a long story. Are you by chance a member of a reciprocal club?"

That's when I remembered my membership card from Whitehorse which still reposed as a curiosity in the recesses of my wallet. Did I have the gall?

"I'm not sure if we have an arrangement with you, but this is my club," I said, handing him the card.

"Whitehorse," he mused, as if examining something exotic.

"Yes," I suggested brightly. "If you should ever visit, I'd be more than delighted to …"

"How long are you planning to visit Sydney?"

"Two weeks," I replied, at which time he floored me with something entirely unexpected.

"Welcome to our club," he said, offering his hand. "I'll have the honorary membership prepared, which you can collect when you come to play."

My triumphant run up to the car served to defuse Rita's displeasure at having been abandoned in the heat.

How did I do it? Simple. "I offered Royal Sydney reciprocal privileges at my home course."

To this day, I haven't a clue what precipitated this secretary's extraordinary deed.

When we arrived at the club the following day, careful not to violate the dress code, I came wearing a tailored shirt and the superbly fitting, canary-yellow slacks Leon had given me in Paris. We had the course to ourselves, which suited me fine as I could hit several balls off each tee to familiarize myself with this exquisitely manicured layout. As soon as we were out of sight of the clubhouse, Rita removed her shoes, and provided commentary the color of which complemented the quality of my effort.

Somewhere along the course, we caught up with a middle-aged couple, who invited us to join them and introduced themselves as Alan and Peggy McGregor. We felt immediately attracted by their openness and unconventionality.

"Dine at the club? With that smarmy lot? Never! You're coming home with us," they insisted, and an instant friendship was born.

Presently, this eccentric and highly original couple brought us up to date about some local rules. To begin with, the slacks I was wearing would never be tolerated on a member, since aggressively garish hues were distinctly discouraged. Ladies were not allowed in the bar, which left the restaurant as the only place where we could have a drink together, but even there the dress code demanded that the men wear jackets, and ladies wear skirts. A welcome advantage was the excellent champagne made especially for the club, which was available for off sales at a moderate price and immediately became our drink *du jour*. We spent our time in Sydney in the company of our exuberantly nonconformist friends, who escorted us around the cultural sights of that intriguing city, regularly took me golfing, and entertained us in their home.

We were eager to see as much of this continent as possible, and since the domestic airline, Ansat, offered attractive rates, we flew to Brisbane. We visited the famous beaches of nearby Surfer's Paradise and the Gold Coast, but it was descriptions of the Barrier Reef that convinced us to make this a destination the following year. Showing my Royal Sydney membership at the Royal Queensland golf club resulted in a free round, after which we returned to Sydney from where we caught TWA to Hong Kong to resume our global pilgrimage.

HONG KONG AND THAILAND

We next flew to Hong Kong, and characteristically, when exposed to something new, we tried to see it all. One of the highlights of the obligatory tour of the teeming harbor was the burned-out wreck of the once magnificent Cunard liner, *Queen Elizabeth*, which lay sorrowfully on its side after a fire deliberately set in an insurance fraud. After tours of the junks, massed sanpans, and jumbo floating restaurants of Aberdeen, it was time to live up to my ambition to play golf at every stop on our itinerary. The only course on the peninsula was in Fanling, which was a two-hour train ride to the Chinese border.

The look on Rita's face as she sat next to my clubs on a railway platform said everything.

The next stop on our itinerary was Thailand. One of the perks of being an airline employee is having access to first-class accommodations at vastly reduced prices. Wherever we traveled, we stayed at Hilton and Intercontinental hotels, which offered fabulous deals. Accordingly, in Bangkok we moved into the venerable Siam Hotel, an ornate example of classic Thai architecture sheltered in a meticulously tended jungle, interspersed with ponds teeming with multicolored fish and populated with tame, Technicolor parrots.

Among our enduring memories is the outdoor restaurant, where bathed in the subdued glow of Japanese paper lanterns, we spent languid evenings sipping exotic offerings from bulbous glasses fussily adorned with tiny paper umbrellas.

We sat absorbed by the sight of immaculately mannered chefs, who collected our choice of live shellfish and crustaceans, placed them in wicker baskets, and after lowering them into a steam bath, spilled the perfectly cooked contents onto serving platters before us.

We loved the look and tenor of this bewitching land, the highlight of which was an extended cruise on the Chao Phraya River, where a succession of exquisite giant golden Buddhas adorned palaces, markets, and temples.

Additionally, the ship proved to be the best platform from which to observe everyday life along the tightly populated banks.

The visit to this country would not be complete without a round of golf, of course, and my inquiries steered me to the Royal Bangkok Sports Club, a singularly conceived layout that straddled a race track. Since the track bisected several of the holes, local rules stipulated that golfers were to cease play for the duration of a race, and this setting remains as the most unusual on which I've ever played.

Inspired with wonder by the richly colorful culture and charmed by the open friendliness of the inhabitants, we boarded our onward connection bound for Delhi.

Rita radiates displeasure at a Hong Kong railway station.

Showing enviable form with a full eight iron. (Gareth Gwilliam photo)

DELHI

The bus ride to Delhi proved to be a microcosm of what would confront us for the remainder of this inaugural introduction to India. From the moment he left the airport, our driver launched into a spirited competition with all other vehicles, as if on a bet. We clung white-knuckled to anything fixed and watched speechlessly as cars, buses, trucks, and motorbikes slalomed through the multitude of ox carts, camels, and rickshaws, which in stark contrast to the chaos around them proceeded with stoic indifference at their steady medieval pace.

Round-eyed with disbelief, we observed the serene detachment of pedestrians who, embedded in their karma, coolly tolerated the passing traffic as it hurtled past them, inches from their bodies, fluttering their garments and covering them in dust. Since approaching vehicles swept past us on both sides, it wasn't until the road narrowed to three lanes that we realized India had appropriated the colonial English practice of driving on the left.

After a night at the Hilton, we embarked on a tour of the city, which left Rita with an impression that remains seared into her memory. It occurred as we approached the steps of the Delhi Mosque. As we threaded our way up through the crowd, Rita was confronted by a harrowing apparition. Facing her stood the unnerving specter of a faceless, living mummy, swathed ominously in a jet-black shroud. It was only a woman in a burka, yet this stygian ghost pierced something primordial within her that continues to haunt her to this day.

It's impossible to explain the efficiency of the jungle telegraph in Indian cities that somehow announces the presence of a tourist in the street, but its effect is immediate and disconcerting. Just stepping out of a hotel to a taxi causes swarms of urchins to materialize and swirl underfoot with upraised hands. The pitiful sight of mothers' imploring eyes as they held mutilated children up to a car's window was too soul-crushing to contemplate. It would take several more visits to India to become accustomed enough to the devastating poverty to allow us to start cultivating a fascination with the history and culture of this infinitely complex society.

TEHRAN

We arrived in Iran full of anticipation. We had eagerly looked forward to visiting this cradle of civilization and planned to spend three days in Tehran and three more exploring what's left of the tombs and palaces of the ancient capital, Persepolis. Unfortunately, the process of disenchantment started early.

We obtained information at the tourist center at the airport regarding the cost of a taxi to the Intercontinental Hotel, but when we arrived, the driver demanded double the price. A mini-row, deliberately disregarded by the hotel staff, ensued in the lobby.

Though under the Shah this was still a secular country where women could wear lipstick, appear unescorted by a man, and parade in European dress, to our increasing chagrin we began to discover an entirely unexpected level of xenophobia.

Information in the hotel was grudgingly offered, and city maps did not exist, but as we hesitantly traipsed on foot through the neighborhood, a mullah politely invited us to visit his mosque. We were genuinely surprised by this unexpected gesture of hospitality, but not nearly as much as by his demand for ten dollars for his guided tour.

Incomprehensibly, taxis hailed in the street might slow down, but on seeing Rita's blonde hair, accelerated away. A disturbing incident occurred when a cab, already occupied by a teenaged schoolgirl, stopped to pick us up. The meter displayed Persian characters, but the young lady spoke some English, which put us at ease. Upon arrival at our destination, the driver demanded a sum that made the girl catch her breath.

"That's ten times the number on the meter," she whispered, which produced a deranged outburst from the driver, causing her to curl up in fear. When we left the taxi, we couldn't help wondering about the fate of the girl who cowered in her seat, overwhelmed by the driver's continuing harangue. This was the last of a catalogue of annoyances that caused us to shorten our stay, but we didn't leave before I vented our outrage with a four-page missive of complaints addressed to the Minister of Tourism. We are still waiting for his reply.

Our flight to Paris included a scheduled stopover in Beirut. It was a tense time in Lebanon, where the usual internecine rivalries and religious differences stood on the brink of the civil war, which would ravage the region sometime later. It was also at this airport that a few years earlier Israeli defense force operatives, not known to take umbrage lightly, blew up twelve airliners belonging to various Arab companies in reprisal for the PLO's temerity to fire on an El Al airplane.

The crew briefed us all before arrival that only departing passengers would be allowed to leave the aircraft, and that picture taking was forbidden, but I couldn't resist snapping some clandestine photos of the manned gun-emplacements that ringed the terminal.

When Leon met us at Orly Airport, after straightening Rita's attire disheveled by Wotan's spirited attempts to set the canine standing high jump record using her face as the bar, we repaired to the apartment to indulge in Maria's French cuisine. A photo I took that evening carries a tell-tale sign of a stress-related cold sore blossoming on Rita's chin, which testifies that the last stages of the trip were not all sweetness and roses.

It was a relief to decompress in Paris by shopping at the markets of the Rue Mouffetard, trying on new clothes from Leon's factory, and relaxing in the simpler pleasures of family, pets, Paris, and each other.

My sketch of Rita and friend.

CITY STAGE LOSES LIP GRANT

The ten-day sojourn in Paris served to rekindle my creative juices, and I was raring to get back to the theatre, but a phone call to Ray changed everything. City Stage had lost its grant.

A group of glum faces met me in the theatre the next day.

The notification from Ottawa had arrived the previous week: Manpower is baffled and is waiting for confirmation.

"We're not the only ones," said Ray. "Perhaps the Liberals have blown all their money on the election."

I'd forgotten that there had been one during our absence. Though Trudeau still clung to power, he now led a minority government and had taken a severe beating in BC.

It was encouraging that Manpower was making inquiries—we were, after all, their pet project.

In the meantime, Ray had a hit running on stage with Jean Anouilh's *Cecile, or the School for Fathers*, a costly production employing six actors, one of whom, I was pleased to note, was Drew Borland. Glenn McDonald not only designed the set but was in the cast, along with Brigid Johnston, Mario Crudo, Alex Moir, and Felicity Roche, an attractive young actress who had appeared in *Playboy* in a spread on the "Girls of Canada."

Ray had already made calculations for a worst-case scenario, which revealed that there wouldn't be enough funds to cast another play. *Cecile* had been on the boards since November 21, but because it was doing well at the box office, Ray decided to extend its run to the end of December.

What to do? There was no plan B. This meant the death knell of City Stage. Intoxicated by our success and thoroughly immersed in this project, we never paused to recognize our vulnerability of being at the mercy of a single benefactor. By mid-December, we had the confirmation: there would be no renewal of our grant.

A Manpower file listing recipients in BC whose grants *were* restored left us thoroughly confused. Why would Ottawa choose such a successful group for the axe? Dismissing desperate measures, such as lowering our wages, reverting to non-Equity casts, or raising the cost of sandwiches and admission, we were ready to resign ourselves to our fate until Martin Keeley, in a spirited attempt at an impersonation of Neville Chamberlain, waltzed in brandishing a piece of paper. It was a newspaper clipping in which the writer appeared to suggest a political motive in the cancellation of LIP grants by pointing out that they mostly occurred in ridings where the Liberals took a beating.

Rushing back to our list, we quickly confirmed the pattern that had escaped us because of an insufficient application of cynicism. We discovered that in the lower mainland, the ridings of Capilano, Vancouver-Quadra, Burnaby-Seymour, and Fraser Valley showed a distinct correlation between the cancellation of grants and the ouster of Liberal MPs. The same was true in Prince George, Kamloops, Victoria, and the Okanagan. We had the smoking gun … now what do we do with it?

We considered checking if this were true across the nation, but soon discovered that somebody had beaten us to it. Either a person with a grudge against the Liberals, or someone like us who had lost a grant, had done a lot of homework. Furthermore, he revealed the sinister nature of this act by pointing out that, to disguise its punitive purpose, not all grants in affected ridings were withdrawn. To make it look fair, some like ours were pulled, even though Mr. Basford, the Liberal MP for our riding, had been re-elected. To us, it seemed doubly unfair to be tossed out with the bathwater.

Conspiracy theories, of which this was a classic, are a bitch to prove, but to victims like us, nothing could be more convincing. Though the pattern was obvious, we had no idea how to exploit it. However, if political skullduggery was in fact involved, this just might tilt the equation in our favor. We knew that something had to be done, and that something was nothing short of getting our grant restored.

Fueled by indignation, we recognized that our first step was to get our cause known. The full frontal attack began with letters to the newspapers—always a satisfying venue to give vent to pent-up vexations, with our suspicions of political chicanery woven unsubtly into the text. Simultaneously, we launched a fundraising campaign.

"CITY STAGE IS INCORPORATED AS A NONPROFIT SOCIETY" trumpeted one of the many signs decorating our window.

"YOUR CONTRIBUTIONS ARE TAX DEDUCTIBLE! OUR GOAL FROM PRIVATE DONATIONS IS $5,000," proclaimed another.

Relying on the powers of petitions as an instrument of democratic change, we commenced canvassing names in support of our quest. Solicitations started with our audiences. Sitting captive in their seats, they suffered patiently through our post-show entreaties requesting them to become signatories to our objectives, the most successful of which were those delivered by Ray, since his darkly menacing demeanor strongly implied that a signature was a condition of being allowed to leave the house.

Like barkers at a strip show, we prowled the block to press-gang into compliance anyone whose resistance fell short of open violence. Lists of names grew quickly and soon covered both sides of several sandwich-boards. A further prong of our attack was to co-opt radio talk show hosts to our purpose, and it was here we discovered that, contrary to our naively held assumptions, not everyone was a convert to our cause.

The most prominent among these was the intimidating voice of an unappeasable Scotsman whose stentorian censure of all schemes scenting of socialism started each morning at 9:00 a.m.—*precisely*. Jack Webster did not suffer fools gladly, which included all who disagreed with his convictions. His signature tactic to dispose of anyone foolish enough to challenge his opinions was to punctuate his rebuke with a climactic slam of the phone.

Additionally, the pathetically meager results of our cash drive exerted a depressing effect on our enthusiasm, which climaxed with our closing show on the last day of December. Though there was much of which we could be proud, our farewell fling was freighted with a feeling of finality. A forensic examination of our finances revealed that we had just enough cash to pay our January rent and for a skeleton crew to wind down this beautiful dream.

Ray, Mary Lou, and John retained a nominal salary, while the rest of us volunteered to go off the payroll, but the devotion developed over the nine months of communal effort continued to keep us together. We knew that evidence of political mean-spiritedness, along with the continually growing list of names and letters of support, were powerful weapons in our armory, but how to make effective use of these assets was unclear.

That our petition should reach an influential person in Ottawa was obvious, but to mail it to the Minister of Manpower with a polite covering letter was an invocation akin to burning incense. What about delivering it in person?

Progressively, the sheer audacity of such an act began to ripen in my brain.

Even if this overture should fail, there was nothing to lose, and since this stratagem was incontestably mine to put into play, the prospect of this intriguing endeavor found roots in fertile soil.

Martin Keely in front of City Stage plastered with petitions.

Gearing up to face the politicians in Ottawa, 1973.

WALTZING WITH POLITICIANS IN OTTAWA

On a soggy Sunday in January, with Rita's blessing, I took advantage of my Air Canada pass, flew to the capital, and rented a room at an attractive airline rate at the closest venue to the seat of power: the Chateau Laurier Hotel.

Ensconced in the comfort of this venerable establishment, I began to lay my plans for the morning. My primary goal was to request a private consultation with the Honourable Robert Andras, who as Minister of Manpower and Immigration was the person directly responsible for our fate.

Freshly shaved, smartly turned out with a Tracker pin jauntily embellishing my tie for effect, I strode confidently into the Minister's office emboldened by the dossier containing 860 names on the petition.

After describing my mission to several levels of underlings, I was eventually ushered into the presence of the Minister's executive secretary. Diplomatically avoiding any allegations of impropriety, I outlined the reason for my visit, which I clinched with an imposing display of my collection.

"You can leave it with me," he said curtly. "I'll show it to the Minister at his convenience."

There was no way that I would allow myself to be disarmed in this manner, so I reiterated that my mission was to gain a personal audience with the Minister. Impossible, I was told. He is not available at this time.

"I am willing to wait," I said, and determinedly took a seat at the entrance.

I might as well have been a statue. I sat ignored for half of the morning, but this sojourn gave me a chance to consider other options. Although I knew that ultimately Mr. Andras was the person who held the key to our future, I began to realize that playing the role of supplicant denied me the use of my most effective weapon: the claim of political chicanery that I was convinced governed the withdrawal of LIP grants.

Employing this argument would be useless with the Liberals. Although members of the Progressive Conservative Party could be expected to be philosophically opposed to LIP, who knows what an opportunity to embarrass the government might spawn?

After quietly departing the Minister's office, I decided to try out this tactic by visiting a selection of Conservative MPs from Vancouver. What prompted me to start with John Fraser, MP for Vancouver South (future Minister of

Fisheries and Speaker of the House) has long escaped my memory, but this choice proved to be nothing short of providential. Following the usual vetting by the executive secretary, Mr. Fraser listened courteously to the reasons for my visit and paid particular attention to the claim of political machinations.

"How are you planning to act on this assumption?" he wished to know.

"Frankly, Sir, unless I can get a hearing from Mr. Andras, I thought I'd see if I could canvass support from the opposition."

I have never understood what prompted Mr. Fraser's subsequent proposal.

"As long as you're here, if you wish, feel free to use the spare desk next to the secretary's," he said. "You might find it useful."

While a warm space, a coat rack, and a telephone proved to be indispensable in the pursuit of my assignment, a sympathetic ear by far outweighed these conveniences. I gratefully accepted this unexpected act of hospitality and moved in for the remainder of my stay, where I occasionally found myself to be the only occupant of the office.

My attempt to speak to Minister Andras that afternoon was met with the now familiar result, after which I continued my rounds with a visit to MP John Reynolds, a PC from West Vancouver. He was equally sympathetic to my revelations, though he wasn't sure how he could be of help. After another futile attempt to see Mr. Andras, I returned to the hotel and called Rita and Ray. Ray was eager to hear the story of my quest, which had so far got me nowhere, but after all, I had just begun.

"Have you thought of trying to see Ron Basford?"

Though Mr. Basford was a Liberal, he was the representative of Vancouver Centre, which included the entire downtown core and was one of three surviving Liberal ridings in the province. As the Minister of State for Urban Affairs, his was a most influential portfolio.

"He is definitely on my list," I told him, and moved his name to the top of my schedule for the morning.

Mr. Basford proved just as unattainable as Mr. Andras, and after politely turning down an offer to leave my dossier, I returned to "my" office.

"How are things going?" John asked.

After bringing him up to date, he invited me to lunch in the Commons cafeteria. It was a singular privilege to be escorted to this hive of our governing body, and I distinctly recall being taken aback by the casual informality permeating this animated arena. The elegantly attired clientele exchanged greetings with hearty familiarity; hands were shaken, backs slapped, and nothing about the prevailing *bonhomie* suggested a mixture of rivals from opposite sides of the House.

John seemed to know everyone, and I was genuinely flattered to be presented like a VIP to anyone approaching our table, particularly when MP Flora McDonald, who appeared warmly disposed to my cause, invited me to see her after lunch. I found her busy office to be imbued with an atmosphere of gaiety, perhaps because it was staffed entirely by women.

This gracious, angular-featured lady granted me an extensive hearing, and like John Fraser made me feel immodestly important when introducing me to her visitors, after which she capped my day by inviting me to Question Period as her guest.

Clutching my pass, I dashed up to the visitors' gallery to absorb the proceedings from a front row pew.

I had no idea that governing could be such jolly fun.

After receiving permission from the Speaker of the House, Members took turns to rise, and encouraged by sprightly rumblings of support from their peers, hurled unspeakable accusations, albeit larded with obsequious politeness, at the opposition; the latter, booing roundly, would return the compliment until order was restored, when the cycle was ready to start over again.

The duty of the Speaker of the House, similar to that of the President at a naval mess dinner, was to find a balance between the need to remain within the strict rules of engagement, while occasionally sanctioning their breach commensurate with the wit of the transgressor.

The difference between the two lay in the degree of hazard faced by the participants. At mess dinners, this was typically limited to becoming the target of a flying bun, whereas Question Period was chronically fraught with the threat of character assassination.

On return to my hotel that evening, I found a message on my phone. Would I be kind enough to contact Mr. Ray Perrault at my convenience, and a number was provided.

With studied courtesy, Mr. Perrault opened by expressing his familiarity with my mission and wondered if I might be free to have lunch with him tomorrow. Would the restaurant in my hotel be suitable? Indeed it would be, I agreed, highly intrigued.

In the morning, I made my customary visits to the offices of Messer's Andras and Basford, and being met with the same rebuffs, returned to the hotel for my luncheon rendezvous. Mr. Perrault turned out to be a distinguished and cultured gentleman with an unexpected interest in our case. He was expansively complimentary of the achievements of City Stage, tisked compassionately at the apparent unfairness of the withdrawal of the grant, but felt obliged to chastise our suggestion that politics played any part in this decision. It was jejune of us, he counseled paternally, to continue trotting out this naïve assumption, which, he cautioned, could prove counterproductive in the end. He disseminated this advice with such disarming charm that it nearly obliterated its patronizing character, which almost vanished completely when he warmly shook my hand, wished me luck, and waved away my insincere offer to pay for my share of the meal.

"Who is Ray Perrault?" I asked John when I arrived at the office.

"Landslide Ray? He was an MLA in Victoria until he decided to run as a Liberal MP and won the Burnaby-Seymour riding from Tommy Douglas by 152 votes—ergo, his nickname. By the way, he lost his seat in the last election."

Aha! This was beginning to make sense. But was he friend or foe?

I believe I may have made more rounds that afternoon trying to gain allies to my suit, but it was now Wednesday evening, I still hadn't been able to get close to my target sources, and I had no inkling of whether I was accomplishing anything at all.

I was no closer on Thursday afternoon following fresh rebuttals from the Ministers when I decided to call Ray Michal.

"What the hell are you stirring up there in Ottawa?" he wanted to know, his voice filled with alarm. "Jack Webster is screaming on the air like a maniac. He's turning his guns specifically on City Stage. This morning he actually used your name. We've been recording his program: 'Georrrge Plawski, dirrrector of City Stage, is thumping on all the politicians' desks in Ottawa; these *arteestes* think they deserve your hard earned money to pay for their epicene frivolities.' Where the hell is he getting his information? Somebody must have briefed him overnight."

The penny dropped; it had to have been Ray Perrault.

"Well, it shows I've got someone's ear, at least" I offered. "I'll keep trying one more day and fly home on Saturday. Nothing ventured, you know…"

In the evening there was another invitation from Ray Perrault. He would like to have lunch with me in the Commons cafeteria tomorrow. Any port in a storm, I reckoned.

"How's your quest progressing?" John asked in the morning.

"You probably know better than me," I said. "I just can't penetrate the defenses of the Ministers, but I'm having lunch with Ray Perrault again."

"Keep on plugging," he encouraged. "By the way, I was going to invite you to Question Period today, but your new admirer beat me to it. Get your pass from Flora's office."

I dropped in on the way to the cafeteria. Once more such friendly grace, as if she owed me a lifetime of favors.

Mr. Perrault was in an effervescent mood; again, he encouraged me to dismiss those unseemly and groundless suspicions and expressed his hope that my trip had been worthwhile. It made it unthinkable for me, in this chummy atmosphere, to try to pry out any connections between him and Webster.

Similar to my visit with John, lunch flowed replete with lavish introductions to people stopping by our table, and I wonder how many future Prime Ministers shook my hand that day. If I was being neutralized, it was an act silkily accomplished with style and panache.

After lunch, I decided on a last-ditch effort to see Mr. Andras, but failing again to penetrate his screen, rushed over to try Mr. Basford. As I stood waiting in line, someone opened a door at the back of the office, where I caught a brief glimpse of the unmistakable bald pate of the Minister.

"My name is George Plawski; I'm here to see Mr. Basford," I proclaimed boldly to the receptionist when my turn arrived. After a brief pause, following what appeared to be a confirming glance from the parliamentary secretary, she calmly informed me that, regrettably, the Minister was away.

I let the statement sink in; this was a *gotcha* moment I was going to savor.

"Very good," I acknowledged, oozing unctuous politeness. "If I may then, I'll just take a seat here until the Minister returns."

I took a chair in the waiting room from where I could see the Minister's door. As I settled in for my vigil, I was sure that, unless there was a fire escape or an ejection seat, nobody could leave that office without me seeing him from my sniper's perch.

I remember the emotions coursing through me during that ambush as if it had happened this morning. For an hour my presence was ignored. I watched as people came and went; phones were answered, papers shuffled, and files filed, but I couldn't help noticing an awkward tension infiltrating the room, particularly in the self-conscious care taken never to open the Minister's door wide enough to permit me a peek inside. In fact, it became increasingly apparent that their fib was causing a general embarrassment.

"Mr. Plawski, would you follow me please?"

It was the parliamentary secretary who materialized next to my chair.

"Come in," said a voice from Mr. Basford's office in response to the knock.

"Mr. Plawski, Sir," the exec announced, shepherding me inside.

"Good afternoon, Minister," I ventured respectfully as I stood in front of his desk.

"Good afternoon," he countered curtly. "Sorry to have kept you waiting. I see that you're here trying to restore your theatre's grant."

"Yes, Sir," I said, simultaneously noticing a file marked CITY STAGE lying on his desk. Clearly, he'd been fully briefed.

"You may leave your dossier with the secretary," he said, nodding at my package.

"Thank you very much, Sir," I said, and sensing that the audience was over, permitted myself to be marched out through the door.

With my head held needlessly high, I followed the exec through a suddenly silent office to the exit where, after handing over my files, we conducted civil goodbyes like parting business associates.

A feeling of emptiness swept over me in the corridor. What had I achieved? I had been dismissed like a captain's defaulter. No commitment was offered, and any feelings of satisfaction on my part were entirely unwarranted.

I could have used a drink, but I wouldn't have missed Question Period for anything.

Following another riveting session of verbal calisthenics performed for the benefit of reporters and Hansard, I made my way to a phone and called Ray Michal.

"Jesus Christ!" he opened. "You've sure stuck a stick in a hornets' nest over there. Webster was apoplectic this morning, telling everyone that you're staying at the Chateau Laurier, implying you're doing it on public funds."

That two-faced Ray Perrault was at it again.

"It's all inconclusive, but at least I got to see Basford today; the dossier is now in his hands. I'm coming back tomorrow."

The night gave me time to reflect on these five whirlwind days. I had no idea if I'd achieved my goal, but what an incredible experience. I mused over the easy access available to our Members of Parliament and how I was permitted to wander through the corridors of power unchallenged, unfrisked, and without even an identity tag.

Fleeting moments of pleasure glow warmly in my memory: recognizing Mr. Stanfield walking alone on a deserted street, who returned my greeting with a courteous tip of his hat; and after John's introduction, the short but amiable exchange with Mr. Martin on the marble stairs of the Parliament building.

My stay at the august Chateau Laurier, where I luxuriated in being just a short, snowy walk away from the core of our parliamentary democracy, was also an undeniable treat.

The most satisfying experience of the visit was John Fraser's extraordinary hospitality. Seen in retrospect, such an act stands as an example of the chasm that separates us today from personal intercourse with our representatives, still possible in earlier times.

Knowing that John would be working in the morning, I armed myself with a bottle of Benedictine, his favorite liqueur, before dropping in to say goodbye. I had not anticipated that such a gift might be a source of embarrassment, but to my relief, after a moment of vacillation, he accepted it as a gesture of personal gratitude, and opening it on the spot, we shared a parting tot.

THE VIGIL COMMENCES

Except for having the satisfaction of knowing that my presence in Ottawa did not go entirely unnoticed, I returned to Vancouver empty-handed. By Monday morning, Mr. Webster was once again in full voice, braying against all recipients of Liberal largesse. Ray played some of the recorded rants that had gained enthusiastic support from a majority of callers, while the few who disagreed were unceremoniously dismissed in his patented manner.

We convened at the coffee shop next door to consider our options. It was imperative that, on the slim hope of a renewal of the grant, we keep City Stage alive. Creative accounting revealed that there was just enough in the kitty to cover the February rent, which would allow us to hold out for a month before dismantling the theatre.

"How come everything's so quiet with you guys these days?" the Greek proprietor wished to know. Reluctantly, we told him. Our neighbor had come around to recognize that he had plenty at stake in our continued existence, and although, in spite of our standing offer, he had never set foot in our theatre, his was one of the most persuasive letters of support in our file.

What about Webster? Was it worthwhile to attempt some damage control by getting on his program? There was nothing to lose, we agreed, so the following morning, as Ray sat ready to record the anticipated debacle, I called the radio station, identified myself as a City Stage director, and stood by to get mangled.

None of us was prepared for the outcome. After a brief introduction, I was allowed several minutes of uninterrupted air-time, during which I described the important contribution City Stage had made to the Vancouver theatre scene. I mentioned how our productions enjoyed critical approval, developed strong support from an appreciative public, and created meaningful jobs. I emphasized that none of this could have been achieved without the LIP grant, and did not stint airing our conviction that the withdrawal of our funding was politically motivated. Emboldened by Mr. Webster's forbearance, I called attention to the unfairness of his innuendo which suggested that my visit to Ottawa was funded by grant money, and offered, if he wished, to show him our financial report.

Webster's was a powerful and influential voice on radio and TV for many years in Vancouver; though he could be merciless with his critics, and remained on principle opposed to programs like LIP, he treated me fairly, let me have my say, and allowed me to escape with my skin intact.

Early in February, someone brought in a newspaper with the announcement of the appointment of Ray Perrault as parliamentary secretary to our unapproachable Minister of Manpower, Robert Andras.

Very interesting. Did this mean the death-knell of City Stage? Was it the key to its revival? Or would it be of no consequence whatsoever?

Life at the theatre now entered a sedentary stage, which reminded me of standby on a tanker base between fires. I put the time to good use working on my games, and enjoyed a few rounds of soggy golf with my friends Gareth Gwilliam and Ken Stephens.

Meanwhile, Linc had finally finished his book. Published with the title *Air Attack on Forest Fires*, it was a stunning achievement. The handsome, hardcover edition came copiously illustrated and offered an exhausting summary of the history and techniques of firebombing. It was the only work of its kind, and deservedly achieved the status of the encyclopedia of the business.

Boxes containing eight hundred copies filled Linc's basement, garage, and most of his living space, and sending out mail orders took all of his time.

With our existence on hold, Rita and I drove to Tofino, where we rented a rustic cottage tucked under the trees barely above the tide-line at the recently opened Pacific Sands Resort. Roughly hewn and equipped with bare essentials, it included a fireplace, a superb view of the ocean, and nightly visits by a stray white cat. In this ideal place to unwind, we jogged in the mornings on the firm gray sand, and the pictures of us next to a beach campfire roasting wieners, which we washed down with Lens Moser Liebfraumilch straight from the bottle, are among our favorites in our albums.

Each sunset, after crossing a precarious stockpile of logs, we climbed to the top of the rocky promontory separating Cox from Chesterman Beach. From this vantage, mesmerized by the power of the sea and slightly giddy from a puff or two, we watched the endless succession of breakers smashing into the rocks below. We wistfully recall the thundering cascades of spray that occasionally rose to bedew us with a salty mist, causing us to laugh uproariously as w embraced on our stony perch.

Idyllic as our West Coast beaches are, the thought of seeing their counterparts in warmer climes firmed up in our imagination. We had already decided to visit the Barrier Reef on our previous journey, so why not combine the trip with stopovers in Tahiti and a sojourn at the Club Méditerrané in Moorea?

It was time to reconsider the course of our lives. Firebombing was my bread-and-butter, which required a commitment of a minimum of five months of the year, plus training time, leaving half a year for everything else. On the off chance that Ottawa should reinstate our grant, this trip to Tofino would be our only getaway before returning to the theatre, after which I would have to go flying again.

We agreed that such a cycle was untenable, which meant that I must make a tough decision. Accordingly, on return to Vancouver, it was with a heavy heart I confessed to Ray and the staff that regardless of what happened, this would be my final involvement with City Stage.

By the third week of February, we resigned ourselves to the futility of this wait and started planning to wind the venture down.

RESTORATION THEATRE, VANCOUVER VERSION

The call from Manpower came around the twentieth of the month:

"Local Initiative Project No. 511696 is reinstated; appropriate funds are to be released forthwith."

Having almost given up, it took a while to catch our breath. We recalled the team, and everyone was ready to go. Wasting no time, we deluged the press with the news, while the posters I displayed in our windows loudly proclaimed our impending restoration.

Though this embodiment retained some of the drama of its seventeenth-century counterpart, it lacked its radical innovation of women playing women's roles, because we'd had the foresight to have done so all along.

Soon the theatre was crowded with supporters and well-wishers, along with actors ready to contribute to the approaching renaissance. Everyone wanted to know how we did it. Nothing to it—a quick word in the Prime Minister's ear and Bob's your uncle, we replied. Though it was clear to us that my visit to the capital played a decisive role, who among the politicians in Ottawa engineered this reversal would forever remain a mystery.

As we sifted various ideas on the appropriate vehicle for our opening, someone discovered that Shaw's one-act play, *Poison, Passion and Petrifaction*, was on the high school curriculum, which would guarantee busloads of students filling the house. Neither Ray nor I particularly liked the play, but the expectation of high attendance for our triumphant second debut influenced our decision in its favor.

We tossed a coin to decide who would direct; regrettably, I won. I engaged the multi-talented Drew Borland to design as well as to act; he would join Keith Pepper and Yvonne Adalian in the cast, but decidedly, this was a piece that did not stir my imagination. The result prompted Chris Dafoe, one of our most supportive critics, to write uncharitably that the play "flopped about the stage like a hippo without bones." The show was richly attended, however, which included a visit by John Fraser, who brought his two young sons and came as our honored guest.

In the meantime, Ray was busy preparing our most ambitious production to date: the musical, *Passionella*. This happy choice originated from the Broadway musical *The Apple Tree*, a trilogy of playlets based on stories by three authors of which this segment had been penned by Jules Feiffer, with music by Jerry Bock and lyrics by Sheldon Harnick. To produce it, Ray fielded our number one team. Designed by Glenn McDonald, lit by John Wood, with costumes by Margaret Ryan and musical direction by Lloyd Nicholson, it would be stage-managed by our ubiquitous Mary Lou White.

The cast starred Toni Sinclair and included Jim McQueen, Victor Young, Ross Douglas, Nora McLellan, and Kathryn Shaw; yes, the same Kathryn Shaw who replaced Antony Holland in 1985 as the artistic director at Studio 58, the Theatre Department of Langara University. Kathryn holds this position to the day of writing, and deserves our collective gratitude for her inspired leadership in nurturing this cradle of talent that continues to fuel every aspect of Canadian theatre.

Passionella would be an expensive production demanding an open-ended run, which meant that there wouldn't be enough time for me to direct the next show before having to leave for my summer job. Rita and I took advantage of this opportunity to spend some time in Paris, which solidified my love affair with that city.

Since I still had some time on my hands when Rita needed to return to work, I detoured home via California, where I visited Bill Park long enough to immortalize his spectacular high-speed dismount from a water ski. I froze him in momentary suspension perpendicular to the horizon just before a succession of skips of increasing magnitude, the final of which plunged the viewers into despair, convinced that his next destination was the infirmary. His grin when we hauled him up into the boat unmistakably suggested that the only First Aid he required should originate from a distillery somewhere in the Caribbean.

1973, RUSTING IN ALBERTA

While I was engaged in the exciting world of political theatre, intriguing events had also taken place on the political front in Ontario. Because the understanding between Kenting and The Ontario Ministry of Natural Resources did not materialize, and Kenting failed to find a buyer for the airplanes, the company signed a last-minute contract in Alberta, albeit at a ruinous rate, and engaged Linc and me to fly them. To our delight, Bill Nash completed our team as the birddog pilot.

I arrived in Toronto early in May and discovered to my chagrin that, like the previous year, the major problems written up in the maintenance log had not been rectified. Since the pilot who had flown the airplane from Winnipeg to Toronto hadn't experience backfiring, this item was considered as fixed. However, the same bellicose tank still protruded from the belly, promising a repeat of last year's control headaches.

After discussing the matter with the company, I consented to accept the airplane in its present state on the condition that we perform a field-fix on the tank before flying fire-bombing missions, provided, of course, that the beast even got me to the destination. It was a pleasant relief to find the engines on their best behavior during my re-fam.

Upon learning that our initial staging-post was to be Calgary, we loaded the machines with the usual overload of spares, and with my long-suffering engineer, Jim Cook, in the right seat, and Bill Nash riding shotgun with Linc, we arrived without incident.

The following morning, a delegation of Alberta Forest Service brass arrived to welcome their new front-line contingent and to inspect their machines. They acknowledged being honored to have the author of *Air Attack on Forest Fires* as the leader of the group and solemnly promised to learn as much as possible from his experience. This was a most encouraging commitment, because up until now, Alberta had failed to understand that the primary mission of air tankers was to be used as initial attack and not as a last resort, which had been their practice.

As soon as the welcome committee left the area, we set about fixing my pitch-up problem. Our solution was not only simple: it was cheap. All we needed were thick slabs of Styrofoam and a pot of glue. Our assembly line formed under the open tanks of my airplane, where Cook cut the Styrofoam into rectangles approximately corresponding to the dimensions of the tank, Linc smeared them with glue and passed to me to press up into the back of the opening. When we were satisfied that our masonry filled about a quarter of the space, we let our work dry overnight, closed the doors, and filled the tank with water. After Bill cut the gummy lumps of glue out of my hair, which otherwise would have attached the helmet to my skull for the duration of the season, I taxied out for a test drop, with Linc in the right seat.

Shortly after takeoff, the right engine thundered its displeasure with a report that nearly propelled Link into my lap. After calming him down, I continued to a safe drop area where, at a prudent altitude, we dropped full flap and set up the airplane for a salvo drop.

Ready to rescue the machine from any post-drop gyrations, we planted our hands on the control columns as I punched the drop button; an easy to control pitch-up with none of the previously experienced nose-dive told us that our engineering feat was a resounding success. However, having witnessed the other aggravating condition, Linc agreed that I should ground the airplane until the problem was fixed.

Kenting obliged with unexpected haste. A Pratt and Whitney engineer flew in from Montreal, who over the next four days systematically changed the carb, the magnetos, and every component aft of the firewall.

Everyone sat with bated breath as I taxied out for a test flight. All was normal on the run-up, but as soon as I applied full power, a vigorous backfire, which I felt as a sharp jolt through the throttle, terminated the exercise.

After performing an Irish stomp on his hat, the PW engineer departed in disgust, leaving us with one last option, which was to change the engine. Since Kenting was unwilling to go to this expense, I faced an unhealthy choice: continue to fly this airplane, or abandon my contract.

Because I was still young, stupid, and convinced of my invincibility, and this symptom was occasional, I agreed to stay with the team. As if to prove the soundness of my decision, when we flew to Fort McMurray, my right engine performed the mission with nary a burp. This state was not destined to continue. My log book records seven aborted takeoffs in the next twenty-seven days, all of them on practice flights, since continuous rains ensured an absence of fires.

This weather pattern had been previously predicted by a First Nations elder with whom Linc had spoken two months earlier.

"It's gonna to be a wet one," he said.

"How do you know?" Linc inquired.

"The beavers are telling us," he replied knowingly.

"What are the beavers saying?"

"They are cutting the trees high up on the banks."

This indisputable evidence made us wonder why Environment Canada insists on waking hibernating groundhogs for its forecasts when the very symbols of this nation are demonstrably more accurate.

In Fort McMurray, we had plenty of free time to explore the drilling sites and marvel at the gigantic Caterpillar trucks trundling around on twelve-foot diameter tires operated by drivers whose salaries vastly exceeded ours, many of whom were women. Our next base was High Level, after which the Forestry took pity on us and stationed us in Calgary.

We knew that the dismal season would put an end to Kenting's venture into fire suppression, especially when our instructions were to return our machines not as expected to Toronto, but to Red Deer, which I accomplished with Linc's very excited twelve-year-old son, Zach, as co-pilot.

CONAIR AVIATION TO THE RESCUE

To be sure of stable employment the following year, I drove to the Conair offices in Abbotsford immediately on my return. As an expanded offshoot of Skyway Air Services, Conair employed many of the original pilots and was principally led by the same management team. Both sides chose to ignore the circumstances of my separation from the parent organization six years earlier, and my application was warmly accepted. Linc soon followed my example, and we would both fly for this company until our retirement, which for me would constitute twenty-five highly enjoyable years.

With employment assured, my primary concern became my mother. Survivor's loneliness is always a most challenging condition, but thankfully, in addition to Rita's care, the Polish refugee who rented her basement suite proved to be a genial and affectionate companion. I encouraged her to renew her participation in the Polish Women's Federation, because the activities of this group, with its help to new arrivals and organization of émigré functions, proved highly fulfilling.

This association of energetic and imaginative ladies, for which my mother served some terms as secretary, would eventually oversee the construction of the Kopernik Lodge retirement home. Before becoming a resident, my mother ran the library; it would become her home, where she would eventually end her long life at the age of ninety-nine.

I next visited City Stage, where Ray's production of the *Diary of Adam and Eve* was in full swing for a five-week run. City Stage had learned a vital lesson from relying on single-source financing. Ray was now obliged to compete with the procession of artists, academics, research scientists, and dozens of charities grubbing for grants from federal, provincial, municipal, commercial, and private sources. This energy-sapping and time-consuming process committed him to longer runs and to hiring guest directors.

Observing the daily working of the smoothly running operation convinced me of the correctness of my decision to leave City Stage. Running a professional theatre cannot be done on a part-time basis. As each fire season separated me further from its culture, the pretense that I could return fresh and ready to pick up where I left off was a pipe-dream. Theatre is a demanding mistress who commands constant coddling. Though I was proud of being the founding director of this now thriving organization, and of my part in restoring the LIP grant, from now on my interest would remain strictly avuncular.

All vacuums clamor to be filled, however, which for me became the preparation of my next triumph, Quarterback. As I continued to work on its development, I became convinced of the commercial possibilities of this game's unique qualities. None of the existing models provided for meaningful engagement of the defense, nor offered a realistic means of judging time. In addition to solving both of these problems, my concept drew the participants into every play in a way that vastly exceeded anything on the market.

In the course of pursuing this venture, I was about to discover some highly revealing practices in the as yet unfamiliar to me field of business transactions.

1973, AUTUMN IN PARIS

Before striking out on our planned journey over the Pacific, an exciting revelation awaited us in Paris: Maria and Leon had bought a new apartment. This inspired move was entirely thanks to Maria, who on learning of its availability, de-railed someone's previous offer by instantly agreeing to the asking price. Conveniently, it was the adjoining corner suite on the same floor.

The 270 degree sweep introduced sunsets to our daily enchantments and expanded the already fabulous view south to Orly Airport. We could now luxuriate in two bathrooms, and Rita and I could have a separate bedroom.

We also visited Leon in La Ferté Milon, the village east of Paris between the Brie producing area of Meaux and the champagne region of Reims, where he managed the garment factory. We explored the nearby remains of a substantial fourteenth-century chateau, visited the Église Notre Dame dating from the same *époque* as its eponymous big sister in Paris, and dined with Leon in a superb vine-covered country *Relais*, which reputedly had been a favorite haunt of Alexandre Dumas Père. We also toured Leon's factory, which employed about a hundred employees and whose primary product was men's slacks. It was amusing to saunter about Paris in Leon's company and visit the venues that carried his creations.

In the Jewish section of the fourth *arrondissement*, the prices were reasonable; shops in the Rue du Rivoli upped the cost considerably, whereas to purchase the same product tarted up with fancy labels from the boutiques along the Rue St. Honoré required the approval of one's banker.

Suspicions confirmed.

As we strolled through the streets of Paris, Rita showed me the landmarks of her youth: her schools, the cafes where she lounged as a student at the Sorbonne, the addresses where Leon and Maria used to work, and her favorite parks. The most important focal points of her interests were the museums. Rita loved art; in her teens, she made good use of her student pass to visit works of artists whom she called her friends. Drawn by her passion, she would frequently do this alone, and the image of this petite school girl wandering in enchantment through the corridors of the Louvre makes me fumble for my hankie.

[Rita was hardly the only one of her family who loved and created art.

Though her mother began designing very late in life, when she did, she employed her skills as a seamstress to produce stunning appliqués. This is a highly demanding and complicated craft which requires stitching pieces of cloth specifically chosen and pre-cut to compose an image. When the motor skills and eyesight needed for this task began to fail her in her early eighties, she blithely switched to painting with oils which she continued to practice into her nineties. The picture which I painted of her holding an example of her stitching appears at the end of this chapter.]

Paris conquers the heart on sight, but seeing it through Rita's eyes made the experience intimate, personal, and instantly ignited my ambition to become more than a transient voyeur. I began to succumb to its magnetism in the same way as the world's artists and writers who over the centuries had made it their home. Searching out their addresses, which I inscribed on large-format maps, became my new obsession. It transformed my walking trips into pilgrimages to destinations once peopled by the architects of this culture. I traipsed these storied streets in the company of friendly ghosts who led me to their garrets, their studios, and their drinking holes, and initiated my enduring fascination with their achievements, their habits, and their loves.

Following a whirlwind passage through Vancouver, by mid-November we were already in Tahiti.

My sketch of Maria holding one of her appliqués.

TAHITI, MOOREA, NEW ZEALAND, AND AUSTRALIA

Our first duty on arrival in French Polynesia was to pay homage to Paul Gauguin, one of Rita's favorite painters, but the museum erected in his name disappointed in displaying little more than paltry reproductions of his work.

After circumnavigating the island's coastline in a rented car, we boarded a ferry to the tropical bacchanalia of the Club Med in Moorea. This was an idyllic hideaway where we lived in thatch-roofed huts in the company of curious geckos that punctuated their spasmodic peregrinations with frozen poses of alert petrification. The white beaches fronting a pristine blue ocean became our home until we had spent the last beads of our necklaces, which served as cash.

On route to Australia, we profited from a ten-hour stopover in Auckland to visit the Natural History Museum, where the inexhaustible collections of local fauna, much of it unique to Australasia, captivated us all day. On arrival in Sydney, we were disappointed to discover that Ansat, the airline that serviced our destinations of the Gold Coast and the Barrier Reef, had most inconsiderately gone on strike.

Deciding to wait it out, we planted roots again in the familiar Texas Tavern, resumed contact with our friends Alan and Peggy McGregor, and dropped in at the Royal Sydney Golf Club, where the secretary graciously reinstated my membership.

Though the strike de-railed the purpose of our visit, our time was hardly wasted. We visited parks, beaches, and museums, where we fell in love with the striking inventiveness of indigenous Aboriginal art. We saw several plays, and while exploring the city, witnessed a police chase that featured the getaway car making its escape toward us along the sidewalk. We barely avoided being hit by leaping sideways against a storefront, but once the car was gone, we couldn't help admiring the agility of the pedestrians, since not a single person lay writhing in its path. I have always loved the Aussies for their carefree, no-worries-mate style, and this trip strongly fortified this impression. After a two week wait, we postponed our intention to experience the Reef to a future visit and flew home via Hawaii.

By early spring, the prototype of my game was sufficiently complete for me to risk its disclosure at the toy fair in Toronto. The site was a dizzying conglomerate of game and toy manufacturers. I demonstrated my game to several companies, and though all admired my offering, they uniformly agreed that my Canadian version was too limiting and encouraged me to try again with its American counterpart. Since this was already in my plans, I returned home and buried myself in this project.

Over the winter we had been receiving disturbing news about Leon's health. Sometime in March, Rita flew to Paris, where she discovered that, like my father, he'd been diagnosed with cancer of the stomach. An operation disclosed that the disease had spread beyond help, and the doctors sent him home. Rita came back devastated by the knowledge that she and her mother were about to be faced with a tragic loss.

1974, FIRST SEASON WITH CONAIR

My eager anticipation of the approaching flying season usually awakened around the vernal equinox. It generally started with the exhumation of the pilot's manual and the stacks of approach plate amendments sent monthly by the Ministry of Transport, which had been collecting dust since the previous fall. I took pride in memorizing all the critical numbers and procedures before showing up for training, a process useful to whet the appetite for the summer's adventures.

It was to be a welcome renaissance of my firebombing career, which had been on hold for two seasons when fire-fighting became subsidiary to concentrating on sheer survival. I looked forward to flying a well-maintained machine supplied by a responsible company, and it pleased me to discover that Al Kydd was to be my check pilot.

While admiring Conair's shiny A26s, my heart skipped a string of beats on the discovery of two overly-familiar outcasts of the breed; it was the pair of Kenting's castoffs that crouched in the grass, impudently pretending to belong to the collection.

"Don't worry, even their numbers are going to change by the time they go on-line," consoled Walt Weslowsky, who was showing me around.

After two hours of training, during which I impressed Al with my silky expertise in aborting takeoffs, I was ready to go.

On the cold and rainy day of May 1, the rebirth of my new career commenced in tanker 22, which I piloted to my assigned base of Williams Lake.

My flying partner was Howie Rowe, an ex-RCAF, CF104 Starfighter pilot, who boasted being the first Canadian to reach one thousand hours in that supersonic machine.

Howie liked to show his log book, into which he had pasted before-and-after photos of his Starfighter. The first showed off the sleek profile of the missile-like machine in flight, while the second offered a view of scrap-metal strewn over a vast area, which were the remnants of the airplane from which he ejected shortly after takeoff. Howie survived because his chute carried him just far enough to miss the fireball of the crash. Howie's mischievously rebellious nature coupled with an easy going, devil- may-care attitude made him a perfect fit as a base mate.

Ten days into the season, Rita called to tell me that Leon had died.

Conair unquestioningly granted my release, and the following day, with a bereavement pass that Rita obtained from her employer, we flew to Paris.

The passing at the age of forty-seven of Rita's mentor and best friend, and Maria's life companion, was an inestimable blow. Alongside his brothers, their families, and his friends, we bid farewell to Leon in the cemetery at Thiers, and then spent a week in Paris trying to digest this loss.

When I resumed my place in Williams Lake, I discovered to my dismay that the machine Linc flew for Kenting was to be mine for the remainder of the season. It was, however, fully refurbished, and I had faith that Conair maintenance would ensure its serviceability.

This faith was slightly dented when news of Al Kydd's close call at Abbotsford was traced to a mechanic's oversight. The A26, for reasons which escaped us all, did not come equipped with engine fire extinguishers. Consequently, the emergency we feared the most was an engine fire.

Fortunately, when his left engine burst into flames, Al was close to the airport, where he alighted with appropriate haste. Though he had his straps undone before coming to a stop, he soon realized that the flames enveloping the left engine made it impossible to climb down the normal way. His only choice was to jump off the nose, in the process of which he broke an ankle. This failed to impair his strong motivation to distance himself from his burning machine, which blew up lustily shortly after Al had crawled far enough away to avoid most of the explosion's effect.

Nevertheless, respect for my new employer rebounded considerably on receipt of my first paycheck, when I discovered that my wages were not docked during my absence.

Tanker 22, my favorite Conair machine.

Firebombing near Williams Lake, 1974.

THE WILLIAMS LAKE STAMPEDE

Williams Lake was a rough cowboy town that dominated the Chilcotin Plateau.

Sometime in June, during the three-day-long celebrations of the annual Williams Lake Stampede, the area metamorphosed into bedlam. Waves of vandalism spread through the town, which caused the merchants, like their counterparts in California waiting for the Big One, to prepare for this occasion with a supply of custom-made plywood screens ready to install on their shop-fronts. Regrettably, this precaution rarely saved the window glass, which was the chief target of the celebrants.

A highlight of this event was a dance held on the Stampede grounds in a space called Squaw Hall. The numerous injuries caused by a barrage of beer bottles flung in over the walls made these premises well worth avoiding.

A spike in the occurrence of forest fires inevitably coincided with the pro-ceedings, which featured a method of ignition locally known as "horse light-ning." This practice was characterized by a succession of bushfires breaking out at the speed of a galloping horse. In anticipation of these eventualities, Forestry routinely reinforced the resident tanker group with the team from Kamloops.

One of the visiting pilots was Ralph Boulton, a man who was universally respected among his peers for his professionalism as well as for his unchal-lenged title as the world's champion belcher, which earned him his nickname, Rotten Ralph. Tall and loose-limbed, Ralph's boyish good looks camouflaged a tough, streetwise upbringing: a useful skill in a place where, for the dura-tion of the Stampede, the very air hung saturated with testosterone-titillating pheromones that elevated the males' latent pugnacity to a hair-trigger setting.

The skirmishes that developed all over town were mere preludes to the main bouts staged at closing time outside the beer parlors.

During my lifetime, the few inconsequential flailing altercations in which I found myself a reluctant participant caused me to develop a horror of physi-cal violence. Consequently, I felt well protected as Ralph and I walked home together from a restaurant when, upon passing the local movie house, we were attracted by a commotion in the lobby. It was caused by two ladies settling a spirited dispute while surrounded by a ring of encouraging males. One of the combatants, already the clear victor of the feud, continued to pound merci-lessly on her fallen adversary, which struck Ralph as unsportsmanlike. Wading unceremoniously into the fray, he hauled the offender off her helpless victim and pushed her aside.

"Fuck off," he bid her politely as he helped her bleeding opponent to her feet.

Expecting a vote of approval from the kibitzers, I was amazed when a swarthy, red-headed punk took advantage of Ralph's inattention and, flying across the room, blindsided him with a vicious punch to the head. The blow sent Ralph, knees sagging, against a wall. Since it was clear that this assailant was about to take advantage of Ralph's incapacitation, without a second thought I jumped in, and nearly coming out of my shoes, smashed the guy with all my strength on the side of his face.

Though my punch had a momentarily distracting effect, the son of a bitch shrugged it off like it was a mosquito bite. Dismissing my killer blow, he refocused on his primary target, by which time Ralph had partly recovered and was ready to deal with his attacker. A brutal exchange followed, with me circling the brawlers like a terrier, prudently holding back my deadly punches in favor of an opportunity to deliver a decisive kick.

Ralph was clearly the stronger, but this bulldog-like aggressor kept coming back for more, and by the time Ralph decked him for good, both were bloodied and gasping for air. I grabbed Ralph and steered his shaky body toward our motel. Unbelievably, a few moments later the redhead was right behind us.

"No, Ralph," I growled, refusing to let him go.

The guy was following but thankfully kept his distance.

"Are you gonna walk away from a fight?" he challenged.

"Hell no, I usually run," I tossed over my shoulder.

That seemed to defuse some of his belligerence; possibly he tabbed me as some wimp who might press charges. We returned safely to the motel, where we treated Ralph's abrasions.

"He would have had me if you hadn't slowed him down," Ralp acknowledged. "I needed that time to recover."

"I'm glad to hear it," I said, soaking my knuckles, but I was already visualizing a swift tactical retreat from any future confrontation.

Ralph continued to dazzle us with his sure-footed accuracy until 1987, when he reluctantly agreed to replace John Truran in France to teach the pilots of the *Securité Civil* to firebomb.

Ralph didn't feel comfortable about this appointment, a fact he revealed to his wife before departure. His apprehensions were tragically realized while flying the Conair-converted Fokker F27 when his student-pilot stalled the machine at low level, killing them both.

One of the significant advantages of being based in Williams Lake was the relatively easy access to Vancouver. Rita could hop on a PWA Convair and be with me in one hour, often arriving in the cockpit jump-seat whenever Ken Stephens was the captain.

On her first visit, we discovered a viewpoint on a promontory high up on the east bank of the Fraser River that presented spectacular views of the sun as it set above the sweep of the valley below.

After the flat expanses of Alberta, the thrill of mountain-flying returned in full force. We covered plenty of ground, from Prince George to Kelowna, from Blue River to Puntzi, and were settling in for a busy season when rains washed out our parade. Typically, we were on one-hour call, which the new invention of beepers allowed us to exploit some distance from the base. This not only put the golf course comfortably in range, but it also allowed me to roam the countryside in search of mushrooms while at the same time charting the presence of grouse in preparation for the opening of the season in September, and all this while I was being paid!

Though Forestry didn't like to spend money on practices, after a week without action it was mandatory to schedule an hour of flying. Howie didn't get far, as shortly after takeoff he garbaged an engine and deposited a pool of pink water in a farmer's field. This made him thoroughly unpopular with the engineering staff, who spent all night installing the new engine trucked in from Abbotsford.

Engineers are a breed apart whom we tanker drivers have learned to regard with deserved esteem. Though they are bound to the same standby schedule as pilots, they have to remain behind to repair our machines long after we've repaired to a bar.

The three engineers on base that year were headed by Mr. Bradley, an elderly gentleman close to retirement, along with Bill Tonsacker, his second in command, whose stunning bikini-clad girlfriend interfered with everything as she sunbathed on base all day. Completing the team was a young apprentice, Francophone Peter Trilsbeck, for whom this was his first season in the field.

After dismounting from his noisy Harley and disencumbering from the obligatory leathers and chains, Peter disclosed a body in fighting trim, topped by a face with a broad smile that revealed a disarmingly sunny disposition and unexpectedly intact bridgework.

Howie Rowe and me.

Motel party in Williams Lake; L to R; Doug Ashton, Howie Rowe, Ralph Boulton, Peter Trillsbeck, and nk.

START OF THE FIREBOMBING *ANNUS HORRIBILIS*

Summer eventually returned to our region in August, and it was good to get back in the saddle again. We were operating out of Kamloops on the second of the month when the news reached us: Conair Chief Pilot Jim Fewell crashed in the DC-6 east of Ashcroft. There were three fatalities. The queen of the fleet in the hands of an experienced pilot … what the hell could have gone wrong?

During a lull in the action, I was called to the phone. It was our CEO, Barry Marsden. Barry had witnessed the crash and wished to convey details of this tragic event to each of his pilots in person. I remember precisely the way he described the accident. As he watched the DC-6 approaching the target, it appeared to Barry that Jim was low at the start of his downwind leg, and that his flight path to the fire would take him uphill.

"I hope it feels better than it looks," Barry said as he watched with increasing concern.

"We're losing airspeed," Jimmy reported somewhat laconically, shortly followed by a much more alarmed, "We're in trouble now!"

"Drop your load!" Barry shouted, but a moment later the DC6 stalled and smashed into the trees. Inexplicably, Jimmy failed to activate the primary safety feature unique to air tanker aviation: to be flying an empty aircraft at the push of a button.

"Call your family to tell them it's not your crash that they'll be seeing on the evening news," Barry counseled.

Barry's personal concern for his employees was typical of his management style, which was much appreciated and uniformly respected by all of us.

The fire season in central BC was now in full force, and during the next three days, I logged over twenty hours and made twenty-eight drops. While our region urgently needed backup, the team in Smithers sat idle, and we knew how they must be chomping at the bit. Eventually, the Prince Rupert duty officer agreed to release his tankers. Two A26s piloted by Lloyd Rauw and Eric Yuill, along with a birddog and two engineers, soon arrived at our base, making Williams Lake a formidable force.

Since we never knew where we might have to spend the night, tanker crews routinely checked out of their motels each morning and loaded their suitcases onboard.

I don't know why the memory of the eye-contact I exchanged with Lloyd as we stood at the motel checkout counter on the morning of July 7 should have registered with such force, but its impact would reach significance a few hours later.

"A fire near Clinton; all tankers and both birddogs required!" Doreen, the dispatcher, announced in her melodic voice.

The visiting tankers were first in the pits. Howie and I manned our machines at our leisure and watched, as Eric leading, they rumbled off to the fire. I was the last to take off, and making sure to maintain the specified altitude that gave passing tankers a five-hundred-foot separation, I saw Eric pass over me on the way back to Williams Lake, but there was no sign of Lloyd. When I switched to the bombing frequency, the birddog's instructions to Howie revealed that we were dealing with two fires.

"Disregard the fire at the base of the mountain, Howie. Your target will be visible at the end of the valley at four thousand feet."

Had I listened on the frequency of the second birddog, which monitored the action from above, I would have heard its air attack officer's report of the crash and his request for backup from the group in Kamloops.

I reported three minutes out, and when I turned into the valley, the picture became clear. Howie was on final to a hot blaze at the valley's western end, the cause of which was the wreckage of Lloyd's machine.

"A quarter long but 100 percent effective, Howie; reload and return."

From my position it looked like a bullseye, but Herb was unfamiliar with such assessments unless confronted by three-dimensional hologramic evidence.

We learned to take it in stride.

Hugging the right edge of the tight, box-like canyon, I reported the target in sight.

"Give me a tight, two-door string to parallel Howie's drop on the uphill side. You'll have to drop in the turn to fly out down the valley. Do you want a lead in?"

"Negative, I have my target," I reported as I finished my bombing check.

We were not yet equipped with a bombing computer, so the interval between door openings was a matter of judgment and experience. I was in a perfect position to set up for a 180 degree descending turn with the target at its apogee.

"*Don't fuck up*," I said to myself, because it would be a long and embarrassing climb for another downwind approach.

All looked good as I opened the doors in quick succession and continued my descent out of the canyon.

"A quarter short but 100 percent effective: reload and return," was the assessment.

I had already written it down.

On the way out, I flew past our original target. Eric had put an accurate load above it earlier, but by now the fire outflanked it and was moving briskly up the hill. It promised to be a long day.

Early in the afternoon, I taxied to the airport terminal building where we used to take fuel before the installation of gas pumps in the loading pits. Peter Trillsbeck and Ross Bailey climbed aboard to check the oil and fill the right wing tank while I serviced the left. Briefly looking up, I saw two tankers on long final but gave it no more thought until I happened to catch Peter staring open-mouthed at the runway. Following his gaze, I saw the extraordinary sight of an A26 sliding to a stop on its belly amid a cascade of smoke, dust, and sparks.

Abandoning my task, I leapt into the cockpit to grab my movie camera and caught a sequence on film of the pilot, who I knew was ex-naval aviator Buck Buchanan, as he exited the cockpit, climbed out onto the wing, and slowly slid to the tarmac. Meanwhile, Howie circled overhead, and after ascertaining that there was enough space to land, set up for an approach.

While I started my engines, someone in a truck sped out to fetch the stranded pilot.

"Is there room by that airplane?" I asked Howie on the radio as he was turning on base.

"No sweat; Buck considerately stopped to the right of the center line," he added, giggling in his mischievous way. Howie passed the wreck without slowing down.

As I lined up for takeoff, I could see that to pass Buck's machine was no problem as long as one hugged the right edge of the runway. We continued to operate in this manner until late afternoon, when someone from the Ministry of Transport arrived. The blur of a fellow rushing to the radio room was instantly followed by a Notam (Notice to Airmen), closing the airport.

Fair enough: it was time to drink a toast to the departed, anyway.

After securing my airplane, I inquired about Buck. Apparently, someone took him to the hospital, from where he soon disappeared. This news disturbed me profoundly; Buck had retired from the Navy after a distinguished career. I wished to pass some words of compassion and solace to this venerable gentleman over this embarrassing oversight, particularly because I knew that he'd been the victim of an incident in the Navy that had unfairly cost him his career.

Sliding into home base.

THE LAW OF THREES

Just like we used to do in the Navy, the day's sad events required a thorough debriefing at a convocation traditionally known as "weepers." The cause of Lloyd's accident was a clear case of pilot error. Inexplicably, he chose to fly his approach too close to the center of the box-canyon, leaving him no room to turn. Buck's failure to complete a crucial item on the landing checklist was inexcusable, but one couldn't help speculating that bombing a fellow pilot's grave was a contributing factor.

"That's two," said Howie sometime into the proceedings.

"Two what?" someone asked.

"Two fatal crashes so far; they always come in threes."

"Jesus Christ, Howie!" we yelled, forcing him into a defensive ball to ward off the pummeling we gave him whenever some outrage like this escaped his lips, but you could hear him chortling all along.

"That's bullshit anyway; a wheels-up counts as one, so you've got your three," someone corrected, trying to put the subject to sleep. The party ended late, but when I turned in, I couldn't dismiss the memory of the morning' haunting eye-contact I'd exchanged with Lloyd.

Two days later, my log book records: "Late call to Malcolm Island; dinner with Rita cancelled." Fate, as we had come to know her, is a fickle tart, fond of regarding family visits as a provocation. Rita's arrivals, however, bore the mark of a curse by practically guaranteeing, if not a base change, at least an overnight stay somewhere else. True to form, after Eric, Howie, and I bombed the Malcolm Island fire at dusk, our instructions were: "Campbell River and stay!"

I'll never forget the following morning's dispatches to Malcolm Island along the Johnstone Strait, where flying at zero feet I passed a northbound cruise ship. There were even more viewers on deck to wave up to on the way back, and by the time I streaked past the third time, the upper decks looked like those of the *Queen Elizabeth* returning loaded with troops to New York in 1945, its passengers clinging to every hand-hold on the superstructure. I expected that my flying mates were doing the same, and could only hope that the abundance of photographic evidence would not lead to tedious exchanges with the Ministry of Transport.

I logged nine hours making seven drops that day, at the end of which Howie and I stayed overnight at Campbell River while Eric flew to Abbotsford to have some glitch fixed at home base.

A cold front swept through that night, which ruined our fun; with no targets left on the coast, Forestry released us to Williams Lake, where we were to meet up with Eric, whose aircraft was now serviceable. The weather forecast predicted low scud to form in the valleys under the overcast, promising to make a VFR trip through the coastal range somewhat exacting.

A26s were not IFR certified, and all flying had to be conducted under visual flight rules.

Howie seemed unconcerned as he watched Wayne and me plotting a zig-zag, low-level course through the valleys.

"I'll see you in Willie's puddle … that is, if you make it," he said as he walked to his airplane. "I've got six chapters of *The Happy Hooker* to finish."

Howie took off while we were still planning our trip.

As was the custom, the birddog took off first, but we agreed not to push the weather and, in case of doubt, to return to Campbell River. As we picked our way cautiously through the mountains toward the flat terrain of the Chilcotin Plateau, I gave Howie a call.

"Where are you?" I wanted to know.

"On the second to last chapter," he giggled. "OK, I am en route to the Williams Lake beacon at fourteen thousand feet; there's a two thousand foot ceiling and good viz underneath; it's the safest way to go."

Sure it is, but flying in cloud in controlled airspace without an IFR clearance demanded considerable *chutzpah*.

Howie had just landed when I pulled up behind him in the pits.

"How was your flight?" I asked.

"Piece of cake," he said. Then with an elfin grin, he pulled me over and confided *sotto voce*: "I lost my airspeed because the fucking pitot-tube froze up, and when the same thing happened to my glasses, I was straining so hard to read the last pages of the book that I missed beacon-passage and had to backtrack some distance before starting descent."

"You are incorrigible," I said, punching his arm as we neared the building, looking forward to an early supper.

A strange silence pervaded the group of base personnel as we came in. Ron Beazley, the base manager, approached us stony-faced and said: "We didn't want to tell you while you were flying; Eric Youill never made it this morning."

Wordlessly, we plunked down our gear and sat to listen to what was known.

Eric had taken off from Abbotsford that morning and was observed passing over Hope at about a thousand feet. The weather in the canyon was shitty, as usual. There was no radio contact, and Eric simply disappeared.

"Everybody's got the rest of the day off," Beazley announced.

We all trooped to the motel and called our families.

The crash site was found the next day near the peak of Mount Stoyoma.

The accident was headline news on all networks that evening: Conair Aviation's third fatal tanker crash and fifth fatality in ten days. Inquiries were being planned, etc.

We were in a sombre mood when some of us congregated in the bar. We wondered if public pressure could make the Ministry shut us down.

"There's your number three, Howie," someone remarked.

His black humor got the best of him.

"Yeah," he said, covering his grin with his hand. "We wiped out the whole Smithers tanker base."

No one had the energy to give him a smack. Maybe this was the best way to take it. It was his gleeful eccentricity coupled with that roguish touch o *schadenfreude* (trust the Germans to have a precise word to describe this attitude) that endowed Howie with his uniquely moulded charm.

Flying resumed the next day, which included an unusual target—a truck on fire. Unexpectedly, Herb, who never awarded bullseyes, gave me two.

As if we hadn't had enough excitement that month, something that we knew had been brewing in the birddog between Wayne and Herb came to a head when Wayne deliberately scared the hell out of his air attack officer with some reckless stunting. Conair fired Wayne on the spot, which pissed off his buddy, the retardant loader, who in a fit of misplaced sympathy tried to sabotage the pumps. Thankfully, the weather remained cool, which allowed Beazley to train a new loader, and Conair to supply a replacement birddog pilot.

Taking advantage of the lull, Rita boarded a PWA Convair flown by our friend Kenny, who delivered her in his accustomed style. As we prepared to sup on the veal stew she'd been cooking all afternoon, the horn went off, but this time fate relented and allowed us to return to base to consume Rita's creation as the sun began to set. The following morning, Rita accompanied me around the golf course to witness my heroics as I scrambled to tie for third in the annual club tournament.

When our standby expired on the last day of the month, we unceremoniously ripped the August page off the calendar and took turns tearing it into shreds.

Rita's picture of me chipping to save a birdie in Williams Lake.

THE CURSE CONTINUES IN CALIFORNIA

When I phoned Rita on September 1, she told me that Ron Thomas had called from Santa Rosa and wanted me to get in touch.

"Bum news, Palawski," was his opener. "We lost Bill Benedict yesterday on a fire near Clear Lake, south-east of Ukiah."

Bill Benedict! Sis-Q's chief pilot and the most experienced tanker driver on its staff. Ron sketched in the details in his usual terse manner: "Got low on approach, hit three oak trees, game over. Dead at fifty-six."

I filled him in with our string of fatalities. Let's hope that's the end of it, we agreed.

I told Howie about it, and of the irony of Bill Benedict surviving the war flying P51 Mustangs in the USAF, only to lose his life in a stupid accident.

Two weeks later, the fires started again with a vengeance. On September 20, I flew over eight hours, making twelve drops across the province from the west coast of Vancouver Island to the Alberta border, finishing up in Kamloops. We continued to bounce around the province until the twenty-sixth, ending up in Prince George.

Ron Thomas got in touch with me the following day.

Unbelievably, there had been another fatality in an F7F, which crashed on takeoff out of Rohnerville. It was Dick Miller, whom I met briefly before leaving California; he was an ex B52 co-pilot who flew operationally over Vietnam. Dick experienced a power loss on both engines on takeoff, waited too long to abort, and crashed into trees at the end of the runway. The most probable cause was his failure to follow the checklist, which stipulates that, for takeoff, the fuel pumps *must* be selected to *high*.

For me, this crash added a personal dimension; it heralded the demise of tanker 23, the beauty in which I checked out four years earlier.

"Don't even go there!" I warned Howie, knowing full well what he was thinking when I told him about the second crash.

Our season finally ended on the last day of September. What a year to be a rookie with this company. I had flown 170 hours and made over 190 drops; however, for the air tanker community, it was its *annus horribilis*.

1974, AUTUMN ON THE RED DEER RIVER

It was great to be home again, to visit my mother and to admire Rita's latest foray into collages, which she painstakingly composed entirely of sea shells or colored beads.

Fall is my favorite season, and this year we were to experience its extravagance from an intimate perspective.

Come and join us on a canoe trip on the Red Deer River, was the gist of Linc's invitation shortly after I got home.

We instantly agreed and flew to Edmonton, where Linc picked us up and drove us to his house in Red Deer to meet his current lady friend, who would be our traveling companion. The plan was to start upstream of Drumheller for a two-day excursion.

Appropriately provisioned with an inexhaustible supply of wine and beer, a friend of Linc's, who would also collect us at our destination, dropped us off at the starting point. Lulled by the soothing ripple of wavelets mussing our canoes, we spent two idyllic days drifting between the golden, tree-lined shores. As we meandered lazily downstream accompanied by flocks of gossiping geese, we breathed in the pristine, prairie-filtered air, which in this area periodically came infused with an agreeable hint of smoldering marijuana.

Reluctantly, we bid farewell to this lyrical sojourn to return to more pressing concerns, the chief of which was to visit Paris and join Maria at the start of her life in the sudden emptiness of her home.

After returning to Vancouver to commence our next adventure in Fiji, my mother told me that Ron had phoned and wanted me to get in touch. Nervously, I called his number.

Un-flipping-believable! His news concerned the crash of *another* F7F in Rohnerville, which had taken the life of Mike Fagan. This eclipsed the accepted norms of the ridiculous.

"There seems to be something wrong with our bloody ships today," commented Admiral Beatty as he watched his fleet exploding around him in the North Sea at the battle of Jutland in 1916. A similar question was forming on everybody's mind: What the hell is going on?

"Looks like fuel mismanagement again," said Ron. "Mike was experiencing power loss on both engines after takeoff, but when he tried to return to the airport, he clipped a tree and rolled the airplane into a ball along with some farm machinery."

And we'd all been thinking that this horrific year was finally behind us.

I didn't call Howie, just to spare myself getting his theory rubbed in all over again, but I did call Linc to tell him that his cherished tanker 22, in which he blissfully plied the California skies, was now a pile of scrap metal.

On analyzing the tragic year, Linc and I concluded that this attrition had little to do with the danger of the job itself. Every fatality had an overwhelming component of pilot error.

Admittedly, it's always risky performing demanding maneuvers in heavy airplanes close to the ground, because this greatly reduces the margin of safety. But following checklists, planning ahead, knowing your and your airplane's limitations, and using judgment learned from previous mistakes should normally suffice to avoid a majority of the tragic results. However, this list would be incomplete without factoring in an important component, which pilots know is always working behind the scenery: luck.

Fickle she may be, and unreliable as well, but sensing her wink as we walk away from an incident that the odds indicate should have had an entirely different result makes believers of us all.

Mulling over this unprecedented season, Linc and I vowed to each other that if we were to crash, it would only happen because of some unmanageable aircraft malfunction. Importantly, we never allowed these events to mutate into feelings of apprehension. Knowing that such emotions would impair our ability to do the job, we dismissed them with conscious determination from our minds.

It was an attitude that guided us to the end of our careers, allowing us never to lose the thrill of the job, and to enjoy the excitement that accompanied each dispatch.

PEDDLING QUARTERBACK IN NEW YORK

It was mid-February, which gave me a month before the opening of the world's most prestigious games fair in New York, where I planned to demonstrate my football game. Though I was still tinkering with new adjustments to further enhance the game with what in the business is known as "play value," I was confident that I had a winner on my hands.

As I engaged in this time-consuming task for the n'th time, an idea exploded in my brain: Why not attempt to interest the American Football Leagues directly? There were two of them operating at the time: the National Football League (NFL) and its competitor, the American Football League (AFL).

After discovering that neither league sponsored a board game, I found the names of their respective commissioners and sent each a letter. The gist of my address was to acquaint them with the remarkable qualities of my concept and to convince them that by accepting Quarterback as their league's official board game, they would be scoring a novel, and most importantly, a potentially highly profitable advertising coup.

The NFL failed to rise to my vision, but the AFL expressed interest in examining my proposal. Accordingly, I arranged to present my model on a Friday morning coinciding with the opening of the fair.

Having arrived on the red-eye, I made my way with baggage in tow directly to the AFL headquarters located near the Grand Central Station, where a secretary led me to the commissioner's office. I was introduced to a tiny shrew of a woman with a pointed face, who registered undisguised disapproval as she watched me unwrap the elements of the game from their protective layers of socks and underwear. When I finally faced her, she floored me with the icy observation that it was customary to arrive at a business meeting attired in a jacket and tie.

The chill that filled the room was further magnified by my answer to her question: "Who is the manufacturer of the game?"

"That's what I'm here to find out," was apparently not the reply she expected.

My listless presentation was equaled by the apathy of my audience, after which the crush of passengers on the subway that deposited me at my customary *pied à terre* of the Wellington Hotel on Seventh Avenue felt like a warm embrace of old friends.

Profiting from the experience, clean shaven and correctly clad in jacket and tie, I made my way to the Toy and Games Fair. A staggering number of exhibitors filled the arena, which thankfully included an information desk. Though I no longer remember the name of the recommended company, the type of its products appeared promising.

Two representatives of the firm to whom I described my product led me to an office, where they watched intently as I demonstrated the process. I remember them looking at each other with raised eyebrows. Armed with their agreement to consider producing my game, and their assurances that a project manager would be assigned to my portfolio, I rushed out of the place in a state of euphoria.

"We are rich!" I announced to Rita as soon as I found a phone booth.

What a year it was turning out to be! The end of the Vietnam War, the linking of Apollo and Soyuz in space, Nixon out of the White House, and the launch of Quarterback: the unlikely but brilliant brainchild of a Canadian tanker pilot, who has never played the game, flying off the shelves all over North America.

I returned to Vancouver ready for a fling. Rita and I spent a few days in Paris before flying to Munich, where we rented a car. Our destination was the Bavarian town of Rothenburg, which according to literature was one of the best-preserved medieval municipalities in Germany. We moved into a cozily refurbished love nest in a cloister from where we explored and fell in love with this walled-city and its remarkable history.

The town owed its pristine state to two disparate events. The first occurred in the early part of the seventeenth century when the population, already reduced by the religiously-inspired Thirty Years War, and further decimated by the bubonic plague, abandoned the area. The second took place in April of 1945 after the American Army surrounded the town. Unwilling to destroy such a historical treasure, the Americans halted their advance and sent a delegation bearing a white flag with an offer to spare the city if the German garrison agreed not to defend it. Countermanding Hitler's orders, the Germans agreed, which once more allowed this fabulous gem to survive.

I was disappointed that no news from the games manufacturer awaited me on return to Vancouver.

Because the process of inventing this game involved a considerable chunk of my life, and since its saga stretches beyond the scope of this narrative, let me put it to bed.

For reasons I have never fathomed, not a word ever reached me from that company. Efforts to interest a manufacturer at games fairs in Montreal and Kansas City yielded no results until the CO of a Vancouver-based manufacturing company suggested that with a Canadian Football League endorsement, he might be willing to produce it.

I approached the league's marketing company, Hayhurst Advertising, who invited me to demonstrate the game in the Toronto hotel where the league management was to meet for a conference. Hayhurst loved the product and insisted on showing it to the CFL management. The league CEO stopped by when the meetings were over, and being equally impressed, authorized Hayhurst to proceed with the arrangements.

It all looked promising until the director of the Vancouver company learned that the price for the CFL logo would be 7 percent of the profit, which caused him to back out of the deal.

Forgive me, reader, if I've exceeded your patience with these repeated plugs of my game. Though Quarterback is doomed to remain unseen in the bottom of a drawer, I don't begrudge the years of effort invested in its invention, because it remains the most original product of my imagination.

1975, WE LOSE HOWIE ROWE

It was the spring of 1975, and I was ecstatic! In spite of my low seniority, I was posted to Kamloops, the most sought-after base in the province. Moreover, my airplane was Tanker 22, the start of my love affair with what would become my favorite A26 in the fleet.

Immediately after my re-fam with Al Kydd, I started a search for accommodations, and soon moved into a fully furnished house whose occupants, both teachers, wished to spend the summer holidays in their cottage on Hefley Lake. The house was barely a mile from the field, but since Rita did not yet have a driver's license, I bought a bicycle to make it easier for her to visit.

The tanker base, which the previous year was just a shack, was now housed in a new air-conditioned building, which in addition to an impressively equipped control center, contained the dispatch room and offices, and boasted a spacious briefing room, comfortable sleeping quarters, a TV room, pool table, and dart board. The crowning achievement was the fully equipped kitchen, whose two fridges, giant freezers, gas stove and ovens would suffice to prepare feasts for a regiment, while an immense brick BBQ large enough to slow-roast a steer stood beneath the trees of the park-like surroundings.

Since no such country-club setting would be complete without a golf course, one lay conveniently provided just across the parking lot. It was the venerable Kamloops Golf and Country Club, the sixteenth hole of which was easily accessed through a thoughtfully provided gate in the fence right opposite the base. I bought an out-of-town membership, and from then on, my stand-by was spent on the golf course within easy sprinting distance from my plane.

The bombing teams consisted of two A26s, three TBMs, and two birddogs. Joining me in the other Invader was Bill Smith, a highly experienced pilot whose conservative personality contrasted sharply with my last year's irrepressible teammate, Howie, who this season was based in Abbotsford and whose company I sorely missed.

Though we had few actions early in the season, one flight was unforgettable. On Friday, June 13, I was flying in moderate turbulence following a valley en route to a fire near Keremeos when, with no warning, some malevolent deity planted a boot on the top of my airplane and drove it viciously toward the ground. My helmet smashed against the overhead canopy, and anything that wasn't tied down flew upwards then scattered in a mess on the floorboards. Unbelievably, the wings remained attached to the airframe.

If this was a spot of warning for whatever commandment I managed to chip or dent when I thought the gods weren't looking, it certainly got my attention. Mechanical turbulence in the mountains was a condition we accepted as part of the furniture. Its whereabouts, frequently on the lee side of ridges, was often predictable, but an unforeseen wallop in clear air could cause severe structural damage. Though none was visible, I informed the birddog that I would only give him single-door drops to put less strain on the airframe, and immediately headed for Kelowna to have my machine inspected.

My respect for the manufacturer's workmanship rose immeasurably when a thorough examination failed to find a single popped rivet, but to avoid possible provocation, I resolved to be extra vigilant when within committing distance of any of the deadly sins, though my tastes tended to gravitate toward the livelier ones.

Two weeks without a target works wonders on the handicap but tends to lower one's morale. The inactivity finally broke when on July 2, the A26 team was dispatched to a fire near Pemberton. I was the first to take off, and as I made my customary "three-minutes out" report, I spotted the birddog circling high above the target.

"Tanker 22, birddog eight," radioed the pilot, "you will see a fire high and to the left of the original target [followed by the altitude and altimeter setting]; put a salvo on that, then it's Abbotsford and reload. We've had to climb up to contact Kamloops."

Radio contact with the base was often impossible from low altitude, so it was normal for the birddog to climb up, but this was usually done after the action was over. Presumably, Ron Beasley was getting another target.

Since I was perfectly lined up for a straight-in approach from my present position, I called: "I have my target," and completed the bombing check.

The smoke, small in size, was at the top of a slight promontory on the edge of the valley opposite the larger original fire, which I saw was already splattered with retardant.

"On final and armed for a salvo," I reported as I completed the usual double-check of the cockpit, but as I dropped the load and flew past the smoke, I caught a glimpse of a puzzling reddish swath on the other side of the fire.

"Abbotsford and re-load," re-confirmed the birddog, switching his concentration to Bill, three-minutes behind me, who was to bomb the lower target.

A sense of unease enveloped me on the way to Abbotsford, fortified by the unusually somber voices of the tower controller and the tanker base dispatcher, and the graven faces of the loaders. Dispatch informed me that a different birddog would be over the fire, flown by Walt Weslowsky.

I contacted him as soon as I cleared the Vancouver control area.

"What was that fire I bombed, Walt?" I wanted to know, internally fearing the worst.

"That was Howie's crash site, George. You wouldn't have been able to see it from the direction you came in. Howie went in half-an-hour before you got there. It was obvious he didn't survive. We'll put your load 180 degrees from your previous shot. Go ahead and have a look at the target."

From this angle, I could see the remains of the wreck tucked neatly under the trees, my retardant covering the area.

It was easy to re-construct Howie's flight-line.

He was paralleling the slope, planning a left-hand approach to the fire which was low to his left on the opposite side of the valley. Concentrating on the target, he flew straight into the peninsula of land dead-ahead. He must have jettisoned his load a millisecond before ploughing into the base of the timber.

I made a full circle, and with the birddog slightly above me on my port quarter, released my load directly on the still-smoking crash site.

"That's a bullseye two-two; Kamloops and stay."

The last instruction was superfluous; I had no intention of returning. A mantle of silence enveloped the base. Rita's concerns mounted exponentially, as did my mother's, whom I tried to console with the fatuous assurance that it's never going to happen to me. Frank Loesser, the composer and librettist of *Guys and Dolls*, was right when he called luck a *lady*—I befriended her early, and she never let me down.

We flew our butts off in July, during which time I logged seventy-one hours and made eighty-two drops. The season came to an end three weeks later.

AFTERTHOUGHT

Flying air tankers for a living not only satisfied my craving for excitement, but provided me with ample time to sample everything this world had to offer. As the years went by, the safety record of the profession progressively improved, as did the remuneration for our work, and the conditions of our employment.

It wasn't always that way. During the pioneering days of firebombing, the thrill and romance of rushing off to fight forest fires in WWII machines caused many of us to admit in private that we would do it for nothing. Unfortunately, the companies that hired us were on to our secret. They were more than happy to offer us the privilege of flying their airplanes, and banked on our addiction to keep us coming back for more. Year after year we did, but the feeling of being exploited progressively started to penetrate our group. Apart from paltry wages, we had no job security, pilots were paid commensurately with their amity with management, and the awarding of desirable bases too frequently disregarded seniority in favor of company discretion.

Some of us insisted that we had to unionize, but not all pilots were on board with this risky proposition. I remembered what had happened in California. Being suspected of just thinking about it meant an immediate bus ticket home.

Four conspirators—Linc, Tom Wilson, Doug Spence, and I—began to send out feelers. We would need a numerical majority and an accredited union to join. Discretely, we began to assemble the former, but the Canadian Airline Pilots Association, the union we thought was a shoo-in to accept us, turned us down flat. Eventually, The International Union of Operating Engineers, which had some experience with a float plane company, signed us on.

With stealth worthy of Le Carré, we succeeded in signing up nineteen of Conair's twenty-five pilots; no easy task, since we were dispersed all over Canada. On September 6, 1978, following the example set by Martin Luther, a Canadian Labour Relations Board Notice to Employees appeared on the Conair hangar door.

The Company threw a fit. In a panic, Conair's first reaction was to try to decertify us. When this failed, they knew that they had no choice but to start negotiations. We pilots had never seen a union contract until Rita managed to obtain one from the Flight Attendants Union. Intoxicated by the sense of our recently acquired power to strike, we filled every section with our demands and flung it on the table as an opener of our first bargaining session.

Predictably, it didn't go well. Subsequent meetings showed little improvement. The impasse now threatened not only our jobs, but the company's existence. Our union rep recommended mediation, to which both sides agreed.

We met in a hotel in Burnaby. The arbitrator appointed to mediate between us was Vince Ready, who sequestered our groups in separate rooms. When he saw the list of our demands, he was horrified.

"There's something you guys need to learn," he told us, "especially on a first contract, and that's the meaning of the word 'compromise!'"

"But Conair wants to give us nothing," we objected.

"They need to learn the same lesson," he said, and from then on, Mr. Ready circulated back and forth between the rooms, chipping away at both sides.

Two exhausting days later, though our list had shrunk to a sad facsimile of the original, Conair's concessions mounted correspondingly. Finally, there was just one item left to settle: the paying of per-diem in Abbotsford.

"No company pays per-diem to its employees at home base, George," Vince painfully tried to convince me, but I was adamant.

"I don't give a damn, Vince. The pilots come from all over Canada, and only one lives in Abbotsford. Conair is exploiting a technicality that's demonstrably unfair to anyone who has to work on this base!"

Vince rolled his eyes but took the argument next door. We wondered if my obstinacy might be a deal breaker.

When Vince returned, he looked deadly serious.

"Sit down, guys. This is most unusual. The company agreed to pay 50 percent. If you don't have the sense to take it, I'm outa here!"

Sense was easy to tap into when presented in this manner. When at three in the morning the Conair bargaining committee came into our room to sign our first agreement, emotions boiled out of every pore. I will never forget embracing Barry Marsden and discovering that, like me, he was on the verge of tears. It may have been a rocky start, but though we had to wait several years for a pension plan, we walked away with a considerable pay raise and numerous other concessions.

Thank you, Mr. Ready. Compromise is a useful word to know, but it was you who taught us to apply it.

Unionizing was good for both groups. Pilots could now consider making firebombing a career: it stabilized the workforce and saved Conair time and money checking out new pilots each spring. Progressively, trust became reestablished between our camps. I chaired the first bargaining committee for a year, after which more experienced pilots took over, and guided by the union, we all started to pull in the same direction.

Unfortunately, accidents continued to happen. During my time of service, Conair lost two birddog crews and three pilots in Firecat* crashes, but the installation of a Stall Margin Indicator on the glare shield cut the attrition in this type to zero.

I continued to fly the A26 until 1979, when at the insistence of Chief Pilot Peter Mitchell, I spent a harried winter buried in aviation manuals studying for an Airline Transport Pilot Rating. Once obtained, this allowed me to fly the venerable four-engine Douglas DC-6, which I did for the next sixteen years.

With four years left before my compulsory retirement, Conair lost the DC-6 contract in BC but acquired one in Alberta. My choice was to follow the airplane or to take a considerable pay cut and fly the Firecat in BC. Since lifestyle for me had always trumped money, I opted for the latter and spent the last four seasons flying out of Kamloops while ensconced in a swanky apartment with a fabulous view of the city.

In keeping with our union contract, I was obliged to retire on my sixty-fifth birthday. I knew it wouldn't be easy. Luckily, on July 16, 1999, we had a target near Kootenay Lake. I was able to complete thirty-five years as a member of this esoteric profession with a pair of bullseyes. The air attack officer, Bruce Noble, wouldn't have dared to call anything else.**

Many of my closest friends came to the farewell party in Kamloops. Bill Park flew in from Oregon, Joe Sosnkowski brought Rita, and Linc drove in from Vancouver. Barry Marsden delivered a farewell address, and I did my best to follow. The hardest part was leaving the family of Conair Aviation. To have been a part of it was both a joy and a privilege.

---

* The *Firecat* was a civilian conversion of the CS2F Tracker, the type I flew in the Navy, which replaced the A26 as the fleet's twin-engine bomber.

** This was my penultimate flight in the Firecat. The last one occurred on September 7, 2012, when Ray Horton allowed me to co-pilot the Firecat from which, according to Linc's wishes, we dropped my lifelong friend's ashes next to the pier at Porteau Cove.

The management and staff, my fellow pilots, and those fabulous engineers with whom I'd developed a particularly warm relationship were all people who had become an intimate part of my life. So were the Forestry personnel, especially the air attack officers many of whom I had known from the start of their careers.

For the first time in my life, I found myself wallowing in the classic symptoms of depression. This ugly and foreign-to-me feeling lasted until Rita taught me the trick of how to get out of the bucket in which my feet were trapped by pulling on the handle. She is the only one who could have done it. It had all been a wonderful adventure that remains snug in my memory with deeply felt affection.

Rita herself had retired six years earlier. We were now free to soar to horizons of our choice, and our first destination to greet the new Millenium was the Antarctic and the Falkland Islands in Lindblad Explorer's RMS *Caledonia Star*. It was a propitious beginning to the rest of our lives.

Dropping Linc's ashes at Porteau Cove, Sept. 7, 2012. Farewell my lifelong friend.

POSTSCRIPT

That you, the reader, have traveled with me all this way flatters me to the core, and I am deeply thankful for your company. As I hope I made it abundantly clear, this *memoramblia* was not designed to serve up pearls of wisdom regarding the purpose of life or the meaning of existence, which has already been so capably covered by Monty Python. It draws instead from my unrepentant fascination with our species, from my addiction to laughter as the most civilizing music in the multiverse, and from a love of storytelling, a habit ingrained in the human psyche since the time of creation.

Since this captivating journey of which I've been fortunate to be a part is rife with their examples, it seemed natural to wish to share my version of them with my fellow travelers.

To have found Rita to embellish this odyssey with love, companionship, and guidance remains its most priceless blessing.

That this chronicle serves to unearth the memory of the remarkable cast of personalities who enriched this grand adventure remains for me a source of particular satisfaction.

ACKNOWLEDGMENTS

I wish to thank my fellow air tanker pilots, Ralph Langemann, Tom Wilson and his wife, Maureen, and John Laing, who along with his wife, Moina, assisted in the early draft of this book.

I thank my friend Ralph Langemann for his reflections on the Budworm Spray Program, and for the hilarious anecdotes which I included in this book.

I also wish to thank my Naval Aviator friend, Jack Ford, for allowing me to use his painting in which fate guided his hand to immortalize the side-number of the aircraft I flew on my last sortie from the Bonnie.

I am deeply indebted to Dr. Peter Lawrence for teaching me how to structure the contents into recognizable paragraphs, to fellow naval aviator Stan Brygadyr for his penetrating commentary on the entire text, and to our erudite neighbor, Stephane Goiran, for the invaluable contribution of his painstaking line-by-line analysis, which prodded me to justify many of my statements and to bring much needed clarity to the rest.

My acknowledgments would not be complete without my sincerest thanks to Friesen Press's anonymous editor whose myriads of red-ink corrections were vital in steering this messy text toward readability.

Finally, my profoundest gratitude belongs to Rita for tirelessly enduring years of internal widowhood while providing for my creature comforts during this travail, which without her daily encouragement had no chance of claiming this ephemeral gossamer of fame.

COVER CREDITS

Cover proposal, sketches of the Tracker and *Bonaventure* by Author.
The Author is the pilot of the A26 dropping retardant.
Final design by Friesen Press.